WAR AND AMERICAN LIFE

WAR AND AMERICAN LIFE

Reflections on Those Who Serve and Sacrifice

JAMES WRIGHT

BRANDEIS UNIVERSITY PRESS

WALTHAM, MASSACHUSETTS

Brandeis University Press
© 2022 by James E. Wright
ALL RIGHTS RESERVED

Manufactured in the United States of America
Composed in Haarlemmer
Cover design by Cheryl Carrington

For acknowledgments of previously published essays, see page 239

For permission to reproduce any of the material in this book, contact
Brandeis University Press, 415 South Street, Waltham MA 02453,
or visit brandeisuniversitypress.com

Library of Congress Cataloging-in-Publication Data
NAMES: Wright, James Edward, 1939– author.
TITLE: War and American life : reflections on those who serve and
sacrifice / James Wright.
DESCRIPTION: Waltham, Massachusetts : Brandeis University Press,
[2022] | Includes bibliographical references. | Summary: "War and
American Life is a book of essays and reflections of a veteran and a
historian who has been an advocate and a teacher/scholar. It considers
American veterans and how our society needs to understand who they
are and what they have done and the responsibilities that follow this
recognition" — Provided by publisher.
IDENTIFIERS: LCCN 2021056166 | ISBN 9781684580996 (cloth) |
ISBN 9781684581009 (ebook)
SUBJECTS: LCSH: Wright, James Edward, 1939– . | Veterans — United
States. | Civil-military relations — United States. | War and society —
United States. | BISAC: History/Military/United States. |
History/Military/Veterans.
CLASSIFICATION: LCC UB357.W75 2022 | DDC 362.860973 —
dc23/eng/20211209
LC record available at https://lccn.loc.gov/2021056166

5 4 3 2 1

THIS BOOK IS IN RECOGNITION OF THOSE WHO HAVE SERVED,

IN HONOR OF THOSE WHO HAVE SACRIFICED,

AND IN GRATITUDE TO ALL OF THOSE INDIVIDUALS

WHO HAVE HELPED ME TO UNDERSTAND BETTER

THESE EXPERIENCES

Contents

III: HISTORY LESSONS

IV: RESPONSIBILITIES

V: CHALLENGES

Do You Know My Brother?

WHEN I WAS DOING THE RESEARCH for my book *Enduring Vietnam,* I interviewed some 160 people. Over 90 percent of them were veterans who had served in Vietnam, and I had specifically sought to find veterans who had served in combat situations. They shared with me some powerful and moving stories.

But I also sought out some family members who had lost a loved one in the war to better understand their experience. Their memories were equally powerful and moving. And poignant.

Perhaps no interview revealed better the compounding human cost of war than one I had in the winter of 2014 with a man who shared his experiences in June of 1969, when he was just completing eighth grade.

He was home alone when he saw a green car stop in front of his house. Two soldiers got out of the car and walked to the house. He greeted them enthusiastically. They asked if his parents were home and he replied that they were out but he thought his mother would be there any minute. He asked them in and said he couldn't wait to talk to them. He told them that he had a brother in the Army. That his brother was a helicopter pilot in Vietnam. And that he would be home the next month. He proudly showed them his brother's picture in uniform and asked, "Do you know my brother?" They did not.

When his mother came home, they told her that they regretted to inform her that her son had been shot down and was missing in action in the Republic of Vietnam. His mother was in shock. The boy was stunned and then ran to a corner and cried. Soon his father came home and joined them, although the boy recalled that he seemed to be in a state of shock.

The next day when the boy came home from a friend's house there were several neighbors and relatives in the house who were all crying. The Army officers had returned and told the parents that his son's body had been found and identified. The young teenager hugged his grandmother and they cried together. His brother had died on June 6, 1969. His father said he would never forget that because just twenty-five years earlier he had gone ashore on the beach at Normandy.

Years later, recalling this interview still stirs my emotions. And it underlines so emphatically the story of war, the tragedy of a life lost far too young and of family and friends who will struggle, remembering that life for as long as they live.

Remembering is a heavy burden. But it is a necessary one, and one we all need to share. In so many ways this book is about my effort to share. And to remind us of our responsibility to support those who have served.

Acknowledgments

THIS BOOK is a compilation of published essays along with excerpts from two of my books dealing with war and its veterans—and its casualties. It also includes sections from several public lectures as well as some original essays I wrote specifically for this publication.

It represents fifteen years of direct work with veterans, and it is informed by reflections of an octogenarian on an adult lifetime of personal involvement with these issues as well as sixty years of study as a historian and a teacher.

I hope readers will understand that there will be some observations or experiences repeated in these pieces. Often this is to preserve the flow of the text. And in some cases there are things that I have thought may warrant repeating! The previously published pieces are occasionally edited but only to provide clarity and consistent style. Within each of the book sections, in nearly every instance the essays and the lecture excerpts appear in the order of their publication or original presentation.

The published essays and the unpublished lectures did not originally include citations (although in the case of the former, editors subjected them to aggressive fact checking!). I hope this absence will not trouble some readers. As a professional historian I am sensitive to this absence, and I hope my colleagues will find the essays important and will recognize many of the sources. The book excerpts that originally included endnotes still have those citations, as does the concluding chapter.

In preparing this book, I am grateful to so many people, starting with those to whom it is dedicated, those who served, and those who helped me to understand better their service. Along with them, I recognize those who waited for those deployed to return. They also served.

I am grateful to President Phil Hanlon and his team at Dartmouth College. They have been unhesitant in supporting my writing and my work. They have encouraged and sustained my activity and my scholarship.

Many people have contributed to the research and writing of these pieces. For over fifty years now my work has been enabled by the support and advice of the staff at the Dartmouth College Library. And for over fifty years I have been in their debt.

The editors of the various journals in which several of these essays were originally published were quite good at editing and helping me to more effectively express my ideas.

I want to thank Sue Ramin of Brandeis University Press for her encouragement and guidance. Doug Tifft of Redwing Book Services has been very supportive. He, Jim Schley, and Alan Berolzheimer have provided exceptional editing and formatting support that makes this a better book. My thanks to them.

My Dartmouth colleagues Matthew Delmont and Jason Lyall, along with Dr. Jill Rough, a Naval Reserve officer and a distinguished visiting fellow at George Mason University, read and commented on the final chapter of the book. They helped me immeasurably in understanding and writing about some of these complicated but critical issues.

Louise Moon has been my assistant—my colleague—for a dozen years and she has provided research support, guidance, and sharp editing to every article, lecture, or chapter in this book. This publication and its various components literally would not have been done without her. A thoughtful colleague, a tough critic, and a good friend.

And Susan Wright has encouraged and supported me for forty years. She has challenged my ideas when they needed challenging and then helped me to improve upon them and to express them better. She cares personally about these issues. Susan is a good reader, a skillful and unrelenting editor. And my best friend. She surely has enabled me to do all the things that I describe here and has sustained me, and guided me, in describing them: My collaborator in my work, in this publication, and in life.

WAR AND AMERICAN LIFE

INTRODUCTION
Semper Fidelis

IN NOVEMBER 2004, I found myself drawn to television coverage and newspaper accounts of a fierce battle underway in Iraq. The Battle of Fallujah would prove to be the largest sustained battle of the war and the vicious street fighting was reminiscent of the Battle of Hue City in Vietnam during the Tet Offensive in 1968.

Marines from the 1st Marine Division were at the center of the fight along with U.S. Army and Navy units, British Black Watch soldiers, and Iraqi soldiers. This battle took place a year and a half after the initial invasion of Iraq, following assurances in the spring of 2003 that all was well and, indeed, that the mission was "accomplished." In April 2004 Marine units had actually fought and succeeded in occupying much of the city in response to insurgents killing American civilian contractors, but under pressure from the Iraqi governing council, they withdrew. The next six months allowed the Iraqi resistance to buttress its forces.

My interest was less with the politics or the military tactics. The photos and accounts of the young Marines fighting there captured my attention and I was stunned by the brutal fighting with major casualties and with so many acts of heroism. The "Second Battle of Fallujah" would finally result in an allied victory, but a costly one. The allies suffered 197 killed and 613 wounded; 95 of the killed and 560 of the wounded were Americans. As many as 1,500 enemy forces died—and up to 800 civilians. All of this was made more real when I learned that a young local Marine, whose father worked at Dartmouth, had been killed in the fighting.

I kept thinking about the fact that these U.S. troops were the age of the students I worked with on the Dartmouth campus, were the age that I and others were when I had served in the Marines over forty years earlier. The local Marine who was killed on Thanksgiving Day 2004 was twenty years old. I wanted to do something, to reach out and show some support. I had no idea what this would be.

I

A few months later, this was still on my mind when I had a conversation with Peter Michael Gish, a Dartmouth alumnus who had served in the Marines from World War II to Vietnam. He was a widely recognized combat artist and when he learned of my interest in doing "something" he suggested I visit the wounded Marines at Bethesda Naval Hospital. I agreed and he arranged for me to do this with a contact he had in the office of the Commandant of the Marine Corps. I scheduled a visit in July 2005.

In so many ways, this trip was a natural step in my life, but in other ways it also represented a circling back. The son of a World War II veteran, I had joined the Marines at the age of seventeen, a natural move at that time in my small-town midwestern world and culture. I found boot camp a challenging and often very unpleasant experience but I came out of it feeling stronger and more mature. I had real pride in being a Marine. I served with the First Marine Brigade in what was the Territory of Hawaii when I arrived there and my unit was deployed to Japan during the Quemoy-Matsu crisis in 1958. I was discharged in 1960 as a lance corporal, proud to have served but happy to be moving on.

The problem was that in 1960 I was not certain what moving on meant. I had always been an indifferent student but now I thought I would like to try going back to school. I enrolled at a local public university and discovered that if I studied, I could be a good student—and even more importantly, that I loved learning. I graduated in 1964, the first in my family to do so. Then having been honored with a Danforth Fellowship I went to graduate school at the University of Wisconsin, Madison. I was in Madison during the height of the Vietnam War. While I had originally supported the war, I came to be very critical of it. I supported Gene McCarthy in the Wisconsin Democratic presidential primary in 1968. The next year, after completing my PhD in American history, I took a position as an assistant professor of history at Dartmouth College.

At Dartmouth I joined the critics of ROTC and agreed with the protestors who organized against the Vietnam War in the spring of 1970, following President Richard Nixon's invasion of Cambodia and the shootings at Jackson State and Kent State. At that time, I went to Washington with a group of Dartmouth students and we met with members of Congress and other officials to argue against the war. In 1971 I began volunteering for the George McGovern campaign.

In 1998 when the Dartmouth board of trustees elected me as the sixteenth president of Dartmouth, probably a good many of my colleagues did not even know I was a Marine Corps veteran. I certainly never hid this but I seldom discussed it. I had come to support with no reservations Dartmouth's reinstated ROTC program and now firmly believed that the military was stronger with more liberal arts graduates serving as officers. In fact, in 2010, after I had stepped down from the Dartmouth presidency, my successor Jim Yong-Kim asked me to go to the Pentagon to see about beginning a NROTC program at the college. I thought it was a great idea and was sorry that finally it did not work out.

In my presidential years, probably most of my Dartmouth generation knew me as someone who had opposed the Vietnam War. But there was one important qualifier in this opposition. I don't recall ever being generally critical of those who served there—except certainly for the individual thugs and criminals like Lieutenant William Calley of My Lai. I never linked all veterans of the war with this horrible conduct and in fact was sympathetic to those who served. It was my concern for those who sacrificed, a concern based on respect and gratitude, that led me to Bethesda Hospital in the summer of 2005.

At the hospital I went bed to bed, talking to the young Marines, nearly all of whom had suffered very serious injuries. These young men—and they were all men on this first visit—were missing limbs, being fitted for prostheses, had skin and features horribly burned or ripped off by explosives, were swaddled in bandages, and many were heavily medicated to deal with the intense pain they were suffering. These images have stayed with me. (I recall a few years later a visit in which the hospital staff showed me a new wing they were opening for seriously injured patients. When I asked about the absence of mirrors in the bathrooms, I was told that they did not want the patients to look at their burned or otherwise disfigured faces unless they were with someone.)

When I visited these Marines, often their parents or spouse were with them in the room. I expressed my support to these patients and encouraged them to think about continuing their education. I described my own insecurity and hesitation about returning to school when I had been discharged in 1960 as a lance corporal. I assured them that they could overcome their own concerns and would do well. I left them a card and if they asked about my current status as president of Dartmouth College, I told them I was the only Marine to serve as president of an Ivy League school.

That July 2005 visit to Bethesda was the first of over thirty times I went there and to Walter Reed Hospital over the next decade. I even had one visit to Balboa Naval Hospital in San Diego, where I had been hospitalized for an injury in 1957. Each visit was the same. I always asked them what had happened and no one ever hesitated to share with me some powerful, moving, and some very scary accounts. I was struck by the fact that only a few knew who had caused their injuries—this reveals so much about the nature and the anonymity of modern warfare with mines and hidden explosives, mortar rounds, snipers, booby traps, and fiery vehicles. I often learned something of their families and we generally discussed their plans for the future.

Very quickly I realized that the wounded veterans with whom I talked—and always any parents who were with them—did have an interest in following up on my suggestion that they continue their education. They sometimes asked me questions about specific schools or programs. I seldom could answer these. One question that focused me on the unmet need was a soldier asking for some basic information about a school near his Texas home: did the dormitories have elevators? He had lost both of his legs in an explosion, so obviously this information was critical to him. I assured him I would find out.

My research and engagement in this sort of information gathering was neither efficient nor effective. Late in 2005, I contacted David Ward, then the president of the American Council on Education (ACE). I told him what I had been doing and said there needed to be someone providing encouragement and advice regularly, someone who could find answers to these specific questions. Since ACE was the largest consortium of educational institutions, it could arrange to connect these hospitalized service men and women with specific schools. I told President Ward that if ACE would initiate a counseling program in the hospitals, I would help to raise money to support it. He agreed and I did raise the money—and I did this again a few years later to continue the program.

President Ward assigned a retired Marine Corps veteran working for ACE to set up this counseling program. He in turn hired a remarkable advisor who had done college counseling for a private high school in the area. She had a son who was in the Army, so she had an interest in this. She was excellent. The Severely Injured Military Veterans Program began in 2007. And several years later when ACE decided it no longer would run the counseling program, I was able to work to enable this counselor and the program to move to the Semper Fi Fund, where she provided the same support.

While my commitment to the injured veterans continued, in the course of my meetings with the individual injured veterans, I also recognized that there were hundreds of thousands of veterans who were not hospitalized and were completing their military service. They also needed encouragement and support to continue their education. The financial support provided at that time by the Montgomery GI Bill was simply inadequate. It was clear there was a need for a new comprehensive program.

Late in 2007 someone connected me with Democratic Virginia Senator Jim Webb, a Marine Corps Vietnam veteran with a Navy Cross and two Purple Hearts. Webb had earlier served as secretary of the Navy, and as a U.S. senator he was a major advocate for a Post-9/11 GI Bill that would meet the needs of these twenty-first–century veterans. He drafted and introduced legislation that would do this. In February 2008 I met with him for a few hours in his Senate office to discuss the legislation.

Senator Webb arranged for Senator John Warner of Virginia to join us for this meeting. Warner, a senior Republican and also a former secretary of the Navy, was a critical figure. The three of us, old Marines, discussed the legislation. The language in the draft bill we reviewed capped the GI Bill payment at the level of the highest public tuition charged in the home state of the veteran. There was significant congressional resistance to doing anything more that would subsidize what critics considered to be wealthy private institutions. I urged these two Virginia senators to consider ways in which private schools could step up and provide their share of the support as well, in order to enable veterans to enroll. I reminded them that each of them had been able to go to a private school on the GI Bill. Republican Senator Chuck Hagel of Nebraska, another Vietnam veteran, joined us for part of the meeting.

We finally agreed on developing language specifying that private colleges and universities would share equally with the GI Bill program in the incremental cost of their tuition as compared with the highest public university

5

charge. Senator Warner called this difference "the delta." For example, if the private school tuition was $10,000 more than the highest public tuition, then the school would provide $5,000 of this difference and the GI Bill would match this amount. Schools would have the right to choose to participate or not. This option became known as the Yellow Ribbon Program.

Despite public support, there was substantial political resistance initially to this overall more supportive GI Bill from members of Congress and from the George W. Bush administration—the Pentagon especially was concerned that a GI Bill that was "too attractive" might result in lower reenlistment rates. I responded that the GI Bill was a recognition of service and while it might encourage higher enlistment rates, it should not be considered a personnel management tool to keep veterans in the service. The service branches should provide opportunities that made reenlistment attractive and should not depend upon the absence of opportunities in the civilian world.

Ultimately the legislation was amended so that those who reenlisted and potentially made a career of the military could pass the benefit to their spouse or children. In June 2008 President Bush signed the Post-9/11 GI Bill. In the summer of 2017 Congress approved an extension of the bill and expanded some benefits and options. One recent report indicated that over 1 million veterans have used the program for their education.

I continued visiting the hospitals until 2013, by which time very few battle casualties were being admitted. That was the good news. But the broader issue remained of encouraging veterans to continue their education. The GI Bill may have provided important financial support, but it turned out that the major remaining obstacle was to encourage veterans to take advantage of this program, to assure them that they were academically prepared to continue their education. Some of these veterans did not come from areas where the common path was to go on to college. They seldom had thought about this option while in secondary schools—their course of study often had not included any of the common college preparatory courses and they likely had not taken any of the standardized college admission tests. I emphasized to them that this was okay because through their studying and training in the military, they had already demonstrated the capacity to be a successful student at the college level. I encouraged those who were doubtful to enroll at a community college or school near their home to get comfortable with the classroom again and to become confident in their ability.

Given that the battle of Fallujah was the catalyst for my beginning this work, it was ironic that a veteran of that battle was an early contact and became a powerful example. I had visited him at Bethesda in the summer of 2005 when he was under medication and we could not have an extended conversation, so I left a card behind. Several weeks later he wrote me to say that he had been thinking about my visit and had decided that he wanted to continue his education—at Dartmouth. I was surprised because in these visits I never directly recruited for Dartmouth—I was not visiting hospitals as an advocate of my school but I aimed to be an advocate for these veterans, to encourage them to go on to school, wherever it was best for them.

So I told this young Marine, who was recovering from gunshot wounds suffered in a street battle, that he should go home and get well and perhaps enroll in some classes to reorient himself with academic work. He did this and after a semester he wrote me and said that he had enrolled and enjoyed the experience and had good grades. I told him he should go ahead and apply to Dartmouth if he was still interested—and that I would fly him up to the campus for a visit so he, a Louisianan, could decide if he would be comfortable coming to school in New Hampshire.

He did visit—along with two other Marines who had been in contact with me. They all applied and were admitted—I did not make any overtures to the admissions office on their behalf. They and four other veterans were the first group to enroll at Dartmouth in the fall of 2007.

Ironically, that young Marine whom I had met at Bethesda had served with and been a friend of the local Marine who had been killed at Fallujah. And compounding the irony, a few years later we enrolled a Marine veteran who had a Purple Heart that he had earned in that very same fight, an ambush inside of a building, where this Marine had died.

The number of enrolled veterans increased over the next two years and Dartmouth became a model for this initiative—but this was partially a default, a result of most other top schools not engaging in outreach and active recruitment to get veteran applicants. I spoke about this need—and opportunity—in some university president forums or meetings and quite frankly was disappointed in the reaction from many of my colleagues.

While most signed their school onto the Yellow Ribbon Program, they were not comfortable actively recruiting veterans. Each had full agendas, of course, and many things they were juggling, so while they were complimentary of my work with veterans, they did not want to take on this additional initiative themselves. That changed fortunately over the next several years.

In 2009 I stepped down from the Dartmouth presidency. In response to questions about my future plans I always replied that, no, I was not planning to write a book and, no, I was not going to teach. I was going to retire and the only thing I was certain about was that I was going to continue to work in support of veterans. I joined the board of the Semper Fi Fund that year, which gave me a place in one of the exemplary veteran service organizations.

I used to tell Dartmouth students that they should not try to lay out careful and structured life plans: that lives were to be lived rather than planned. No one could predict the twists and turns of life—or the opportunities that they would encounter. I should have learned this lesson myself. Over the next several years it turned out I did return to the classroom, teaching in consecutive years a history senior seminar on war and veterans, an experience I enjoyed immensely. And I did write a book about veterans in American history and began to write op-eds regarding our national debt and responsibility to those who have served. I followed this with a book about those who served in Vietnam. I continued to work in support of veterans, but this work took on a broader advocacy role.

My return to my roots as a historian began unintentionally in that first year following my presidential service. Because of my work with veterans, officers at the Vietnam Veterans Memorial Fund asked me if I would speak at the Vietnam Veterans Memorial in Washington on Veterans Day in 2009. I was honored to be invited and accepted the invitation with pleasure. Also, the chancellor of the University of California, Berkeley, asked me if I would deliver the annual Jefferson lecture there. His advisory committee had recommended that I might talk about my work with veterans over the previous five years.

Preparing for and delivering these two presentations challenged me to think more broadly about the state and status of veterans and the history of our nation's relationship with them. It also moved me to consider what

I might contribute to our national understanding of and our obligations to those who had served.

At the Vietnam Memorial on a cool and drizzly Veteran's Day morning in 2009, I was struck by the number of Vietnam veterans who assembled there. And I was moved by looking at the front rows in which were seated Gold Star mothers, there to remember their sons and daughters. I spoke to them about a couple of names on the wall and described who they were, and reminded everyone that we had an obligation to make certain that others remember that these were more than names engraved in stone. These markings represented individuals whose lives were full of dreams and plans. Collectively and individually, they tallied the human cost of war. I knew after this experience that I wanted to work to remember the human face and cost of war. And to remind others of these inevitable consequences.

At the University of California in Berkeley early in 2010 I decided to do more than describe my work with veterans. I told the organizers that I was a historian and wanted to look at veterans in American history—who they were and how we recognized them. Or failed to recognize them. This had not been my area of scholarship and I was interested in learning more about this history, this legacy. In my presentation I talked some about Vietnam veterans, fully aware that I was doing this on a campus that forty-some years earlier had been a center of antiwar protests. This audience included local Vietnam veterans as well as veterans of the antiwar movement—and many, a majority surely, who had no personal engagement in those distant debates. I concluded my survey of the subject by urging people to remember that: *"those who serve at risk on our behalf should never again feel that the gratitude of the Republic for their sacrifice is dependent upon the popularity of the war we have asked them to fight."*

I had not really focused at this point on what I would do next to support and encourage and remember veterans. But shortly after the Berkeley program I was having a conversation with a good friend, a historian, and spoke of my frustration in discovering while preparing that lecture that there was no updated overview of the public perception and treatment of veterans in American history. She told me that I had expressed this several times so that maybe it was time to quit complaining and write such a book myself. That conversation became the catalyst for my work on and publication of the book *Those Who Have Borne the Battle: A History of America's Wars and Those Who Fought Them* (Public Affairs Press, 2012).

Writing that book expanded greatly my knowledge and understanding. And it focused my work more sharply. While working on the chapter about the Vietnam War, I recognized a story there that I really wished to learn and to tell in greater detail. My personal evolution over those years in the 1960s had moved from supportive veteran to critic of the war, along with my recognition that those who served there had seldom been recognized as anything other than drugged-up psychotic accomplices in an ill-advised war, or as drafted victims of a war machine. As veterans they had been too often pariahs or embarrassing reminders. I thought their generation deserved better.

So I set out to write a book that would focus on those who had served there—and those who had sacrificed in the war. My focus was on the Vietnam combat experience. I interviewed veterans and family members. I read personal accounts and recollections. And I went to Vietnam and walked the battlefields. I dedicated my book *Enduring Vietnam: An American Generation and Its War* (St. Martin's Press: Thomas Dunne Books, 2017) to those who served: *"The difficulty of this American generation's war and the controversies it engendered made their willingness to serve, and the sacrifices that they made, the greater and not the lesser."*

In the book I remained as critical of those who sent the Baby Boomer generation off to this war as I had been in the 1960s. I pointed out the savagery of the war and the cost borne by Vietnamese civilians. But I also described the cost borne by those young Americans who served, mostly bravely and well, a cost that continued to tally well after they came home to an ungrateful nation. If they came home. My greatest satisfaction from the book has been the response I have received from the veterans of that war.

Along with these two books I was also publishing op-eds two or three times a year. This work, my seminar teaching, and a number of public lectures and events at universities and other forums moved me back to the history teacher phase of my professional life. But I was a history teacher with a sharp and constant focus and goal: I sought to remind readers and students of the cost of war, to introduce those who bore that cost, to encourage veterans to continue their education, and to point out the responsibility that citizens must assume to support those who serve on their behalf.

I have often reminded people of George Washington's insistence that every citizen owed financial support (taxes) and service to the defense of democracy. In the twenty-first century the vast majority of Americans have provided neither.

The All-Volunteer Force provided a highly professional military. But it was not one that most Americans knew or, quite frankly other than brief acknowledgment, wished to know much about. This was a challenge for an old teacher, a challenge involving much more than a class in a seminar room. I wanted people to understand what it was we were asking these servicemen and -women to do. And what our responsibility to them was.

This book provides a compilation of some of my presentations in this effort to explain, to teach, to prod. Each individually picks up on a theme or experience or reflects on some anniversary or marker. Together they tell a story, a series of stories, of forgotten veterans of a forgotten war, the Korean War, of the need to come to terms with the sacrifice of the Vietnam generation, and of the hidden costs and consequences of those who have served, too anonymously, in this century's wars as part of the nation's all-volunteer military force.

The pieces that follow are separated into five major categories. The first, "Reflections," shares some more personal, autobiographical writings that describe my own background as a veteran. In these accounts I reflect upon my experiences, my journey, personal and intellectual, to a commitment to work as an advocate for and as a student of veterans in America.

The next group is about "Advocacy," and focuses on reminders of the shared obligation we have to provide educational encouragement and general support for returning veterans. This advocacy and counseling work was my major focus in the period before 2009, and I have continued to remind citizens and public officials of our debt and responsibility. I include here my welcome and salute to a group of student veterans when I spoke to them at a national meeting in 2019. In this piece I remind them that their service is not finished. Our republic, our civic culture, needs citizens and difference makers who have demonstrated their willingness to step up and to serve.

The third group, "History Lessons," includes some of my work to understand better the veteran experience and to share some lessons from history. In these I sought to learn and then to remind readers of wars past, of the changing nature of war in my lifetime, and of the way we need to thank those who have served—and to remember those who did not return. It has become far too easy to ignore what they are doing, or to offer a quick "thank you for your service" acknowledgement. We must never forget that they are sacrificing on our behalf. I recall an interview that I had with a Vietnam veteran. He said that everyone ignored his service when he first came home. But now, he said, everyone wants to say, "thank you for your service." He observed that this was the equivalent of saying "God bless you" when someone sneezes. He pointed out that no one really thought God was going to extend a blessing to you for sneezing. And no one was really thanking him for his service. Each were learned recitations. Obviously, it is unfair to dismiss every expression of gratitude as a perfunctory salutation. But his skepticism, his cynicism, was well learned.

The fourth group, "Responsibilities," is a collection of articles and presentations that represent the convergence intellectually of my legacy as a veteran, my efforts as an advocate, and my training and perspective as a historian. They tell stories and offer reflections on America's wars from the Civil War to engagements in Syria. The causes of these wars and the strategies, or the absence of a military strategy, may vary, but the cost is constant. In these essays I do sometimes question the political decisions that lead to war. However, my theme is not antiwar but is about urging those who make decisions about engaging in war to think about the consequences. To recognize that once begun, they will have less control over the war's evolution. And I urge policymakers to consider the goals—and the means to meet these goals: if the objective is political and not military, what can the military accomplish?

The concluding section, "Challenges," features two of the book's newer essays and seeks to look forward in light of history, including recent events.

A STORY I HAVE TOLD a number of times illustrates and perhaps symbolizes why working with veterans is so important—and so satisfying. And why I persisted with all of the cajoling and nagging and encouraging that is described in this book. It is about climbing mountains together.

In 2009 as I was preparing to step down from the Dartmouth presidency, I determined that I wanted to climb Mount Moosilauke, a mountain to the northeast of the campus that the college owns and that is an important part of the Dartmouth story. In my fortieth year at the college, I decided it was time to do this. I was approaching age seventy but was relatively fit, or at least thought I was, and knew it was not considered a difficult climb—or, as I learned, it was those younger and/or more fit than I who thought so. My wife Susan signed on eagerly to go and I invited a few Dartmouth students and some friends to join us. Fourteen of us set out on a pleasant May morning, Memorial Day weekend, for this trek.

Among the students, I had invited two Marine veterans to climb with us. One of them was the Fallujah veteran whom I had first met at Bethesda in July 2005. He was doing well in his class work and insisted he was physically able to take on this hike. Before we began I joked to the two Marines that they had a special assignment: to remember that Marines don't abandon other Marines out along the trail!

Very quickly I realized that I was not in as good physical condition as I thought I was—and the trail was much steeper than I anticipated! This was not going to be just a walk in the woods. We each had a small backpack with some food and water and a few clothing items. Nothing substantial or heavy. But as I lagged at the end of our group, I saw these two Marines staying back with me and watching me. They had taken their assignment seriously! After a bit they asked if they could carry my pack. I replied dismissively: of course not, I could carry my own pack! A half hour later when they asked that question again, I quickly pulled off my pack and handed it to them.

We reached the summit, slowly but certainly. I slowed our pace but everyone was patient with me. And we all enjoyed the stunning 360-degree vista, from the Green Mountains of Vermont to the White Mountains and up to Franconia in New Hampshire. The trip back down was on a different trail, an old carriage road, and certainly easier. When we arrived back at the base lodge I sat for a few minutes in the shade of the lodge, looking up at the mountain with a new appreciation. And the Marine I had first met at the hospital came over and sat with me and returned my pack. I thanked him and as we looked up I asked if, when we first met in that hospital room four years earlier, he ever thought we would climb a mountain together— and that he would assist me, would carry my backpack. He acknowledged that he had not imagined such an outing.

Life is filled with mountains—and with surprises. I vowed that day never to climb a mountain again. I thought of that vow, along with the ones not to write a book and not to teach again, five years later when I stood at the top of Dong Ap Bia in Vietnam, the mountain that American soldiers knew as Hamburger Hill. I had climbed it with difficulty in the heat and humidity of late-summer Vietnam, along with an American veteran and two North Vietnamese Army veterans of the battle. I was as proud of doing this as I was of climbing Moosilauke, perhaps even more proud at age seventy-five. But my greatest pride in all of this was not my own modest physical accomplishments but comes from the pleasure of knowing that the young Marine who was wounded in Fallujah and climbed a mountain with me graduated from Dartmouth and completed medical school and is now an emergency room physician. He wanted to give back.

It is a good reminder of those who keep on giving: those veterans who served our country as volunteers still have much to contribute. And it is the responsibility of the rest of us to understand who they are and what they have done, and then to encourage them, to enable them to continue to contribute to the nation.

Semper Fidelis, "Always Faithful," is the motto of the Marine Corps. Marines and Marine veterans often express to each other this or the more common "Semper Fi" as a shared salute, a bond. But I have learned well that Semper Fidelis is more than a slogan: it is a commitment, a lifestyle, and it is a commitment that is extended to all, not only to other Marines. And this commitment to serve and to support is shared by many others. *E Pluribus Unum.*

I

REFLECTIONS

Cannons in the Park

2012

I GREW UP in Galena, Illinois, an old Mississippi River town that was settled in the early nineteenth century for its lead mines. While the mining continued, Galena evolved as a commercial port. By the first half of the twentieth century Galena was surrounded by farms and some viable zinc mines, but its days as a center of commerce were behind it. The Galena River tributary into the Mississippi filled in with so much sediment that steamboats no longer could come up to the warehouses and docks. It was and remains a historic town, remembered as Ulysses Grant's home at the beginning of the Civil War.

Within days of my birth in August 1939, World War II began in Europe. Though I am technically considered a member of the "Depression" generation, I believe there should be a special classification for those of us whose early childhood memories are of wartime mobilization rather than of the Great Depression.

In 1940 my father went to work at the Savanna Army Depot, a weapons proving ground and storage depot located some fifteen miles away. In 1943, thirty years old and the father of two, he was drafted into the Army. He reported in January 1944 and by August he was in Europe, serving in the 723rd Railway Operation Battalion in the northern France, Rhineland, and central European theaters. Eventually achieving the rank of sergeant, he received Bronze Battle Stars but was not directly involved in any hostile action.

I strain for a memory of him leaving—I do have an image of a train, I think at the Burlington Station in East Dubuque, Illinois. He and my mother were both crying. I clearly remember his return from Germany and his discharge in December 1945. He brought me a souvenir, a German military knife. I still have it but it has been in the back of a drawer ever since I learned the still-painful symbolism of the swastika shining on the handle.

My mother worked during the war in a defense plant that made batteries. I visited her there, a hot and dark place, heavy with black powder, where women sat at long benches doing things that were unclear to me. She would come home aching tired, literally black with the carbon dust, and would soak in the bathtub.

She and my brother and I saved recyclable goods and used ration books and even participated in air raid drills, with closed shades and all lights turned off. It was a war, but to a five-year-old, it became all part of normal life. I played with metal soldiers and built model airplanes—I was very proud of a P-61 Black Widow that I built and painted. I still have photographs of my brother, Bob, and me in military uniforms, one in which we were saluting, another of us holding toy rifles. I am sure my mother sent copies of these to my dad in Europe.

When she was free, my mother would walk with us across the old Green Street bridge to Grant Park. We would play there on the swings, the slide, and the seesaw. Overlooking this playground was the park's small manicured hill. A bronze statue of General Grant stood in the middle of the field on top, facing south, with places like Shiloh, Vicksburg, and Appomattox inscribed on the base. A large obelisk stood nearby, dedicated to all from the county who served in the Civil War. By one count, there were more than 2,900 men from a county with an 1860 population of slightly over 27,000.

Several cannons sat on the edges of the hill, war trophies from the Spanish-American War, World War I, and, of course the Civil War. These were always magnets to children and I was no exception. We climbed and played on the cannons as much as on the playground equipment.

Later I would learn more about these weapons. The small cannon, a Blakely Rifle, was the first rifled cannon used in battle in the United States when South Carolina batteries fired it on Fort Sumter in Charleston Harbor on April 12, 1861. The Confederate Army used the cannon until near the end of the war, when it was captured by General William Sherman. A Galena Lead Mine Regiment served with Sherman when he took the weapon at Cheraw, South Carolina. At the initiative of one of these Galena veterans, the Blakely found a home in Galena thirty years later, a trophy in the park honoring General Grant.

When we walked to the park we had to cross Illinois Central Railroad tracks. A one-armed crossing guard stood there in a little booth, and would hold up a sign telling pedestrians to stop or proceed. His name was Jake Gunn. He had lost an arm as a young man in a railroad accident, and it seemed natural to learn that he had once met General Grant. Eight other Galenians served as generals in the Civil War, an impressive contribution from a city that then had some eight thousand people. History seemed to hang around.

I had a sense that all of the fathers in Galena were in the armed forces during World War II. Then it seemed that they all came home at once, with a tremendous sense of energy and enthusiasm. Except for those who didn't return. Of the 798 Galenians who served during the war, eighteen died, a substantial sacrifice for a small town then of 4,100 people. The 1940 census recorded that there were only 580 males between the ages of fifteen and thirty-four living in Galena. A number of the men who served and those who were casualties obviously were from nearby farms and rural communities, identified as Galenians but not counted there for census purposes. By any count, of those who had gone to war, many had made the ultimate sacrifice.

Few of the returning veterans, including my father, talked much about the war. Some had served with the Army or the Marines on the Pacific islands, some went ashore on D-Day and fought at Bastogne, while others parachuted behind lines or had been shot down and captured by Germans, or engaged in naval battles. I would learn of this later, from others, seldom from the men themselves. They were neither teaching about war nor really talking about it. Perhaps because of this, I retain a vivid image of one soldier who had served in Europe showing a few of us some horrifying photos he took when his unit liberated a concentration camp.

When I reflect on this now, I think of how natural it all seemed to be in a community of veterans. There was little sense of militarism or of taking pleasure in war. It was simply part of our history, our culture perhaps, and our life. I would later understand that small midwestern cities such as Galena had always recorded high proportions of their young citizens serving the nation's wars.

FOR MY CULTURE and my time, joining the military was a natural step. The Cold War shaped an expectation of war with the Soviet Union or other Communist countries. We had been conditioned by the nuns at St. Michael's and by the newspapers to prepare for conflict. The draft provided one major tangible reminder of this preparation. One scholar, George Flynn, said that among young American men, serving in the military was "close to universal through 1958."[1]

Certainly what we called "going into the service" was a normal rite of passage, more so perhaps for those of us who had never really thought of continuing our education. It was a part of the transition from boyhood to manhood—and it was clearly a pathway on which few girls could walk. Military service seemed a normal choice, along with sports teams, the pool hall, job opportunities in factory, farm, or mine. This all reinforced the male-dominated culture. Moreover, there seemed to be few interesting options available to me. No one in my family had a college degree and in my school days I had no expectation of continuing to college.

With a peacetime draft still in operation, we had an incentive to enlist at a time of our choosing and in a preferred service. I knew I wanted to be a Marine. Of my 1957 Galena High School graduating class of sixty graduates, twenty-five of us were boys; five joined the Marines, just a few weeks following our graduation. I was seventeen. Six of my classmates joined the Army, the Navy, and the Air Force. That number of eleven was far more than the four or five boys from the Class of 1957 who went to college, at least immediately out of high school.... I have a picture of the five Galena Marines posing at the Iwo Jima Memorial in Arlington, Virginia, as part of our high school class trip to Washington, D.C.

This was all part of the culture of the post–World War II years. Ron Kovic wrote that when he met the Marine recruiters in their dress-blue uniforms on Long Island, it was "like all the movies and all the books and all the dreams of becoming a hero come true."[2] Philip Caputo grew up in suburban Chicago and recalled that joining the Marine Corps "symbolized an opportunity for personal freedom and independence."[3] In the pre-Vietnam years there was little thought of cost or consequence. Caputo and Kovic would encounter serious levels of each. My generation, just a few years older, did not. No one ever fired a shot at me and I never had to fire at anyone. Just three years after I joined the Marines, my younger brother enlisted in the Navy; he was also seventeen years old and just out of high school.

As a Marine, I certainly stayed out of trouble and followed the rules, even if I found them often petty and learned that some of the non-commissioned officers I met enjoyed being petty. I resented for years a particularly cruel and stupid drill instructor I had. In time, I achieved the rank of lance corporal, not very rapidly, nor with much distinction. A strength of the Marine Corps has been its training and discipline; sharpening these things in peacetime, while an essential activity, was boring at best.

It was only with later reflection that I realized what a critical and empowering interlude this was for me. While at Keesler Air Force Base in Biloxi, Mississippi, I flinched at the embedded racism of Mississippi in the late 1950s. My unit, Marine Air Group-13 of the 1st Marine Brigade, was stationed at Kaneohe Bay, Hawaii; we were shipped out on an LST (a U.S. Naval vessel, Landing Ship, Tank), the *Tioga County*, LST 1158, on temporary deployment in Atsugi, Japan, during the Quemoy-Matsu crisis of 1958.

From Atsugi, I was able to watch occupied Japan begin to step with some assurance into a new world. I saw this from a base that still had underground facilities from its service for Imperial Japan during World War II, including a training base for Kamikaze pilots. I watched U-2 planes take off from the base for "weather reconnaissance," and I would learn a few years later that the squadron my unit replaced, Marine Air Control Squadron-1, of Marine Air Group-11, was the outfit to which Lee Harvey Oswald was assigned. I was in his barracks while he was down in Taiwan—shortly afterward, he would go home. My unit returned to Oahu, again via an uncomfortable and crowded LST (the *Tom Green County*, LST 1159) in time for the celebration of Hawaiian statehood on Waikiki Beach.

In my formative late teen years, I saw much of the world. I encountered racism in a Marine Corps that was still dealing with desegregation. I also met and developed friendships with young Marines from all over the country and I served under some impressive officers and non-commissioned officers who had been in World War II and in Korea. I developed a sense of discipline and self-confidence, the ability to work within and with a group toward common goals—although surely my St. Michael's School nuns had taught me self-discipline as effectively as any Marine drill instructor!

When I joined the Marines I had no real life plans. I thought this experience would give me a few years to put off working in the local mines or factories. I never had any expectation of staying in the Marines for a career. This reflected the culture of the time: if most of us expected to serve, very few thought of doing so for any more than the minimum time required.

One of my high school classmates stayed in the Air Force for a career. Other than him I knew very few from Galena who served for more than their original enlistment. The military was part of our life, but only briefly.

When I was discharged after three years, still not twenty-one years of age, I decided I would go to college. I was curious to learn and I was eager to explore. Once I started going to school I never stopped. I enjoyed history and thought I would like to be a high school history teacher. I worked hard and turned out to be a good student. Faculty encouraged me to think of a doctorate and upon graduation I received a Danforth Fellowship. In 1964 I commenced a graduate program in American history at the University of Wisconsin, Madison.

IN THE SUMMER before I went to Madison for graduate study I was working in the Birkett mine as a powderman, setting dynamite charges. My ground boss had persuaded me to do this, saying a former Marine must surely know how to handle dynamite; I assured him I had never touched it. He said I could learn and the clincher was when he offered me twenty cents more an hour, $2.35, for the assignment. I left the backer position on the drill machine and picked up a handmade powder knife. We had our lunch breaks underground and in August of that summer I recall that we talked briefly about the reported attacks on U.S. Naval vessels in the Tonkin Gulf of Vietnam. The other miners expressed general support but not much real interest when the Americans hammered coastal North Vietnam with air attacks. I basically shared these feelings, but not in any reflective way.

During my first year at Madison, the Vietnam War ramped up significantly. I do not recall any strong reactions when President Lyndon Johnson sent some Marines ashore at Da Nang in March 1965, the first introduction of American combat troops to Vietnam. Within a short time, however, Madison was roiled by protests against the war. My own view evolved from apprehension to concern, and then to opposition. I did not join actively in protests; I was older and was focused on my program, but I was sympathetic with these activities. David Maraniss in his book *They Marched into Sunlight* captured well the on-campus emotions and views in those years. I knew several of the former students he had interviewed and remember vividly the demonstrations.

By 1967 I had turned strongly against the war because it seemed so strategically wrong and so horrible in its casualties. I never joined in any criticism of the U.S. forces serving; I was concerned about them and what they were being asked to do. I was worried about the Marines encircled at Khe Sanh and in fact wondered if I knew any of them. Later it was easy—I would say essential—to criticize Lieutenant William Calley and his platoon. But I never assumed that they were truly representative.

WARS ARE by and large transitory things, occasional distractions perhaps, for those who are not fighting them and whose loved ones are not fighting. The less realistic the broader society's image is of combat, the easier it is for society to put the reality of war behind. What is missing, then, is a clear understanding of what society has imposed upon some of its young citizens, what their countrymen have asked of them. Those who served will not put it behind.

War is about national strategy and national defense and patriotic pride and geopolitical calculations. And it is about misunderstandings and miscalculations, stupidity and malice, and sometimes about the consequences of accidents. War is about strategic agendas and epic battles that define nations and shape history. War is about courage and heroism, but it is also about pain and suffering and sorrow and tragedy. But combat, the process of actually fighting a war in the dirt and the mud, in airplanes, or upon ships at sea, is about those who finally are sent out to implement these national strategies—and they have more immediate concerns than the national goals or considerations.

People in combat become consumed with tactical problems and personal needs. In the final accounting, combat becomes intensely personal. Within the framework of an immediate tactical military objective, within a military unit with clear hierarchy and crisp differentiation of authority and of responsibility, combat is about simply staying alive, about protecting and aiding those in your unit, and about deadly confrontations with those who share with you the impulse for their own self-preservation. A study of those who fought in America's wars confirms the constant "overriding desire to survive" regardless of the purpose of war or nature of combat.[4]

Most veterans attribute their ability to engage in combat to simple fear as well as pride—no one wants to let others down or appear to be wanting in the necessary courage to engage. It is essential to suppress reason, at least civilian reason. Karl Marlantes served in Vietnam as a much-decorated Marine officer who received two Purple Hearts and a Navy Cross. In his book *Matterhorn* he wrote of yet another order to take yet another hill from the North Vietnamese army: "It was all absurd, without reason or meaning. People who didn't even know each other were going to kill each other over a hill none of them cared about." The main protagonist, Second Lieutenant Waino Mellas, admitted that he "couldn't figure out why they didn't just quit." In a statement of resolution, or resignation, or simple inertia, that has echoed from combat since the Trojan War, Mellas already knew the response, his and his men's, to the question about quitting: "Yet they wouldn't."[5]

Combat veterans then return home. They must suppress their combat experiences in order to successfully return to civil society. But even if they are successfully suppressed, they cannot be forgotten. Each of these tasks of learning and unlearning comes at some cost and the cost is an intensely personal one that is not borne by society.

AMERICA'S COMBAT VETERANS have been called up from their civilian lives to do what were sometimes remarkable and sometimes distasteful, and always dangerous, things. They have served and too often been forgotten, except as abstractions or as historic stick figures. Their families and neighbors know them of course as real persons—even as they seldom truly know what it was these real persons just experienced. Since 1973, in the era of the All-Volunteer Force, when the military is an even smaller percentage and less representative part of our population, firsthand experience with the armed forces is even more rare. Fewer families and fewer neighborhoods know anyone who has served in the current wars.

IN A DECEMBER 2009 visit to American troops in Iraq and Afghanistan, Secretary of Defense Robert Gates said to troops near Kirkuk, Iraq, "One of the myths in the international community is that the United States likes war. And the reality is, other than the first two or three years of World War II, there has never been a popular war in America."[6] Each war in American history had support at the outset, although there has also been major opposition to each, excepting World War II. That war likely sustained support until the end, although costs and goals gradually became a little less clear in the public mind. In any event, in a democracy, wars need to maintain public support in order to be sustained; the idea of "popular wars" might best be left to fiction or to totalitarian regimes.

WHEN THE BLAKELY CANNON was formally accepted at Grant Park in Galena in 1896, one of the park commissioners noted that these monuments were a "sure means of keeping alive the martial spirit which has been awakened by past triumphs."[7] It is not clear that the cannon ever evoked such feelings. They did not for me and for my generation. Cannons rest quietly in many parks in many places in the United States. They are souvenirs and trophies. But removed from their bloody context and spiked from ever again thundering their lethal intent, they are as silent as statuary and as inviting as playground equipment. They also should serve as reminders that war can touch quiet places and peaceful communities.

These weapons say little about the horror of war, but juxtaposed upon our peaceful playgrounds and parks, they whisper that it is best to remember some things that many would prefer to forget, or even never to learn. Let the children play, but also allow the rusting ordnance to provide quiet reminders. Wars are not games and they surely are not pleasant experiences for those who fight them. This book seeks to help us to remember that.

NOTES

1. George Q. Flynn, *The Draft, 1940–1973* (Lawrence: University Press of Kansas, 1993), 230.

2. Ron Kovic, *Born on the Fourth of July* (New York: McGraw Hill, 1977), 73. Even though Ron Kovic is several years younger than I am, his chapter 2 seems so similar in many ways to my experience, but obviously my boyhood was more rural. And of course my military service was not marked by the horror and sacrifice that his was.

3. Philip Caputo, *A Rumor of War* (New York: Holt, Rinehart and Winston, 1977), 8.

4. Christopher H. Hamner, *Enduring Battle: American Soldiers in Three Wars, 1776–1945* (Lawrence: University Press of Kansas, 2011), 207. For a recent personal account of this experience, see Karl Marlantes, *What It Is Like to Go to War* (New York: Atlantic Monthly Press, 2011).

5. Karl Marlantes, *Matterhorn: A Novel of the Vietnam War* (New York: Atlantic Monthly Press with Berkeley, CA: El Leon Literary Arts, 2010), 343.

6. Quoted in Elisabeth Bumiller's article "Defense Secretary's Trip Encounters Snag in Two Theaters," *New York Times*, December 13, 2009.

7. Galena and U. S. Grant Museum website: https://www.galenahistory.org/research/civil-war/the-blakely-of-grant-park/ (accessed August 1, 2011).

The Old Corps:
Boot Camp Memories

June 2021

I ENLISTED IN the Marine Corps with four of my classmates and friends in June of 1957, just a few weeks after graduating from Galena High School, Galena, Illinois. It seemed a natural and an exciting step at the time. We thought we were ready. The Marines were an important part of our culture. We had all been impressed by the stories of the seven or eight boys from the Galena class of 1953 who had joined the Marines. We were brought up on the John Wayne, *Sands of Iwo Jima* culture and, if not great readers, we had all read Leon Uris's *Battle Cry* and had seen the movie with Aldo Ray and Tab Hunter and watched the depiction of battles at places like Guadalcanal and Tarawa. At age eleven, I had been moved by newspaper accounts of the Marines fighting their way out of the Chosin Reservoir during the Korean War.

In that early summer of 1957, we were set to go—although none of us knew exactly what we were going to do. We weren't marching off to war. It was peacetime. I just knew it would be an exciting interlude before I went to work in the mines or a similar life. And in our time and culture it was both a rite of passage and an honoring of a commitment to serve.

The nearest Marine Corps recruiting office was in Dubuque, Iowa, across the Mississippi River from Galena. The Mississippi essentially divided Marine boot camp assignments—those enlisting from west of the river were sent to the Marine Corps Recruit Depot (MCRD) in San Diego and most of those to the east of the river were assigned to Parris Island, South Carolina. The latter was the more famous place, more infamous, organized as a recruit-training base prior to World War I. San Diego was established following that war and was a major recruit-training facility during World War II. As Dubuque enlistees, we were heading to California.

We flew out of Des Moines, Iowa, on a charter plane as part of a group of around sixty recruits—a special Iowa platoon. Before leaving we watched the Iowa premiere of the movie *The D.I.*, starring Jack Webb as a tough drill instructor, which gave us all something to think about on that long plane ride. I had never been on a plane before and I doubt that many others in our group had. It was an overnight flight, with a stop in Tulsa for refueling.

We arrived in San Diego at dawn. Marine green buses were there to take us to the base. And when we stepped down from the buses, wiry Marine NCOs started shouting at us to move. The shouting never stopped. Nor did the moving. Those first days were a blur of physical exams, haircuts that left us bald, standing in lines to receive Marine utility uniforms and basic supplies, orientation sessions, and mailing all of our civilian clothes and belongings back home.

Then we were moved as a group to the Quonset huts that would be our homes. Our drill instructors met us and greeted us with undisguised contempt. They told us how inconsequential we were—"maggots" and "shitbirds" were common descriptions—and they regularly shared their despair in their assignment, the hopeless task of turning us into Real Marines. We were shouted into lines and ordered to run as a group from place to place. We learned to shout back, "Sir! Yes Sir!" to every command. And over the next days we were drilled repeatedly on the basic steps of marching sharply and perfectly coordinated as a group.

We learned how to make the beds on our flimsy bunks. The drill instructors showed us the showers and the toilets and taught us how to use them properly. They showed us the laundry racks. They marched us to meals at the chow hall and hurried us through these brief refuelings. We were surrounded by sand and glaring sun and heat. We slept lightly and were roughly wakened by a drill instructor beating on a trash can and shouting before dawn. We were forced to write home regularly—and assure everyone that all was well. And we waited so eagerly for "mail call," when letters from family and friends would sometimes bring tears to our eyes. We missed them more than we had ever anticipated.

The drill instructors were consistently unpleasant—really quite nasty. The physical conditioning, the learning to march correctly, the pace of the days, were overwhelming. There were no "well done" acknowledgments but instead constant reminders of how few, if any of us, were capable of being

Marines. The drill instructors emphasized that in combat Marines had to depend upon each other—and that they would never want to depend on any of us. Obviously breaking down our sense of go-it-alone independence and teaching us an instinctive, confident, we-can-count-on-each-other interdependence was their goal.

There was physical intimidation and some abuse. Drill instructors would push and hit recruits on the arm or back, occasionally slapping them. The only response was "Sir! Yes Sir." And perhaps a scripted confession was insisted upon: "Sir! Private Wright is a screw-up that does not know how to march. Sir." There was no place in the dialogue for excuse, explanation, and surely not for argument.

Over sixty years later, I still recall one incident very well. I was in the Duty Hut—the home base of the DIs, when one of the assistant DIs, a wiry bully of a sergeant, said, "Wright, get me a cup of coffee." There was a coffee urn and cups nearby. I brought a cup to him, but I carried it by the rim rather than the handle. He looked at me with feigned horror: "You fucking asshole, you fuck-up, look at you holding the cup with your filthy hands around the rim where I will drink. I will not drink anything that has been touched by your filthy fucking hands." He took the cup and held it over my head and dumped the hot coffee on my head. Then he told me to get the fuck out of there and put on a clean utility uniform.

I left the Duty Hut nearly in tears. Not from the pain—the coffee had been hot but not scalding—but more in humiliation and anger. This drill instructor never let up on me—he punished me regularly and hit me often. And in our second week of boot camp we were all required to take a physical fitness test. Failing the test meant that you were sent to a special fitness platoon where you stayed until you could pass the test and then you were reassigned to a different training platoon. Anyone who missed more than a few days of training for whatever reason was "set back" to another platoon.

At our fitness test, the drill instructor who poured the coffee on me watched me and hounded me. He held onto my belt when I tried to do the required pull ups. And he took the score cards we carried and changed my score. It was certainly the case that I was not in great physical condition. But he made certain that I failed the test. I still recall packing up to leave my Quonset hut to be marched to the fitness platoon. My four Galena friends could not really say goodbye because such things were not permitted. They nodded or winked or gestured. I was again on the verge of tears and they were clearly saddened.

I spent the minimum three days in the Special Fitness unit and, with no impediments, immediately passed the test and then was assigned to a new recruit platoon, one week behind my original platoon. We marched and ran and scurried through obstacle courses. We had classroom sessions on all aspects of our training and on Marine Corps history. We were finally issued M-1 rifles—no ammunition, of course, and these rifles were kept in an armory rack in one of the huts. But we learned all about the weapon: I still recall the description we learned to recite about these special pieces of equipment: a gas-operated, air-cooled, clip-fed, semi-automatic, shoulder weapon. We learned especially how to keep it clean. We were reminded that our lives could depend upon us having a clean and functioning weapon. And even more importantly, the Marines with whom we served were depending upon us and the functioning of our weapon. We learned to disassemble and reassemble the rifles, including finally with our eyes blindfolded. I sometimes imagine I could still do this with an M-1.

In the fourth week we left San Diego to go to Camp Matthews. Above the small town of La Jolla, this was the home of the Marine rifle ranges. Camp Matthews was a tent encampment. Hilly and windy and hot and sandy. It had been the training site for the Marine Raiders during World War II and not much had changed in the twelve years since that war. We marched and duckwalked up the hills—I recall two of them that Marines knew as "Little Agony" and "Big Agony." Duckwalking or running in cadence up these hills was agony. We learned to do it almost effortlessly.

(An aside—Camp Matthews is now the site of the campus for the University of California, San Diego. When I visited there some years ago a faculty friend who was hosting me took me on a tour. We found the two Agonies! And the old mess hall/administration building remained as some sort of campus facility.)

Camp Matthews was a better experience than the routine of the Recruit Depot. We were focused on our weapons and how to use them. We finally were able to fire them—and needed to clean them perfectly after use. I was not a good shot as it turned out, somewhat surprisingly. I had grown up hunting around Galena—squirrels, rabbits, ducks. But always with shotguns. The controlled careful squeeze of the trigger on the M-1 was a different experience. I never really mastered it until on a rifle range at Camp Zama in Japan a year and a half later.

At Camp Matthews I had my second setback. It was a Sunday afternoon, perhaps in my second week there, that we had an organized "game." It was a physical competition and one of the tests was called "chicken fighting." I had a smaller Marine riding on my shoulders and we competed against another pair, with the goal of pulling the competitors down to the ground. We were pulled down and my nose slammed against my own knee, a trauma increased by the weight of the person on my shoulders. I bled badly and my nose was clearly deformed. The drill instructor took me to sick bay where I was diagnosed with a broken nose and they decided to send me to Balboa Naval Hospital in San Diego. So, I packed up and left another platoon.

The three or four days at Balboa were like a vacation. Clean and comfortable beds. Ice-cold Coca Cola, and time to sit around. But at the end of this interlude I was hauled back to Camp Matthews and assigned to another platoon, this one a week earlier than mine in the schedule. So I had to meet new people again—not that anyone really had the opportunity to form friendships in the highly regulated routine of boot camp. We finished our three weeks at the rifle range and went back to San Diego not by buses but by marching down. It was probably ten or twelve miles and I recall that buses took us the last three or four miles rather than marching through the city streets.

The last stretch of boot camp was different—after the rifle ranges the drill instructors treated us a little differently (of course I was with my third set of drill instructors!). We marched more crisply, proudly synchronized, and were allowed to shine the buckles on our boots and wear our utility trousers bloused at the top of the boot. We learned to chant as we marched, in time with the cadence of "Heels. Heels. Heels." We sang the popular song, "Honey Babe," often with improvised lyrics. Our DI even arranged for us to be recorded, marching, heavy heels in unison, and singing an adaption of the old Scottish ballad: "Drums in my heart are drummin' / I hear the Corps a'coming / My bonnie Gyrene Corps is comin' for me." There was a greater sense of pride. Maybe we would be real Marines after all.

We had some more advanced training—including introductions to such things as hand-to-hand combat. This was quite an experience as well. Many of the instructors were small and wiry, athletic, tough, and fit. And their emphasis was that with the right techniques you could handle someone bigger than you. So they often pulled me out of the ranks as one of the bigger recruits to demonstrate this. They would taunt, "So—hit me!" And I would start the motion to do this and suddenly find myself on the ground or in a painful hold from my smaller opponent.

We also had bayonet training—using pugil sticks, padded sticks that we learned to swing and thrust and poke at and push our opponents. The obstacle courses became harder—but we seemed to handle them better. The runs were longer but we seemed to be able to run longer. The only occasional acknowledgment of a good routine was that the drill instructor would order us "At Ease!" And then say, "The Smoking Lamp is Lit." This meant everyone could light up a cigarette. And most of the members of the platoon smoked. I did not—both of my parents did, most of my classmates in high school did, including the four guys that joined the Marines with me. Then even though I had never liked cigarettes, in boot camp I irrationally decided that this was the only treat we received. So I started smoking. Cigarettes were a dime a pack in the PX. There were no filter cigarettes then so when we would finish a cigarette we would "field strip" it—tearing the paper off of it and letting the unsmoked tobacco float down to the sand. We would wad up the paper and put it in the sand, where it would decompose.

Even after Camp Matthews, boot camp remained a physically challenging experience. We were all in better condition than we had ever been in our lives. It was not enough. Punishments, individual or platoon-wide, included being forced to run to exhaustion. And then some more. Pushups—"Give me twenty-five!" Duckwalking and wall sits or squats. Even when one individual was guilty of a misstep, the punishment generally was aimed at the entire platoon. We were taught that each of us was responsible for the entire group. Drill instructors trained us relentlessly and they continued to strike and push at us.

It was an interesting time in the Marine Corps. The year before there had been an incident at Ribbon Creek at Parris Island when a Marine Drill instructor took his platoon on a night march down to the marshes. Six recruits drowned that night and there was a major investigation of the incident and a controversy about how drill instructors treated recruits.

Old Marine heroes like Chesty Puller came forward and said it was essential that Marines learn discipline. But the Marine Corps did upgrade its training of drill instructors and attempted to regulate the procedures better. My drill instructors resented this.

I recall on the night or so before our graduation from boot camp our drill instructor, a veteran of the Chosin Reservoir, talked about this new order of things and said that they were pushing them to make us "pussies" rather than Marines, but that he was always going to make his recruits Marines regardless of what the paper pushers said. He dismissively said that now the rules makers were saying they couldn't even hit recruits. He walked down the ranks and asked some of the Marines there if he had ever hit them. When he came to me, he started to ask that question, then he stopped and laughed and said he didn't need to ask me that. He had struck me a number of times. I never saw anyone punched in the face with a fist, but I often experienced slaps or shoves or punches to the stomach that doubled me over in winded pain.

One postscript to the experience. I was in my last week or so of boot camp when I was in the Duty Hut and there, laughing and talking to my current drill instructor, was the one who in my first platoon had dumped the coffee on my head. He noticed me and remembered me. He said, "Hey, Private Wright, have you learned how to serve a cup of coffee?" I replied, "Sir. Yes Sir." And he said, "Well, let us see—get me a cup." I went to the back where the coffee urn was and got him a cup and brought it to him, holding it properly by the handle. He said, "Well, I guess you have learned one thing in boot camp, you fucking Screw." I was dismissed. As I walked out, I carried a very, very gratified inner smile. When I had gotten his cup of coffee in the back of the hut, I had spat in the coffee.

On graduation day, we marched proudly in review on the parade field, the "Big Grinder," and graduated from boot camp. Then carrying all belongings in our seabags, we boarded buses to go to Camp Pendleton for three weeks of intensive infantry training. It would be a rigorous and physically demanding exercise. But after boot camp we were considered Marines—the emotional abuse and bullying were over. Mine had been a thirteen-week experience rather than the regular eleven-week program.

Inconsistent as it may seem given my experience, I took pride in doing this, in being a Marine. In many ways the natural reaction probably of a teenage boy who had been subjected to a very intense physical and emotional ordeal and had completed it well, physically fit, disciplined, and proud.

Fifty-five years after I graduated from boot camp I was invited back to Marine Corps Recruit Depot, San Diego, where I was honored to serve as a Parade Review officer for a graduating class. I spent part of the day touring the place. Few things were familiar. The Quonset huts had been replaced by modern barracks.

There were still pugil stick exercises—I asked the Marine leading the tour why they still did this. I said I doubted that Marines had fixed bayonets for battle in a long time and surely were not doing it today. He replied that it was a different generation: that recruits of my era had grown up in a world that was more physical, marked by more fighting and scuffling and rough games. Today, he said, many of the current recruits had probably never been in a fight, so this was to get them used to hitting someone and being hit. Certainly, the young recruits I watched were exchanging heavy blows.

Before the graduation parade I was taken to meet the commanding general of the MCRD. We had a very pleasant conversation. I said to him that fifty-five years ago I had gotten on a bus to ride out of that gate and I vowed, "I will never set foot on this fucking place again." I asked him if fifty-five years was sufficient to meet a pledge of never again. He smiled and said that, yes, he thought it was. And he welcomed me back to MCRD. I was pleased to be there.

Visiting Vietnam

2017

IN EARLY SEPTEMBER 2014, I stood at the top of Dong Ap Bia in Vietnam's A Shau Valley. Bordering Laos in the northwestern part of the old South Vietnam, this steep and imposing mountain was Hill 937 on U.S. military maps from the Vietnam War period. Local Montagnard tribesmen called it "the Crouching Beast." The American soldiers who fought there knew it as "Hamburger Hill."

For eleven days in May 1969, units of the 101st Airborne Division had fought North Vietnamese regulars, largely from the 29th Regiment but also the 6th and 9th Regiments, for control of this hill. Today there is a memorial at the top placed there in 2009 by the Socialist Republic of Vietnam celebrating "a victorious place." Yet in fact it wasn't their victory, at least not then, not in that battle. The Americans prevailed, but the North Vietnamese returned. Six years later they would occupy Saigon and win the war.

I was on the hill forty-five years later because I was writing this book on the Vietnam War. I was part of a very small group that included two North Vietnamese Army (NVA) veterans of this 1969 battle. I had met them that morning in the nearby village of A Luoi, and they quickly accepted my invitation to join me in a climb of Dong Ap Bia. Our group also included an American army veteran who had served there at this time but not in this battle, as well as two young Vietnamese men. One was the son of a southern Vietnamese man who fought with the National Liberation Front (NLF), known as the Viet Cong, and the other the son of a soldier with the South Vietnamese Army, the Army of the Republic of Vietnam.[1] The latter had spent some time in a reeducation camp after the war ended. I had been traveling through Vietnam battle sites because I wanted to see the places where Americans fought, especially in May and June 1969.

The contrasts between that distant war and modern Vietnam are everywhere. At Cu Chi, the extensive old tunnels are preserved as a tourist attraction, and there is a gruesome display of punji stick traps and other devices used against the Americans. The old airstrip at Dak To in the Highlands, where the 299th Engineers had fought against North Vietnamese forces based in Cambodia, is still desolate, barren and deteriorating. The bunker where nine American soldiers died had been filled and leveled, with manioc growing nearby and local farmers drying it on the old runway. Mutter's Ridge up above Highway 9 continues to be a forbidding-looking place, in the midst of equally forbidding places, known by Americans who fought there as Razorback and the Rockpile.

Outside Hanoi, on the street adjacent to the lake where jagged fragments of a B-52 remain jutting from the water, is a restaurant called Cafe B52. In English, the sign promised that inside, in addition to coffee, wi-fi was available. And south of Da Nang, a cemetery is at the spot on the road where an army chaplain and five others died when their vehicle struck a mine in June 1969. This cemetery contains and celebrates the remains of National Liberation Front and North Vietnamese Army soldiers who died in the "American War."

Southwest of Da Nang we spent some time in and near the area the marines called "Dodge City." It indeed was a place filled with gunfights. South of Hill 55, I wanted to visit a rice paddy where Billy Smoyer was one of nineteen marines in Kilo Company of the 3rd Battalion of the 7th Marines who died in an ambush on July 28, 1968. Billy was a star hockey and soccer player at Dartmouth who had joined the marines upon graduation. He came from a comfortable New Jersey family and probably could have deferred or even found an exemption from service. Instead, he said that the war shouldn't be fought only by the sons of miners and factory workers. I buried a Dartmouth hockey puck in the rice paddy where Second Lieutenant Smoyer died less than four weeks after arriving in Vietnam.

In a tragic coincidence, a Dartmouth classmate and friend of Billy Smoyer's, Duncan Sleigh, died in another ambush less than five months later just two miles away. Duncan was in Mike Company of the 3rd Battalion of the 7th Marines. They lost fourteen men in that ambush and Second Lieutenant Sleigh was awarded the Navy Cross posthumously for his effort to shield a wounded marine from another grenade. The marine survived but Sleigh did not. I buried a small New Hampshire memento in that rice paddy.

North of the pilings from the old Liberty Bridge, four of us were looking across a field at the slope where several U.S. marines died on May 29, 1969, on the last day of Operation Oklahoma Hills. A smiling teenage Vietnamese boy stepped out of a house and waved to us. Then his grandfather came out and greeted us and invited us in for tea. He had lived in that house for his entire eighty-five years. He served during the war with a local NLF unit. He told us that in the 1960s, during the day he farmed and at night he fought. Looking out from this home, looming above this peaceful place, remained the heavy and dark green hills that Americans called Charlie Ridge. The U.S. troops seldom went there and never stayed long. As we walked along the pathway from the home of this veteran, we passed a group of young children playing. They smiled and shouted proudly in English, "Hello!" And one flashed the common V fingers greeting, ironically evoking the American antiwar peace sign.

But Dong Ap Bia has remained Hamburger Hill—very steep, more than three thousand feet high, red clay and rocks, slippery after a summer shower that began our trek. Jungle heat and humidity slowed our pace. Modern Vietnam has hardly touched this place. After the 1969 battle, soldiers described the hill as looking like a moonscape—artillery and bombs and herbicides having torn and burned trees and undergrowth. The land, at least superficially, had now recovered. Double- and triple-canopy growth had returned, with incredibly dense foliage and shrubs, much of which would have been familiar to those men of the 187th of the 101st Airborne who hurried from their helicopters there on May 10. Now the Crouching Beast was silent, or at least the chaotic sounds of war had been replaced by a cacophony from unfamiliar birds and animals and insects.

NOTE

1. The National Liberation Front was commonly called the Viet Cong by Americans. The term was a contraction of the Saigon government's description of these forces as "Viet Gian Cong San," or Vietnamese Communist Traitor, which was shortened to "Viet Cong" by most Americans, probably with little sense of it being a pejorative term. I use NLF except when quoting from participants and observers. I use NVA to describe the North Vietnamese Army (this force also was called the People's Army of North Vietnam, or PAVN). I use ARVN, the common contemporary name, for the Army of the Republic of Vietnam, the South Vietnamese regular army.

A Generation Goes to War

M Y BOOK *Enduring Vietnam* is about the generation that grew up in post–World War II America and about their war. During the 1960s, and likely even more so as the years have passed, many of them would reject the ownership implicit in calling the American War in Vietnam "their war." But it was that generation's war. As youngsters, most joined older generations in supporting it at the outset and, still essentially as youngsters, many finally served in it. If not always eagerly or even willingly, they served. They may legitimately deny responsibility for starting the war—their parents' and grandparents' generations did that for them—but they cannot deny that this war marked them profoundly. And they marked the war. It was *their* war. This generation is often called the Baby Boomers, a description that I use descriptively but somewhat reluctantly when considering this subject, since there is something light and flippant about the title and there was nothing light and flippant about their war.

I have sought primarily to understand and to tell the story of those Americans who were the war fighters, perhaps a half million or six hundred thousand men over eight years of regular ground war, approximately 25 or 30 percent of the more than two and one half million U.S. troops who served in Vietnam. As the war went on, increasingly they were Baby Boomers. These men—and the women who served with them in medical or other combat support specialties—were fully and not peripherally a part of their generation. And they were on the ground for their generation's war.

In addition to these combat troops, there were roughly two million Americans who served in noncombat missions, and their contributions and service were substantial. They worked to sustain and protect the fighting force and to advance the overall mission of support for the South Vietnamese government and people. And many of them served in vulnerable posts or took on exposed assignments that could at any time have subjected them to an attack by the enemy.

37

Over ten million Baby Boomers served in the armed forces in the 1960s and early 1970s. Nearly 27 million young American men reached eighteen, draft age, between August 1964 and March 1973. More than 2.2 million of them were drafted and 8.7 million enlisted in military services. Nearly 10 percent of the men in that generation went to Vietnam.[1] As the war went on in the 1960s, draftees as a proportion of those serving in the military increased. But the majority of those who served enlisted, willingly as volunteers or less willingly in response to or in anticipation of a draft call. Most were not deployed to Vietnam but were posted elsewhere at U.S. bases or at sea. They too served when called, were always on standby for Vietnam deployment, and their service is a part of their generation's account.

The images of the 1960s that resonate today are of Woodstock, youthful rebellion, of a generation leading protests against the war, against authority, and against convention, embracing new musical sounds considered revolutionary, of a time remembered romantically as the decade of "Peace and Love," of the Beatles and of the Age of Aquarius, and, indeed, of times that truly were a-changin'. But it is necessary also to remember that many of that era also have a powerful memory of the thump-thump-thump of helicopters flying over the hills and treetops of Vietnam and the smell and feel of rice paddies or of humid jungle.

More young Americans in the '60s died in Vietnam, over 58,000, than went to jail for refusing to serve in the military or moved to Canada to avoid serving. This book is about the experience of those who served—not to impugn those who protested what they believed was an unnecessary or unjust war, one that was sometimes immorally cruel in its execution. After all, it turned out that they were largely correct. But there is more to their generation's story—and their generation's war—than that. For the Baby Boomer generation not only challenged the war, they also experienced it. And that experience, on the ground in Vietnam, was far more complex and more nuanced than persistent stereotypes of atrocities committed, of mutiny and fragging and antiwar activities in a haze of drugs. Each of these images came to have some basis, especially in the last years of the war, but by no means can they stand as fair generalizations of the conduct of most of those who served.

The American War in Vietnam was a powerful force in American life. But for most Americans it was more metaphor than experience. "Vietnam" was a word used to describe a policy, an engagement, to refer to a distant, mysterious place. Vietnam represented an unpleasant activity occurring on behalf of the United States. It represented something increasingly considered negative in the decade of the 1960s.

A friend recently returned to Vietnam to see again the places where he fought in late 1968 and early 1969. He particularly wanted to visit the rice paddy where a close college friend and hockey teammate, Billy Smoyer, died. He shared with me his reflections on this as well as an exchange he had with a high school classmate, whom I then contacted. The veteran observed that "my story is one small paragraph in that much larger history of our generation at war that was, for many only part of our '60s upheaval." His high school friend wrote him:

> Your time in 'Nam resonates with me, quite deeply. Like many of our generation, Vietnam was at the center. From 1965 to 1975, Vietnam seemed (to me) the black hole around which that decade floated. The music, the protests, the drugs, the clothing, the long hair, the changes in academic curricula, the attitudes towards the "Establishment," Chicago in 1968, Watergate, Nixon, Nixon's resignation, LBJ not running for re-election, McGovern, free speech, Woodstock, Altamont, rights for Blacks and women, environmental concerns, open sexual mores...seemed to float around the darkness that was Vietnam. Like many, I spent a number of years making sure I did not go to 'Nam.

Educational and then a medical deferment enabled this man to avoid serving in the military. He continued his education and then began a life-long career as a high school English teacher. But "then, in the late '70s, the dark hole that was Vietnam began to almost haunt me. In trying to understand who I was, and what those ten years meant and how they formed and informed me." He devoted himself to learning more about Vietnam—but always with the recognition that like the blind men trying to define an elephant by touch, it is hard to ever truly know this "black hole" that touched and haunted all of his generation.[2]

By focusing on the American on-ground experience, it is not my intention to obscure or challenge the sharp criticism of the assumptions, judgments, and, yes, the deceit that led the United States into that war. The war was conducted with ambivalence and uncertainty, conditions exacerbated by very general and shifting objectives, and by restraints and conflicting instructions from Washington based upon political rather than military calculations. Senior policymakers never provided an honest public assessment of the war's progress and its costs. In the field, the war officially entered into on behalf of the Vietnamese was carried out too often with indifference toward the residents of the country or even with willful cruelty in which the noncombatant Vietnamese civilians were innocent casualties. It would be shameful to minimize these things, just as it would be slanderous to many good men to suggest that all American troops behaved as indifferent or willful thugs.

As a number of critics then and scholars later have agreed, among the Baby Boomer generation the burden of American military service and even more specifically of combat service was not equitably shared. The sons of blue-collar families, African American, Hispanic, and Native American young men were disproportionately out in the jungles of Vietnam. And while many, increasingly more as the war went on, were not eager to serve, it was also the case that not all were there as reluctant draftees. These young men were often serving because of their sense of patriotism and obligation, of what many considered their responsibility; some served because they hoped that military service could expand their future opportunities. Despite the inequities, a large part of an iconic American generation served there—and served well. If it was largely a blue-collar war, it surely was not uniformly one. College students and college graduates were also on the front lines. And by no means only as officers.

The Vietnamese were more than background, more than a tragic Greek chorus, hovering over the Americans fighting in their country. After all of the arguments seeking to support political and moral positions, after all of the sweeping generalizations and exaggerations, the American War in Vietnam was marked by high numbers of innocent victims. Of course, that is true of any war, but the best calculations are that a million or more Vietnamese civilians died between 1965 and 1975 as a result of the war. Some have tripled that figure.[3]

The American War largely was a war without front lines. It was built around small-unit actions intended to surprise the enemy or lure them into attacking. And battles were not so much won as they were concluded.

Temporarily concluded. The objective was to kill enough opponents to dissuade the enemy from continuing the war. These kinds of activities do not lend themselves readily to standard war story narratives, to tally sheets listing battles won. In the accounts of great battles in American military history, there are no examples from Vietnam.

Absent tangible military goals, it was hard to produce tangible military results. So the great debates during the war—and since then—about its conduct have often focused on the metrics that the military and their civilian leadership developed to measure "progress." Winning hearts and minds is not a measurable result, at least not one that generates periodic scores and tallies. The U.S. military was more sophisticated than the stereotyped image of an obsession with "body counts" suggests, but it surely used these as it struggled to find the real light at the end of the long tunnel. Vietnam had no benchmarks remotely comparable to those of the army sweeping from Normandy and on to Paris in the summer of 1944. There were no headlines shouting of territories won, of happy villagers cheering their liberation. There was no iconic flag raising such as at Iwo Jima in 1945.

In the late 1960s, the growing dissent against the American War in Vietnam focused on costs and consequences. Critics increasingly pressed the case for recognizing moral costs and moral consequences. As the scale of U.S. involvement grew, and the nature of the fighting intensified, as the war in Vietnam became the American War in Vietnam, so did the volume of reports and accounts from that country. These led to increasingly negative public attitudes toward the war and, for some, perceptions of the men fighting it.

The popular depictions of the soldiers and marines on the ground changed from 1965 to 1970, from original views of heroes in the jungle fighting to protect democracy. Certainly from 1965 onward, this narrative shifted as more Americans came to be critical of or at least uncertain about the wisdom of the U.S. buildup and expansion of combat operations. In order to mobilize the forces for this expanded engagement, the Pentagon needed to increase significantly the number of men drafted. This meant that draftees constituted a growing part of the U.S. forces just as American casualties increased markedly. As there were more draftees among the killed and wounded, some common perceptions of the troops deployed to Vietnam moved from heroic freedom fighters to innocent young men dispatched to fight a mistaken war, a cruel and tragic war.

Finally, by late 1969, especially following the public disclosures of the My Lai massacre of several hundred Vietnamese civilians in March 1968, some accounts depicted the Americans no longer as victims but as eager perpetrators of the war, perpetrators often high on drugs. Although neither innocent victim nor cruel participant was a majority public view, these nonetheless often were dominating ones. Each was a condescending and grossly distorted generalization.

Among the more than 2.5 million American servicemen and -women in Vietnam, some may have fit easily into one or another of the stereotypes, but surely most did not. Many of those who served may have been unwilling, but they did not consider themselves hapless victims nor were they racist psychopaths. But they nonetheless came home quietly and stepped aside quickly, except perhaps for those who joined in antiwar activities. Most did not join in the protests, even those who shared some of the views of the group. Even though the American War in Vietnam likely had proportionately as many individual acts of courage and bravery and sacrifice as any other war, there was relatively little enthusiasm for publicizing these accounts—or, revealingly, perhaps even less interest in hearing them. The result was a hard and impersonal war narrative with few publicly celebrated military heroes, and an often difficult and lonely homecoming. U.S. Army Lieutenant William Calley, convicted of leading the massacre at My Lai, is the most recognized name of those who served in the field in Vietnam. Yet most Americans would be hard-pressed to name even one person who quietly and honorably served.

For those who served there, Vietnam was a pretty basic world in which they focused on survival as a daily goal. Participants in all wars do that, of course, but in Vietnam it became harder to project this personal goal, to imagine the daily experience, within a broader and grander set of military objectives serving critical national needs. Except for a brief period at the beginning, the American War in Vietnam lacked a nationally endorsed feel-good, big-story narrative in which the personal accounts could fit and be warmly embraced by a grateful nation.

SERVING IN VIETNAM was of course a burden. Despite popular tales of romance and heroic and often bloodless drama, serving in any war is a burden. But perhaps unlike any other American war, having served in this war also became a burden. It is hard ever to feel pride for serving in your nation's war if it is always described as a negative example, as a war that should not have been fought—or, if fought, should not have been fought the way that it was. Or should not have had the embarrassed conclusion that it did. It is hard to express pride to those who were not there if the most commonly remembered event of the war was the massacre of civilians at My Lai. So the veterans of Vietnam tried to fade quietly back into American society.

NOTES

1. Lawrence M. Baskir and William A. Strauss, *Chance and Circumstance: The Draft, the War, and the Vietnam Generation* (New York: Knopf, 1978), 3–5.

2. Warren Cook, "My Vietnam Reprise," shared with author; e-mail exchange with Edward Yasuna, April 26, 2016.

3. There are many powerful accounts of the Vietnamese experience. Especially compelling is Viet Thanh Nguyen's prize-winning novel *The Sympathizer* and his subsequent nonfiction book, which I encountered only as this book was going to press. *Nothing Ever Dies: Vietnam and the Memory of War* is a thoughtful and provocative reflection by a Vietnamese American whose family left Vietnam in 1975 when Viet was only four years old. "The majority of Americans regarded us with ambivalence if not outright distaste, we being living reminders of their stinging defeat" (*The Sympathizer*, 113). He wrote in *Nothing Ever Dies*, "This is a book on war, memory, and identity. It proceeds from the idea that all wars are fought twice, the first time on the battlefield, the second time in memory." He observes that for him the "metonym for the problem of war and memory is what some call the Vietnam War and others call the American War. These conflicting names indicate how this war suffers from an identity crisis, by the question of how it shall be known and remembered" (4).

Veterans Day 2009 at the
Vietnam Veterans Memorial Wall

Washington, D.C.

I AM HONORED TO join here with so many who share a commitment to remembering.

For the past few years I have worked with veterans wounded in Iraq or Afghanistan to encourage and enable them to pursue their dreams through education. Today we remember those who did not have an opportunity to pursue their dreams.

I grew up in a mining town, Galena, Illinois. With four friends I joined the Marines in 1957 at the age of seventeen—to keep me out of the mines for at least a few years. When I returned in 1960, I decided to go to college— but I needed to work in the mines while in school. My boss when I worked underground was Clarence Lyden. He was a good boss, a good man, who had received a Purple Heart while serving in the Army in World War II. He encouraged me to become a powderman, setting dynamite charges, in order to earn twenty cents more an hour. I did take on this assignment and continued to study—and was a student teacher back in my old high school.

One of my students in an English class was Clarence Lyden's son, Michael. I remember him as an energetic, pleasant, hard-working young man. A few years later he was drafted and went into the Army, where he became a sergeant in the 101st Airborne. Already holding a Purple Heart, Michael died on May 15, 1969, in Operation Apache Snow at a place we remember as Hamburger Hill.

This wall records the sons—and daughters—of many miners, factory workers, and farmers. And so many others. The wall contains the names of fifteen graduates of Dartmouth. I did not know any of them. But I came to know well the father, the sister, the brother, the classmates, the coach and teammates of one.

Bill Smoyer grew up in comfortable circumstances in New Jersey. At Dartmouth he was an All-Ivy soccer player and a star hockey player. He was by all accounts a gracious and generous young man, a gentleman. And he joined the Marines in order to go to Vietnam because he believed that wars should not be fought only by the sons of the miners, farmers, and factory workers. He was in Vietnam for only two weeks on July 28, 1968, when his platoon was caught in an ambush while crossing a rice paddy at An Hoa. Second Lieutenant Smoyer and eighteen other members of Kilo company, 3rd Battalion 7th Marines, were killed that Sunday.

Who knows what Billy Smoyer and Mike Lyden would have done with their lives? Mike may have gone back to work at the Kraft Foods plant in Galena—he did not want to follow his dad into the mines. His old teacher here believes that whatever he did he would have done well. Billy Smoyer was a history major who may have gone into business—but all attest that whatever he did, he would have tried to make a difference for others.

Late this past summer my wife, Susan, and I visited Normandy, where we spent a lot of time walking through the American cemetery at Colleville. The white marble crosses and Stars of David filled the hillside with a sense of order and tranquility—and whispered of lives lost. We walked among the graves for some time, reading the names, observing where they were from and how old they were. We thought of lives cut short and of dreams unrealized and wanted to know more about them.

Casualties of war cry out to be known—as persons, not as abstractions called casualties nor as numbers entered into the books, and not only as names chiseled into marble or granite. We have carried in our memories the stories of those recorded here. But memories fade—as do those who remember. We are graying. After all of us who knew them are gone, the names on this wall will endure.

It is essential that the Education Center planned for this site sparkle with the human records of those whose sacrifice was forever. We need to ensure that here, in this place of memory, lives as well as names are recorded. Lives with smiling human faces, remarkable accomplishments, engaging personalities, and with dreams to pursue. We do this for them, for history, and for those in the future who will send the young to war.

Walking the Hill They Died On

June 2019

IN SEPTEMBER 2014, I made the first of three trips to Vietnam. I was writing a book to tell the story of Americans who fought in the war. I had interviewed many veterans who served, and now I wanted to walk some of the ground marked by major American combat.

Traveling with a small group along the canals and waterways of the Mekong Delta, I began to understand what men meant when they called it a scary place. We also spent several days in what had been called I Corps, the military's designation for South Vietnam's northern region, where we visited battle sites at obscure places like Needlepoint, The Rockpile, and Mutter's Ridge, as well as the more well-known Khe Sanh and Hue. Then four of us set out from Hue for the A Shau Valley and afterward traveled down to the Central Highlands.

With me was Vietnam veteran Bruce Jones, who served in the U.S. Army and was now a guide with Military Historical Tours, which helped organize my trip. We had a Vietnamese guide and interpreter, Tran Thanh, and a driver. Our first stop in the A Shau Valley was Dong Ap Bia, a mountain labeled Hill 937 by the U.S. military and known by the soldiers as Hamburger Hill, where more than seventy Americans died and hundreds were wounded in a brutal battle fought May 10–20, 1969.

On our journey to the mountain, we met with three North Vietnamese veterans of the battle in the village of A Luoi. I interviewed them, and two accepted my invitation to join our climb up Dong Ap Bia on a trail maintained by the Vietnamese government. We saw no one else on the hill that day.

After a brief rain shower, the path was steep and slippery. Stone steps helped in some of the steepest or most difficult places. Bruce counted 922 of them. As I stumbled and slid and sweated, I wondered how the young men of the 101st Airborne Division had clamored up the hill in 1969. Knowing they were more than fifty years younger was not a sufficient explanation—I wasn't carrying fifty or more pounds of equipment and ammunition. It took ten days for the soldiers who reached the top. We did it in about two hours, but no one was shooting down at us. Some of the American units that arrived on the first day of battle suffered 70 percent casualties.

Our trail went up the eastern side of the mountain, while the sustained fighting and the initial landing zone were to the west, nearer Laos. The west side didn't have a road or trail when we were there, and the Vietnamese warned us to avoid that area because of unexploded ordnance. Climbing through the dense jungle, we would sometimes pass old tree trunks with bullet holes and large puddles of water in bomb or artillery craters. Occasionally the two North Vietnamese Army veterans pointed out a small squared hole, what U.S. troops called a "spider hole," a camouflaged opening that probably led to an underground network of enemy tunnels and storage areas.

At the top, we sat at the monument the Vietnamese built to commemorate their "great victory." I decided not to remind the North Vietnamese veterans that there was no great victory for them, certainly not on that hill in May 1969. I asked what they had learned from the eleven days of intense combat. They learned they could stand and fight against American firepower. But they also came to respect our soldiers. All these years later, they still could not believe that these young Americans, despite heavy casualties, climbed the hill day after day to assault the North Vietnamese bunkers.

This year, 2019, as we mark the fiftieth anniversary of the Battle of Hamburger Hill, is a good time to reflect on the soldiers who fought with relentless determination until they defeated the enemy force. The battle captured the attention of people back in the States. It became a focus and symbol of much of the controversy about the Vietnam War as the American public debated whether lives had been senselessly lost fighting over a hill that U.S. forces abandoned shortly after their victory. Regardless, the battle reflected the remarkable courage of the generation that fought and sacrificed there.

Before our small group at the hilltop monument began the walk down that September day in 2014, I shared a story. After my service with the Marines in 1960, I went home to Galena, Illinois, an old mining town. Among other jobs, I worked in zinc mines, including time as a powderman setting dynamite charges. My boss, Clarence Lyden, was a Purple Heart World War II veteran. His son Michael was a bright, engaging young man. I liked him a lot and was deeply saddened when I learned that he had been killed at Hamburger Hill on May 14, 1969, while serving with the 101st Airborne's 187th Infantry Regiment. He was hit by a rocket-propelled grenade and died instantly.

I interviewed some of the men who served alongside Mike, a sergeant well-regarded by his platoon and by his platoon leader, who saw him die. They said he was a good soldier and a natural leader. Mike's family shared his correspondence, and there's no indication that he spent a lot of time thinking about the cause. Mike was focused on his men, his own safety, and coming home.

After I told the North Vietnamese veterans about Mike, I pulled from my pocket a piece of lead sulfide, about one inch square. The Latin name for this cubed form of lead is galena. I picked it up while working in Galena's Graham mine fifty years earlier. I had kept it on my desk for many years, and now I had a new home for it.

I buried that chunk of lead sulfide on the top of Dong Ap Bia. Mike Lyden never made it to the top of the hill, but now a piece of his hometown is there. I am confident that the galena will outlast the red clay of that desolate mountain in Vietnam.

II
ADVOCACY

Honoring Veterans

October 2007

O<small>N</small> S<small>EPTEMBER</small> 23, 2007, the new Ken Burns series on World War II aired on public television around the country. As we remember that generation and all it accomplished, let us not forget our current generation of veterans from the conflicts in Iraq and Afghanistan. I fear, in the midst of the debate over troop levels, exit strategies, and assessment of the war's progress, that we have lost sight of the men and women who are fighting this war. To be sure, there is deference to them, but too often they are seen as abstractions, as numbers and not individuals, as heroes or helpless pawns. Those who gave their lives are remembered for but a moment, except in their hometowns. Those who have been seriously injured seldom even have the moment.

In early August, I visited Balboa Naval Hospital in San Diego. Fifty years ago, as a seventeen-year-old Marine, I had suffered a minor injury during boot camp and spent a few days at Balboa.

Nothing looked familiar but the overall experience was similar to the ones I had a few weeks earlier at Walter Reed and Bethesda hospitals: experiences that were both inspiring and overwhelming. Over the last two years I have made multiple visits to military hospitals to talk to wounded veterans about their experiences and hopes.

So as we talk about exit strategies, let's be sure that we address in a far more engaged way those whose exits will be aboard medical evacuation aircraft. Predictably we will forget about them soon after the war is over—most will slip back into the anonymity of their lives, and, as far as many are concerned, happily so.

However, the education and rehabilitation programs provided by the government to enable veterans to make that transition need to be enhanced significantly. It is time for a new GI Bill. This is a national debt—and a wise national investment.

The difficulties and conditions at Walter Reed stem from a simple set of facts: We misjudged the duration of the conflict and the number of troops it would require, and the extent of the casualties we would sustain.

While debate about who voted how four years ago and projections about who would withdraw at what pace are important, they surely have little impact on the treatment of veterans. The medical and military officials at the hospitals I have visited care deeply about their patients, but they are overwhelmed by the numbers of casualties and are struggling to address the shortcomings highlighted last year. The Dole-Shalala Committee recommended much-needed changes in veterans' treatment. But problems remain. I spoke to a young Marine several days ago who is waiting for a wheelchair.

Improvements in body armor have ensured that more casualties survive. However, though vital organs are protected, limbs are vulnerable and head injuries are nearly epidemic. I have listened to young soldiers and Marines, as fluids seeped through their stumps of limbs, explain how they first learned their leg or arm was not there; to a National Guard single mother with cognitive impairment who missed her three children; to a mother wiping the head of a son who could not respond even as she assured him he would be fine; to a father, with his hand on the shoulder of his son in a wheelchair, who acknowledged that the family had lost everything to Hurricane Katrina, "but my boy is alive and I now know what is important in life."

The wounded veterans are real people—not objects of condescending sympathy nor abstracted heroes. They don't consider themselves heroic. (For the most part, they simply want to get on with their lives.) I have rarely heard them express anger or blame. Clinically, many will suffer from Post-Traumatic Stress Disorder, but young men in the military are not likely to admit to being depressed, nervous, or scared. As one young man who had lost both legs up to his torso said with an embarrassed grin, "I was depressed for a while, but now I have got over it." He said he suffered his injuries ten days before.

Remember that the GI Bill at the conclusion of World War II enabled that generation to contribute to society. Let us focus as well on the sacrifices, needs, and the remarkable potential of this generation of veterans.

The New GI Bill:
It's a Win-Win Proposition

May 2008

WHEN I WAS A YOUNGSTER in the Midwest in the years after World War II, many people still called Memorial Day "Decoration Day," acknowledging its roots as a national day of mourning for the Union soldiers who had died in the Civil War. After World War I, the day became a time to honor all those who had died in uniform. For the past several years, however, it has been an occasion to remember the men and women who have died in Iraq and Afghanistan, and to think of our obligations to those who are still serving overseas or recovering at home.

Although national support for the wars is as limited today as it was for the Vietnam War in the 1960s and '70s, most people acknowledge that the policies that have taken us into the Middle East are not the fault of the men and women in the military. Yet few Americans realize that the young people who are serving their country in Iraq and Afghanistan will not receive the kind of assistance that their grandfathers received when they returned from World War II. Educational benefits for the current generation of volunteers, whether they served in the regular military or in the Reserves or National Guard, are seriously inadequate. The original GI Bill covered the full cost of a veteran's education, but today the maximum assistance covers only 60 to 70 percent of average tuition—not room or board—at a public four-year university. In the coming days, Congress will consider a new GI Bill (S.22), sponsored by Senator James H. Webb, a Democrat of Virginia, that will provide the support veterans deserve.

The idea of providing returning veterans with benefits as both a reward for their service and as a means of enabling them to reintegrate into civilian life dates to the early history of this country. Revolutionary War soldiers received military pensions, land grants, and other forms of care, depending on their service and its location. After the Civil War, Union soldiers (but not, until much later, their Confederate counterparts) received pensions. In anticipation of the large numbers of returning American troops from World War I, the government developed a comprehensive package of veterans' benefits that included disability payments, pensions, rehabilitation, and vocational training.

President Franklin D. Roosevelt, faced with the prospect of some 15 million returning military personnel from World War II, signed the GI Bill, in 1944.

Formally known as the Servicemen's Readjustment Act, the GI Bill provided tuition, room, and board, as well as incidental expenses for books, to any veteran who attended a four-year college or university, a two-year college, or a trade school. The bill, which applied to both women and men and provided benefits regardless of race, was initially opposed by some of the leading educators of the day, who worried that it would open up their institutions to unqualified applicants.

Opening up the academy is exactly what the bill did—although the veterans proved to be more than qualified. In the first year alone, one million of them used the benefit to attend college. Within a decade, eight million had attended college or vocational school. Colleges and universities across the country saw great expansions of their student bodies and increasing numbers of veterans in their classes. In 1947, at my own institution, Dartmouth College, 60 percent of the members of the incoming class were veterans.

The law was largely responsible for the development of a new middle class, and it not only helped the returning veterans but also expanded American higher education. The "greatest generation" may well have made its greatest contributions as educated, resourceful, and creative civilians in the sixty years following the end of World War II. Before that, only one in sixteen Americans had a college degree, compared with one in five by 1970.

Yet despite the overwhelming historical success of educational benefits for veterans, such support for those who served in Iraq and Afghanistan has, unfortunately, proved to be an unnecessarily complicated matter. Remarkably, Congress allowed the legislation for the new GI Bill to sit for a year with no action on it. The three major arguments of those opposed: the expense of adding another entitlement program; Pentagon concerns that reenlistments might suffer if too many people left the military to pursue higher education; and reservations by some in Congress about providing federal tuition dollars to wealthy institutions.

The estimated cost of the Webb bill is $45 billion in the first ten years. We spend that much in less than six months in Iraq. Veterans' benefits are a cost of war, and support for them should not be held hostage to reenlistment targets. While reenlistments might indeed decline, a new GI Bill could also encourage more young people to sign up for military service.

Indeed, one of the military's greatest problems right now is declining enlistment. A more generous GI Bill would only improve the numbers and quality of enlistees. Access to higher education will give enlisted personnel the opportunity successfully to reintegrate into civilian life—and will provide our country with another generation of well-educated citizens.

As I write in May 2008, the new GI Bill enjoys support from fifty-seven senators and 275 members of the House. It has been endorsed by virtually every veterans' group and by major higher-education associations. Passage should be assured—but it is not. President Bush has threatened to veto any attempt to add the bill to his $108-billion funding request.

Our campuses are quieter than they were in the Vietnam era, so it might be easier for some people to forget the sacrifices of our Americans in the military. Now is a good time to remember them—and to recall the responsibility we share to those who represent us. American colleges and universities should help meet that responsibility by urging Congress and the president to support legislation that will give veterans the educational opportunities that they have more than earned. Maybe this Memorial Day, as we mourn those whose sacrifice is forever, we can thank and invest in those who have survived and now wish to move on with their lives.

The Yellow Ribbon Program and Private Colleges and Universities

February 2, 2009, in Washington, D.C.

Two weeks ago many of us sat mesmerized before our televisions as we watched the inauguration of the United States' forty-fourth president, Barack Obama. Regardless of individual politics, it was a moving occasion—the sight of the first African American taking the presidential oath forty-four years after the Voting Rights Act of 1965. I told some students that I was not so sure that their generation could fully appreciate what this moment symbolized. I had spent a winter in Mississippi fifty years ago when I was an eighteen-year-old Marine from a small town in the Midwest and was shocked by what I encountered. President Obama's inauguration indeed marked a different world in ways that most of us could not have predicted then. The substantive work of extending to all equality and opportunity is surely not finished, but the symbolism as well as the accomplishment this occasion represented should cause us to pause in shared pride.

While watching I reflected on what a privilege it is to be a part of a nation capable of redressing injustice within its own borders and unafraid of adapting to meet the challenges of a global economy. We are fortunate to live in a place that holds freedom of thought and speech among its core values—two values central to the lives of academics—and a country with an unparalleled tradition of intellectual leadership.

As you well know, with privilege comes responsibility. Higher education remains one of the most important paths to individual success and a critical means for national achievement and the attainment of global understanding. If our country is to succeed and to play a positive role in an international context, we must ensure access to postsecondary education for all our citizens. Accomplishing this will be both one of the greatest opportunities and the biggest challenges we will face in the twenty-first century.

My focus today is on but one of the tools and the means to move us to our goal of expanding access and opportunity.

It is my hope, and indeed my expectation, that we will meet this challenge and that the Post-9/11 Veterans Educational Assistance Act of 2008, including the Yellow Ribbon Program, will play a significant role in this endeavor, as did the 1944 Servicemen's Readjustment Act (or GI Bill) for previous generations.

As a historian, I cannot resist the opportunity to speak about the 1944 GI Bill. I want to talk about its consequences for the veterans who received benefits and to consider the impact it had on higher education institutions and our country as a whole. The broad positive impact of the bill makes a compelling case in support of the current GI Bill and the Yellow Ribbon Program.

From 1942–1944, the years of the GI Bill's development, President Roosevelt's attention was largely on wartime strategy, but he could never drift too far from thinking about the postwar economy. The Great Depression was still fresh in the minds of many Americans, and most anticipated that when the war ended the country would again be plunged into a financial crisis. The Servicemen's Readjustment Act was among the many proposals developed.

It called for the development and expansion of educational and training opportunities for veterans. While Roosevelt and others recognized that the Readjustment Act would help veterans resume educations disrupted by the war and serve as a means to thank them for their service, they primarily viewed it as a means to strengthen our economy. The author Keith Olson wrote, "To prop up the postwar economy Congress could have poured money into corporations, as it did in the 1930s…; it could have created jobs, as it did during the New Deal…; it could have curtailed the profit motive and moved toward a planned economy…. Instead, Congress chose… the veterans." It was, by today's terminology, a stimulus plan!

Regardless of the initial intent, the results went far beyond what anyone could have predicted. Thousands—then millions—of men and women suddenly had the financial means to attend any institution that would admit them on their academic record. For the first time, education was no longer for the wealthy and white alone. Institutions once considered off-limits to all but the elite were open to all, for few institutions could refuse qualified students when the government guaranteed payment of their bills!

Unsure of the reception awaiting them upon their return from war, African American vets found that they had more options than ever before—although surely not enough. Many schools relinquished their quotas on Jews, although not always without additional pressure to do so. Of course, increased access did not end discrimination in all areas of life, but it did alter the social climate on and off campus. It paved the way for our current understanding of the important role access and diversity have in the learning environment and for the heterogeneity and pluralism that we celebrate and defend today.

What we have described as the "greatest generation" did not earn that distinction simply by their role in a difficult and costly war. They were more than warriors. That generation fundamentally came home from the war and set about to shape American life—economically, culturally, politically, and intellectually.

Initially, the numbers utilizing the educational benefit were small—about 8,000 in the first year of the program—but by the fall of 1946, as a result of significant demobilization of the military, over a million veterans were enrolled at a college.

During the next ten years, veterans continued to enroll in high numbers, and as a result the number of total college enrollments, including veterans, increased by 75 percent. Unprepared for the massive numbers of veterans enrolling, many colleges and universities rushed to hire faculty and expand facilities. In a number of states, new institutions and consortiums were formed in order to meet the demand.

Among its significant achievements, the original GI Bill helped usher in what has often been called the "knowledge society." It was a process that had been underway, but slowly and without a clear vision. Down through the late nineteenth century, American colleges and universities had largely served to transmit received wisdom and classical knowledge. A college degree had limited practical meaning but a college education was a mark of culture. Beginning with the Land Grant College Act, the Morrill Act, of 1862, this changed, and often dramatically. And public institutions began to emphasize the role of research and creating knowledge as a core purpose of the university. In the nineteenth century, private institutions, including my own, were slower to value curiosity and to encourage faculty and students to challenge received wisdom. Perhaps down through the Depression, private education still focused primarily on transmitting knowledge to those who would constitute the cultured class.

By the end of the Second World War in 1945, just as veterans were pouring onto our campuses, government sponsorship of research and interest in public health greatly increased. Regional universities, such as Stanford, grew into major national and international research universities with the aid of federal research dollars. Innovation, creativity, and the abilities to analyze were of paramount importance, not only for faculty work, but also for a student's success in the job market. Work as we knew it changed, and as a result, the four-year degree became an essential tool for individual access—and we became certifiers as well as educators.

Of course, there were other forces influencing the shape of our society at the time the GI Bill was expanding the student population—and causing students to have an expanded set of ambitions. The civil rights movement and the women's rights movement, scientific and technological advances, and ever-changing international relationships helped to direct growth in higher education and this country's future. But we cannot underestimate the contributions made by the veterans. Enabled and encouraged by the GI Bill, they made this a stronger and more inclusive society.

Some sixty years later, we stand at another critical moment in our history. The worldwide financial crisis has affected every aspect of our lives. I am sure all of us feel the reverberations on our campuses. State and national support for higher education has been declining as a percent of revenue for years. Society depends on our schools for advancements in knowledge, for practical contributions to economic innovation, and for credentialing and enabling our young people—and society supports this essential work less generously. Our private schools may have different revenue sources, but the changing demand and our capacity to meet it have changed. And our society is losing the race to maintain our competitive edge in many arenas.

In his inaugural remarks, President Obama noted: "Our time of standing pat, of protecting narrow interests and putting off unpleasant decisions—that time has surely passed. [W]e must pick ourselves up, dust ourselves off, and begin again the work of remaking America." His plan for this remaking includes an investment in science, healthcare, and technology, and a rebuilding of our infrastructure, both physically and intellectually. To do this, the U.S. will need increased numbers of citizens with a post-secondary education.

Unfortunately, today there are many signs that the pipeline for educated workers is broken. Today, only about 67 percent of students graduate from high school, and college completion rates have also declined. Thirty-five years ago the United States ranked second internationally in terms of workers with a college education. Now we are eleventh. In December 2008, the College Board Commission on Access, Admissions, and Success in Higher Education, of which I was a member, released its report, "Coming to Our Senses: Education and the American Future." In it, we asserted that to reclaim our position as a leader in education we must make sure that 55 percent of young Americans complete a two-year degree or higher by 2025.

To achieve this, we need to find ways to help the estimated 1.7 million to 3.2 million academically qualified students who will not earn a four-year degree this decade because they cannot meet the financial costs—or even when financial support is available, who have never been *encouraged to believe* they can secure a college education and those who simply do not have the counseling and information needed to make informed decisions about applying and enrolling in a degree program. Fortunately, through the Post-9/11 Veterans Educational Assistance Act of 2008 (the new GI Bill), we have the capacity to bring a significant subset of both populations into our institutions.

The Higher Education community, led by NAICU and the American Council on Education (ACE), worked with veterans' groups and many other individuals and organizations to secure passage of the legislation. There was significant resistance from the administration at first. But in June of 2008 President Bush signed the new legislation, including what was called the Yellow Ribbon section whereby institutions with tuition rates higher than the state cap can look to share some or all of the incremental cost with the Veterans Administration (VA). Beginning this next August, most continuing students who are veterans will seek to transition their benefits from the Montgomery GI Bill to the Post-9/11 Bill, and others will take advantage of their educational benefits for the first time through the new GI Bill. There could be a 20 to 25 percent increase in the number of enrolled veterans—currently there are 350,000 enrolled under existing VA programs—and this could be greater, and almost surely will be in the future.

The bill covers the cost of any public institution's undergraduate program and provides a monthly housing allowance and book stipend for all veterans. However, the institutions most of us in this room represent charge undergraduate and graduate tuition rates higher than the tuition benefit cap, leaving a balance for veterans to pay or for colleges to cover through institutional aid in partnership with the VA. As college and university endowments continue to suffer during the current financial crisis, the number of schools that are comfortable signing onto the Yellow Ribbon Program may be decreasing. None of us are comfortable with incremental expenses at a time when we need to cut costs substantially. If many of us do not participate, this places a greater burden on veterans who wish to attend more expensive schools, a burden that most of them cannot meet. Let me urge you all to join in this program.

The Yellow Ribbon Program provides more flexibility for institutional participants than is immediately obvious. Signing onto this does not obligate your school to contribute the maximum amount, half of the difference, to all veterans who enroll. It provides a dollar-for-dollar match of *up to* 50 percent of the difference between the highest undergraduate tuition at a public institution in its own state and its own tuition.

Your campus can choose at what level you will participate—what percentage of the cost difference you will cover—and you may choose the number of veterans you will enroll under this program. Colleges must enroll annually and can change their level of participation and the number of veterans accommodated.

For those institutions that are concerned about participating in the full 50 percent match, I would urge you to run the numbers with care. There is in this program the possibility of federal support for up to 75 percent of the tuition cost of the veteran—your obligation would be the remainder. And these students would bring support for additional expenses with them. I would urge you to join in the program and to limit the numbers if you are apprehensive rather than limiting the amount of support for each student. The latter puts the burden on the student. Your participation underscores support for veterans and affirms that they are welcome on your campus.

As I have learned over the last several years, it is not enough to sit back passively and expect veterans to come to us. It is my observation after several years of talking to veterans—largely wounded veterans, to be sure, but I think they are pretty representative in this regard—that the financial barrier is only part of what is keeping them from thinking about higher education. They have in some cases never been encouraged to think about this and they have often come to believe they would not be welcome. We need to step up to remedy this. This requires us to remember that these are not conventional students being encouraged and supported by high school guidance counselors, teachers, and parents. They need encouragement. They need information. They need help in applying. And they need us to be flexible.

We have an opportunity to think carefully about how our practices and policies either deter or encourage veterans to join us on our campuses. We have done no less for other underrepresented groups as we have sought to fulfill our educational missions, and I believe it will take less work than some fear to make a similar effort for veterans: posting information in a central location on your website; identification of a coordinator or contact person who can address specific needs of veterans; development of workshops to help students, faculty, and staff understand the experiences of veterans; accommodating the needs of these particular students; and possible partnerships with your closest VA hospital or other veterans' organization. These are all manageable steps we can take toward creating an inclusive environment for veterans—as is enrolling in the Yellow Ribbon Program.

Each of your schools will have to come to its own decision about participation, and for those of you with graduate programs or differing tuition levels, there may be different levels of participation. Last week I read some of the public comments posted in January about the proposed regulations, and I know that there remain unanswered questions related to the administrative work they will require, both for the Department of Veterans Affairs and for institutions. Among other questions, there are concerns about what "fees" will be covered, about how "need-based" financial aid can relate to this program, about the current requirement that schools "waive" tuition rather than use scholarship programs, and about the ways in which multiple schools within a single institution can have different plans.

These are all important issues to consider, and over the next several months they will have to be addressed. Even then, it is likely there will still be concerns to be worked out over the first year of the program. Last week I had the opportunity to talk to Keith Wilson, who is the director of education benefits at the Veterans Administration and is responsible for developing the regulations for administration of the new program. He will join us tomorrow for a session on the Yellow Ribbon Program. I am impressed by his commitment to find a way to make this work—for the veterans and for the schools.

All of our schools are privileged, to be sure some more than others, but we are all enabled by government grants and protection and by the tax-advantaged support of individuals. With privilege goes obligation—and we do here have an obligation to recognize those who have stepped forward and have served the country. But there is more than that—beyond privilege and obligation, we all surely do feel a commitment to make our school the better and the experience of our students the stronger.

That need introduces one additional reason for participating in the Yellow Ribbon Program that I have not yet addressed, and it is perhaps the most compelling of all: the students themselves. At Dartmouth we have several Iraq and Afghanistan veterans who have joined us in the last two years; they now number nine. Probably six of them have Purple Hearts and three or four had major injuries. I counseled a few of them before they applied, and one of them I first met when he was in a hospital bed suffering from gunshot wounds suffered in a firefight in the Battle of Fallujah. These students are exceptionally bright and engaging young people.

If they stand apart from their peers in any way it is to their credit: their GPAs are at or above the average. Several have already earned honors. Their professors report they rarely miss class and are diligent and timely in the completion of all work. They have tended to take many history and government classes and are particularly interested in international affairs and languages. They are active in all aspects of campus life, and last year they formed their own student veterans' association. Other students have enjoyed having them as classmates. They are a wonderful addition to our classroom discussions and to the campus environment.

We expect several more veterans will matriculate at Dartmouth next fall. These students have and will continue to enrich our campus, as did the veterans who came to Hanover before them—dating back to the fall of 1945.

There are many compelling reasons for us to proactively support access to higher education for our country's veterans. I would argue it is the right thing to do for them, an important thing for us to do for our nation, and the wise thing to do for our institutions. This is a wonderful opportunity, a trifecta you should not let pass you by!

Veterans Day Is for Remembering—
and for Looking Ahead

November 2012

V ETERANS DAY 2012 is an occasion to pause and do what we should do every day—remember those who have served and sacrificed. This year, coming on the heels of a national election, we also need to resolve to address some tasks ahead.

The president and Congress will need to determine just how to draw down our forces in Afghanistan. They must define the nation's military objectives for those forces who will serve there over the next two years. They must also do far more to support those who return.

This is also time to consider how the United States will remember those who have served in Iraq and Afghanistan—and memorialize the now more than 6,600 who have died in those two wars. These veterans themselves and the families of those who were lost should have the primary voice in determining the form of national memory.

The form and voice of memorializing have varied significantly over the years. Following World War I, there was a great emphasis on "living memory"—public facilities and infrastructure. Since World War II the focus has been more on physical memorials—but each of the three national memorials completed in this period has had a quite different theme.

This Veterans Day we celebrate the thirtieth anniversary of the Vietnam Veterans Memorial on the National Mall. Today the Vietnam Veterans Memorial is a national treasure, visited by over three million people annually. In 1979 Jan Scruggs, a Vietnam veteran, proposed a memorial honoring those who had sacrificed there. It moved forward remarkably quickly and in 1982 it was dedicated. But quickly does not mean it moved easily: thirty years ago critics found it somber and unheroic. Ross Perot led criticism of the memorial and Tom Wolfe wrote in the *Washington Post* that the memorial was "a tribute to Jane Fonda" and to antiwar activism.

The Vietnam Memorial broke from the iconic, heroic, memorial pattern by remembering the individual lives that were lost. Of course, most local monuments dating from the nineteenth century featured the names of those who had been lost in the wars. For many in 1982 the model of the ideal memorial was the Marine Corps Memorial a few miles away in Arlington, a Felix de Weldon statue based upon the Joe Rosenthal photograph of the Marines raising the flag on Iwo Jima in 1945.

This Marine Corps Memorial did not mention the 22,000 Marine casualties on the island—including nearly 7,000 dead. It did not indicate that three of the six men raising the flag later died on Iwo Jima. Critics of the Maya Lin design persuaded Secretary of the Interior James Watt to approve the Vietnam Memorial only upon the condition that the site would also include a statue and an American flag. Frederick Hart, who created the "Three Infantrymen" statue, had studied with de Weldon.

In the early 1980s some Korean War veterans proposed a memorial for their forgotten war. In 1986 Congress approved fundraising for a site on the mall, across from the Vietnam Memorial. General Joseph Stillwell was the chair of the group of veterans who planned the memorial. He did not live to participate in its dedication in 1995. The Korean War veterans sought to remember all who had served, as well as the 36,000 who had died in that theater. Colonel William Weber, a leader of the Koran Veterans group, said, "It's not a memorial of grief. It's a memorial of pride." Black granite walls display sandblasted images of men serving in Korea. The memorial features nineteen figures walking through a field. Their expressions show the faces of men in combat. The wall at the end of this grouping memorializes those who died in that war. Currently there is sentiment on the part of many Korean War veterans to add the individual names of the fallen at the site.

The last of the three modern war memorials created is that of World War II. It is ironic that it was the last completed given that it was the first war—and it was of a scale that finally engaged nearly all Americans and was concluded with a clear sense of victory. In 1987 Roger Durbin, a veteran of the Battle of the Bulge, proposed a memorial to the war. It took six years for Congress to authorize the memorial and seventeen years to complete it. Durbin did not live to see the memorial. Neither did eleven million other World War II veterans. At the groundbreaking for the memorial, war hero

Senator Bob Dole said his generation was moving "from the shade to the shadows."

The World War II Memorial is more traditional than the other two postwar memorials on the mall. The Vietnam Memorial honors sacrifice and the Korean War Memorial evokes the experience of war. The World War II memorial records the triumph of democracy. It remembers successful campaigns and victories. Four thousand gold stars, each representing 100 Americans who died, symbolize the cost of those victories.

This Veterans Day is a good time to initiate a conversation about a memorial to those veterans who have fought our wars in Iraq and Afghanistan, our longest wars. We still do not have a monument to World War I and its 53,000 battle deaths. The last living veteran of World War I, Frank Buckles, hoped to see such a memorial. He died in February 2011. We can do better than this. Jan Scruggs and the Vietnam Veterans Memorial Fund intend to honor these latest comrades in the interim in the new Education Center.

Iraq and Afghanistan veterans need to tell us how they want our nation to remember their wars and how to memorialize those who died in these conflicts. There is no clear model. And perhaps they will want to move beyond granite and marble. But the human face of these wars needs to become part of our nation's memory—wars do have real human costs. Forgetting wars is bad history. Forgetting sacrifice is irresponsible history.

What Does America Owe Its Veterans?

November 14, 2012, in Springfield, Illinois

M Y MOST RECENT BOOK is titled *Those Who Have Borne the Battle.* You will know this is language adapted from Lincoln's second inaugural address—affirming, at the end of a cruel war, the nation's obligation to those who served. It was perhaps one of the most eloquent addresses of this remarkably eloquent man. And he concluded it with generosity—and with resolution: "With malice toward none; with charity for all; with firmness in the right, as God gives us to see the right, let us strive on to finish the work we are in; to bind up the nation's wounds; to care for him who shall have borne the battle, and for his widow, and his orphan—to do all which may achieve and cherish a just and lasting peace among ourselves, and with all nations."

President Lincoln reminded the nation that the end of a war initiates rather than concludes the national obligation to those who fought.

MY GENERATION observed the World War II veterans, including my father, return home, their war saluted and celebrated. These veterans seemed to fit easily into the heritage of the "citizen soldiers" rooted in our national narrative beginning with the American Revolution. We considered this the American way of war. Rather than a professional military, throughout our history when the republic was threatened Americans moved from farm and factory and shop, put on uniforms and picked up the weapons of war. As soon as the war was over, they moved quickly back to their civilian pursuits. On the eve of World War II, presidents from George Washington to Franklin Roosevelt had affirmed this model.

George Washington during the Revolution spoke of the obligation of all citizens. "Every citizen," he stated, "who enjoys the protection of a free government, owes not only a proportion of his property, but even of his personal services to the defence of it."

This principle of obligation, a belief shared widely by the revolutionary generation, became a cornerstone value—moreover, we even began thinking it was factually the case. From Lexington and Concord to Gettysburg to Belleau Woods to the Battle of the Bulge, American citizens have stood at the ready to any who would challenge us.

In 1940, when European war threatened to engage the United States again, Senator Bob Reynolds of North Carolina warned Hitler not to take lightly American boys who grew up with squirrel rifles in their hands.

As someone who did grow up as a squirrel hunter, on the hardwood bluffs and hills outside of Galena, I have to acknowledge that it never occurred to me that I was prepared to take on a Panzer division. Needless to say, that is not the point, nor is it the theme of the national narrative: Americans are reluctant warriors, but they are ready when called upon. In the telling, they have stepped up for their country's wars and as soon as they are able, they return to their civilian lives.

In truth this story was always a bit exaggerated. Washington expressed great frustration with the militia during the Revolution. Most of the colonies had to resort to all sorts of devices to get enough men mobilized for war.

The Civil War was marked by bonuses and bounties, community and group pressure, and finally by a draft. Early on in that war, recruits from all segments of society enlisted with a sense of optimism and naivete about the duration and bloodiness of the war. World War I had a draft as well—and it was largely successful in placing in the field an army that represented a cross-section of American society.

But World War II really was an example of the power of the citizen soldier—there was a massive mobilization. By war's end on land and sea and air, Americans fought bravely and well in a cruel war.

The 12 percent of the country in uniform represented a more significant proportion of the population than any previous wars except the Civil War. The mobilization was induced by a massive compulsory draft, to be certain—but one widely accepted and applauded.

From the Korean War on, those who fight America's wars have been increasingly less representative—no longer is there much mention of, much pretense even, of the citizen soldier. The Korean War draft was marked by deferments, exemptions, and enlistment options.

Vietnam had even more of these options to avoid or delay the draft. With college deferments common it was described as the blue-collar war. And by act of Congress and the support of President Richard Nixon in 1973, the United States initiated the All-Volunteer Force. That is the state of the military today. There is no more emphasis upon service as a shared obligation. And surely no political figure ever reminds us of General Washington's insistence that citizens of the republic owe some part of their property when the nation is at war. There are no taxes designated for support of these wars.

Today we no longer think about shared obligation, about taxes or representativeness. Over the last several years I have tried to introduce those who fight and sacrifice today, to put a human face on them—the hidden 1 percent of our population.

Secondly, in my work I also have tried to describe, especially from the Civil War onward, some fundamental changes in the scale of war, resulting cruelly in impersonal, an almost abstract, scale and scope of tragedy: the increased anonymity of war. In ironic ways, as few of those serving are known—outside of their family and their community—they have all become "heroes."

Two examples underline the scale of tragedy of modern war: the battle of Gettysburg and that of Iwo Jima. At Gettysburg, in July 1863, 170,000 men fought for three days. There were over 50,000 casualties, nearly 8,000 dead.

On the small but strategic island of Iwo Jima, held by Japanese forces, 30,000 Marines went ashore in February of 1945. They suffered 22,000 casualties—nearly 7,000 dead. This means that 29 percent of the Marines killed in World War II died on Iwo Jima. And essentially all of the 20,000 Japanese defenders were killed.

Modern wars are robbed of individualism. And political leaders and narrators describing these wars of great sacrifice increasingly do not dwell so much on sacrifice but on purpose, or a common heroism. They sometimes are trying to hide the human costs of these wars—but they also are suggesting that the individual accounting is secondary to the shared purpose. The rationale, the reason for the war, not the cost in blood, becomes paramount. Two iconic examples of this are the dominant historical descriptions of the battle at Gettysburg and Iwo Jima.

Let us consider President Lincoln's Gettysburg Address.

Four score and seven years ago our fathers brought forth on this continent a new nation, conceived in liberty, and dedicated to the proposition that all men are created equal.

Now we are engaged in a great civil war, testing whether that nation, or any nation, so conceived and so dedicated, can long endure. We are met on a great battle-field of that war. We have come to dedicate a portion of that field, as a final resting place for those who here gave their lives that that nation might live. It is altogether fitting and proper that we should do this.

But, in a larger sense, we can not dedicate, we can not consecrate, we can not hallow this ground. The brave men, living and dead, who struggled here, have consecrated it, far above our poor power to add or detract. The world will little note, nor long remember what we say here, but it can never forget what they did here. It is for us the living, rather, to be dedicated here to the unfinished work which they who fought here have thus far so nobly advanced. It is rather for us to be here dedicated to the great task remaining before us—that from these honored dead we take increased devotion to that cause for which they gave the last full measure of devotion—that we here highly resolve that these dead shall not have died in vain—that this nation, under God, shall have a new birth of freedom—and that government of the people, by the people, for the people, shall not perish from the earth.

These remarks are considered one of the finest eulogies in our history. And they are—but think about them for a moment. In these moving comments there were no names, no heroes, no blood.

President Lincoln knew better than any American that the Civil War meant awful personal losses. He met with wounded veterans of some the bloodiest battles that had ever been fought and expressed his gratitude and support. Observers noted his sad and haunted eyes. When the ambulances returning the wounded soldiers from the Siege of Petersburg to D.C. passed him, he turned away stricken, uttering, "I cannot bear it. This suffering, this loss of life is dreadful."

He walked in the funeral procession for women who died in an arsenal explosion in Washington and saw their distraught family members desperately pushing through the crowds to seize the coffins.

When Lincoln delivered his Gettysburg address, some bodies of the dead soldiers were visible in shallow graves. The smell of death was in the air.

Nonetheless, Lincoln does not dwell on the sacrifices of these people, each of whom had a story, dreams, and aspirations, but instead seeks to clarify the purpose for which they died. A purpose for which others must be prepared to die. The Gettysburg Address is less a eulogy than it is a rededication.

He urged Americans to make certain that the fallen have not died in vain—in less deft hands than President Lincoln's, where a broad national purpose required sacrifice, too often this language reverses the equation: sacrifice itself defines purpose.

The iconic Marine Corps Iwo Jima Memorial is another example of heroic memory. When the Iwo Jima monument was under consideration in the 1950s, there was some controversy over the idea of a traditional statue. Some arts committees fought the concept, but this was really no contest pitted against the politically strong Marine Corps and given postwar sentiment. Felix de Weldon received the commission to construct a statue in Arlington based on Joseph Rosenthal's photo of the flag raising on Mount Suribachi on Iwo Jima. The base listed heroic Marine battles. There was no mention of the thousands of casualties. No indication that three of the six identified then as raising the flag did not leave the island alive. The human sacrifice was abstracted.

The Vietnam Veterans Memorial on the Washington Mall is an outlier in the modern era—it itemizes the human cost and whispers of sacrifice. And of course, there was some real controversy over this memorial because it was considered unheroic. The later Korean War Memorial on the mall, with its larger-than-life statues of men moving across a field, evokes the experience. And the World War II Memorial affirms the triumph of democracy.

So in most regards these memorials and eulogies serve less as memorials and more as monuments, reminders that grand national purposes require sacrifice, and that those who step up are heroes. With the exception of the Vietnam Memorial there is little reminder of the human cost.

Today an unrepresentative military fights and sacrifices on our behalf— and they serve in wars in which it is harder to describe the purpose, the rationale. Anonymity in these wars is not a result of the scale but because most Americans don't even know those who fight.

But these are real wars to those who fight them. As wars always have been and always will be.

The Challenge of Memorializing
America's Wars

May 2017

E ACH MEMORIAL DAY, tourists descend on the nation's capital to visit memorials and monuments honoring members of the U.S. armed forces who've died defending their country. For the family and friends of the fallen, the act of remembering is daily—as is their grief. This distinction between public acknowledgment and private grief is captured tangibly in the sites on the National Mall.

Often the terms "monument" and "memorial" are used interchangeably to describe the iconic sites in the nation's capital, but there is a difference. The *New York Times* recently cited philosopher of art Arthur Danto's definition to illustrate this distinction: "We erect monuments so that we shall always remember, and build memorials so that we shall never forget." While memorials are a source of remembrance, monuments seek to celebrate the purpose, the accomplishments, the heroic. They evoke the cause. As the Global War on Terror Memorial Foundation campaigns for a site to honor those who've died in Iraq and Afghanistan, its members will likely have to grapple with these definitions in deciding what exactly it should be.

In March 2017, Representatives Mike Gallagher and Seth Moulton introduced legislation authorizing a study and fundraising for a new national memorial. The bill also exempts the memorial from current law, which states that a memorial can't be authorized until at least ten years after the war has ended. The Global War on Terror Memorial Foundation is leading the initiative. In an interview with the *San Diego Union-Tribune*, Andrew Brennan, the founder and executive director of the group, argued that "we have met the historic burden context," in light of the thousands of those who have died, been wounded, or deal with post-traumatic stress. But memorializing wars while confronting and remembering sacrifice can be a complicated endeavor.

74

The Vietnam Veterans Memorial Wall provides a striking example of this. The wall, inscribed with more than 58,000 names of servicemen and -women, has become a major attraction in Washington, D.C., and plans are now well underway for an adjacent education center that will provide information on the individuals the wall records. But bringing the memorial to fruition was fraught with conflict. The tension that divided supporters of the memorial thirty-five years ago stemmed from two key questions: How does a nation remember its wars? How do we memorialize our war dead?

On July 1, 1980, Congress authorized the Vietnam Veterans Memorial Fund and allocated three acres on the National Mall near the Lincoln Memorial for its construction. The Memorial Fund, led by Vietnam veteran Jan Scruggs, the originator of the initiative, raised over $8 million with the support of nearly 300,000 individual contributors.

The design review committee selected the design of Yale University architecture student Maya Lin. Lin proposed a polished black granite wall with the inscribed names of the Americans who had died in the war. The proposed wall, with no decoration, not even a flag, provided a stunning tally of loss. Many of the early supporters of a memorial were troubled by the absence of any recognition of heroic service.

Vietnam veteran Jim Webb found it nihilistic, ignoring the honor and courage of those who served. Ross Perot, one of the early advocates of a memorial and a major financial contributor, called it a tombstone, and Tom Carhart, a Vietnam veteran, described it as a "black gash of shame."

The Vietnam Veterans Memorial leadership accommodated much of the criticism. They agreed to display prominently an American flag and commissioned Frederick Hart to design a statue that would stand nearby. With these modifications, Interior Secretary James Watt approved the plan. Hart's "Three Soldiers" statue was dedicated in 1984. The 1993 dedication of the Vietnam Women's Memorial recognized the thousands of women who served courageously in Vietnam. The wall—and the two accompanying statues—completed a site that many, including nearly all of the early critics, came to consider special, even sacred.

Today, the Vietnam wall cries out eloquently the magnitude of sacrifice, nearly 500 feet long, marked by line after line of chiseled names. Each name, in turn, whispers the record of a single life lost, and invites its own private memorial. The ground below has been personalized by mementoes left behind—and by many tears.

The celebration of warriors and their sacrifice is at least as old as classical Greece. According to Thucydides, Pericles eulogized the Athenians who died in the Peloponnesian War as men "who preferred death to survival at the cost of surrender." He judged them as the valiant dead who "*proved worthy of their city.*"

Memories of patriotic sacrifice enrich national pride: The courageous dead were worthy of their city or their country. Now the survivors must be worthy of them. It is not necessary to go back 2,500 years to Athens to affirm this. In 1863, Abraham Lincoln stood at Gettysburg, on ground still stained by death and in air filled with the stench from shallow graves, and eulogized the dead only in the most general terms. He provided no tally of cost, focusing instead on the purpose of their sacrifice. He promised, "that from these honored dead we take increased devotion to that cause for which they gave the last full measure of devotion," and assured that "we here highly resolve that these dead shall not have died in vain."

Lincoln mourned privately even as he resolved publicly. More recently, the Marine Corps Memorial in Arlington, dedicated in 1954, reflected this patriotic resolution. The Felix de Weldon statue, based on the Joe Rosenthal photo of the six Marines raising the U.S. flag at Iwo Jima, provided a stirring tribute to the Marine Corps—and to the World War II generation. The base quotes Admiral Chester Nimitz: "Uncommon valor was a common virtue." There is no acknowledgment, however, of the more than 6,800 Americans who died in that battle, including three of the six men who raised the flag.

There has been a democratization of memorials since the nineteenth century, when town squares and public plazas were marked by resolute figures, typically generals, and usually on horseback. From the Civil War onward these public places generally included a tablet or statue base that listed the community members who served—and those who sacrificed.

National memorials, meanwhile, continue to illustrate the tension between statue and base, between the several goals of heroic celebration, honoring service, and remembering loss. Dedicated in 1995, the Korean War Memorial features a striking tableau with nineteen stainless-steel statues representing American troops warily crossing a field, bounded on one side with a black granite mural showing the experiences of and honoring those who served.

In the years since it was completed, Korean War veterans have worked tirelessly to include the names of those who died in this war. In October 2016, President Barack Obama signed the Korean War Veterans Memorial Wall of Remembrance Act. Now the Korean War Veterans Memorial Foundation is raising funds to add a laminated glass wall including over 36,000 names of those who died in the conflict.

The World War II Memorial dedicated in 2004, on the other hand, is monumental in a traditional sense. It includes granite pillars and arches representing the theaters of operations, bas-relief sculpture, two poles with American flags, a plaza, a pool, a fountain, and a wall with 4,000 gold stars each representing 100 Americans who died while serving in that war. These stars are symbolic, abstract, not personal—they project the scale of loss, though not the individuality of sacrifice.

It is a memorial but it is also emphatically a monument. None of the other memorials on the mall, completed or proposed, has sought to be so large and magisterial, traditionally monumental even.

Apart from the triumphant scale, this merging of forms is what the Vietnam Memorial became when the representational statues joined Lin's memorial wall. It is what the Korean War Memorial will become when the Wall of Remembrance is completed. And it is what the Global War on Terror Memorial Foundation will be tasked with as it presses forward with its site.

Recognizing those who served is important. But to do so without honoring those who sacrificed, as individuals and not as numbers, would provide an incomplete narrative of war. It is their narrative that Americans salute today. And need to remember every day.

American Veterans and
the National Obligation

May 17, 2018, in Washington, D.C.

In 2018 the U.S. Congress, with bipartisan unanimity, approved an extension and expansion of the 2009 GI Bill legislation. This was an important step.

It may provide an incentive to serve and a fully deserved acknowledgment of having done so, enabling veterans in their transitions back to civilian life. But it is also an investment in the future of the republic.

The ranks of the American military today are filled with volunteers. They do not represent the nation demographically, tending to be more rural than urban, more heartland than coastal, largely from blue-collar and middle-class backgrounds. They tend to come from military families. They constitute less than 1 percent of the population. American engagement in Iraq and Afghanistan are the first extended wars in American history with no designated tax to pay for the war and no service requirement. So much for George Washington's reminder that if it is necessary to go to war, then all citizens should support it with their treasure and with their service. Not anymore. Not for these wars. The vast majority of us go on with our lives.

Those who have served in the twenty-first century are the best educated of Americans to serve in any war, better educated than their age group as a whole. The armed forces today expect at least a high school education. Unfortunately, a high school education is insufficient in this modern economy.

The recent pattern of veterans having higher unemployment rates than nonveterans was largely the result of their educational background rather than their military service.

The Post-9/11 GI Bill offers them an opportunity to set a course for their future. But I learned early on in my conversations that while it was essential to provide the financial support for veterans to continue with their education, the prior, and sometimes more difficult, counseling need was to encourage them to do this, to assure them that *they could* do this.

While nearly all of those who have joined the all-volunteer military may be high school graduates, many did not take the college preparation courses. They probably have not taken the standardized SAT or ACT exams. They often feel unprepared for higher education and some of them may not be ready. But I have no doubt that they all can be ready. Counseling and convincing them of this is essential, as is follow-up support to encourage them to pursue and succeed.

We have a national need, an obligation to try to encourage all students who have never been encouraged. They can do this. And here is where those young women and men with military experience may draw on greater self-confidence.

But there is another part of the military experience that we need to understand. Humans learn as infants to remember two constant things: to look out for themselves, avoiding any threatening risks—don't go there, don't touch that, look carefully—and not to harm others. The latter is more than parental guidance, as it is emphasized under threat of law as well as moral code and religious teachings.

When a very small fraction of our citizens, in the late teens or early twenties, are mobilized for war, they must learn to suppress these fundamental instincts and principles when the situation demands. They must be willing to put themselves in harm's way, without question or hesitation. And they must be willing to bring harm to others, lethal harm, without any delay or moral reflection.

When they return to civilian life, they are told to return to their first rules, to forget that which they have just learned, and to wipe from their memory contrary experiences. In each instance, this is impossible. The vast majority of combat veterans do return to civilian lives successfully. But they never forget their experience. It is a difficult transition. Some do not return as successfully as others. And these veterans are a matter for our focus today.

We need to know the experience of war from those who were there before we can begin to understand it; to know how profound their experience is. As a Vietnam veteran, army combat photographer Dick Durrance recently described it.

They risk their lives;
They face terror;
They lose buddies in battles.
And then they come home...
Where they have to square what they had to do as warriors
With what they are expected to do now that they are home.
It isn't easy.

Veterans who are imprisoned for committing a crime face many of the same problems that nonveterans face in transitioning back to civilian life following their release: problems of employment, of acceptance, of reentering American society while encountering suspicion. And finally of avoiding recidivism.

This path is harder to avoid if individuals encounter a society that has little confidence in a good outcome. These problems may be compounded for veterans who have been released. They confront dual and reinforcing stereotypes.

The current "Ban the Box" initiative to encourage prospective employers and college admissions applications to discontinue asking questions about criminal convictions is an interesting effort. It is reminiscent of Vietnam veterans in the 1970s not acknowledging their military service on job applications.

We have come a great distance medically since Post-Traumatic Stress Disorder (PTSD) was recognized as a clinical disorder affecting veterans forty years ago. That journey is not over. And the distance remains even greater in accomplishing social acceptance of this mental health condition.

The medical and the legal recognition of PTSD has been so important. We discuss it more openly now. But I also worry that this ironically has buttressed another cruel stereotype, that of the socially unhinged veteran. The Vietnam veterans encountered the *Taxi Driver* and *Apocalypse Now* deranged psychotic veteran image. The 1970s were not kind to the returning veterans from an unpopular war.

In the early '70s on the TV show *Kojak*, Telly Savalas confronted a series of brutal homicides. He told one of his detectives to find out if there were any Vietnam veterans in the neighborhood of the crimes.

PTSD, a companion of all wars—read Odysseus—was not even diagnosed as a clinical condition until 1979. Before that, veterans with problems were categorized as suffering from the Vietnam Syndrome. As if it were an isolated condition of this whining group of "hippies"! World War II veterans told them to grow up and get over it: "*We* did." But of course, not all did. It was called "combat fatigue" or "shell shock" then. The Vietnam veterans spoke of nightmares becoming daymares. One said, "If those other people had to spend just one night inside my nightmares they would fall to the floor with tears in their eyes." They endured and they have contributed much more to our national life.

One thing we have learned is that veterans will speak more candidly, more personally, about their experiences with other veterans. Some of the best counseling sessions involve a group of veterans sharing their stories and encouraging one another.

If post-9/11 veterans have not had to contend with the same nasty, degrading stereotypes in popular culture, they still have had too often to encounter wisps of the fear and prejudice that remain. And here the reinforcing fear and prejudice and suspicion that confronts them as former convicts *and* veterans can be even harder to escape.

If this is their difficult assignment, I have confidence in them. But we, American society, have a role as well. We still do need to thank them for their service and recognize this is not a throw-away gratuity. They need a hand, not a handout. We still need to recognize what they did on our behalf, even if they have stumbled since. They still have much to offer.

These veterans have worked effectively with others of different backgrounds, assumed personal responsibility and accountability, functioned in complex organizations in an advanced technological environment, and confronted dangerous situations while respecting people of different cultures. They have learned discipline and restraint and self-confidence—and tolerance.

They have observed—and offered—sacrifice for a greater good.

I am impressed by the options that sheriffs and wardens such as those speaking here today ... have created to help veterans. Their counseling and their living units allow veterans to connect with each other, which is an essential step toward their reconnecting with society. The report that is released today (U.S. Department of Justice, National Institute of Corrections, *Barracks Behind Bars: In Veteran-Specific Housing Units, Veterans Help*

Veterans Help Themselves) and this gathering address the value of these programs.

These veterans have met their obligation. Now we have an obligation to reach out to them. They will benefit from our support, of course—as we have already greatly benefited from theirs. And we and our society will be the better if we are able to help them to succeed. It is truly a win-win. A delayed reciprocal: We have got your back.

Welcome: Fall Meeting of the Ivy League Veterans Council

October 5, 2019, at Dartmouth College
in Hanover, New Hampshire

CURRENT VETERANS face a different economic and occupational world from that of your parents and grandparents. Veterans could come home from Vietnam—as they had from Korea and World War II—and look to get a job at a local factory or mill. They could assume that if they did their job, if they worked hard, they would have job security with health benefits until they retired. And then probably have a retirement package to supplement Social Security.

It would not be wise to make such an assumption today. A degree, undergraduate and sometimes advanced, is now often a requisite for a good job or for entry into the professions. And job security is not a lifetime guarantee.

After we secured the Post-9/11 GI Bill in 2008, I realized that, including the Yellow Ribbon Program, we had addressed one of the major financial obstacles to veterans pursuing their education. I am not saying that the support was adequate in all cases. It was not. And I am surely not claiming that all schools recognized the special financial needs of veterans. You do not fit into the conventional models for dependent high school graduates entering college.

But with the 2008 legislation the basic financial aid system was in place, to be enhanced and extended over the next decade. Schools, often far too slowly, came to recognize their opportunity and their obligations. The major challenge then was to convince veterans that they could take advantage of these opportunities, and to navigate the admissions system—including at the very best schools. And for all educational institutions to open their doors and resources to veterans to make that successful.

Your generation of veterans is not a cross section of American society. You tend to be from more rural or small-town backgrounds, more from the South, the Midwest, the Mountain West. Many come from families where military service was a tradition, and veterans today tend to be from blue-collar or middle-class backgrounds.

Many who have served likely attended high schools where it was not assumed that all graduates would go to college. And veterans tended not to have been enrolled in college prep programs—and in fact, many did not even take the standardized ACT or SAT examinations.

So even if the basic financial support system was in place, a more fundamental problem remained. To encourage, enable, and empower veterans—to assure them that, yes, they can do this. And they could do it at any of the elite schools in the country.

I think that convincing veterans of their academic potential is the obligation that institutions of higher learning and counselors share—and we need to work harder to do this. It requires active recruiting. We need to encourage our admissions offices to be more focused and imaginative in recruiting and encouraging veterans.

Once enrolled, it requires us to recognize the differences in age and background and the needs of veteran students. It has been my experience that veterans are far less likely than their classmates to complain or demand an adjustment in procedures.

Recruiting and encouraging and enabling veterans to pursue their education is not some sort of condescending "thank you for your service" gratuity. The GI Bill may provide an incentive to serve, but it is not a gift. It is a fully earned benefit for those who have served the country, one that aids them in their transition back to civilian life.

But there is more. Let's be clear. We—our schools and this republic—are the real beneficiaries of your enrollment. You enrich the campuses and the classrooms where you study and the organizations you join. Our schools and your nonveteran classmates are enriched intellectually by your presence. You are role models. And there is even more. You are not finished serving this country.

A few years ago I wrote an op-ed pointing out that if today's military volunteers do not represent the nation demographically, they do not represent it attitudinally either. In recent years there has been an unfortunate marked decline in this nation in a shared sense of civic engagement—and of civic responsibility. Our national discourse has often been reduced to a contest of individuals or groups pursuing their self-interests and maligning and dismissing the needs and interests of others. Ideology and partisanship have come to represent and to channel these goals. Political figures promise and do not ask for sacrifice—except for the young they send to war.

You who volunteered to serve stand for something different. There was no draft conscripting you.

You know how to serve as a team member. You have worked effectively with others of different backgrounds, followed orders and also assumed personal responsibility and accountability, functioned in complex organizations in an advanced technological environment, and confronted dangerous situations in environments of total mutual dependence. You have learned discipline and restraint and self-confidence—and tolerance. You have represented this nation in undertakings that emphasize respecting those of different cultures. You have observed—and offered—service and sacrifice for a greater good.

We need you to continue to serve and to make a positive difference. We so badly need the voices of Americans seeking to continue to serve their country. Their entire country.

So your education is not only an investment in your futures. It is a necessary investment in the future of this republic. Your tours of duty are not over. Your colleges and universities are beneficiaries who need to shout out with pride the value of your contributions to their institutions and remind everyone of the promise you offer to the world. You have already made a down payment on that promise.

III

HISTORY LESSONS

We Are Always Rewriting Our Past— We Must

July 2020

P RESIDENT DONALD TRUMP celebrated Independence Day 2020 on July 3 in South Dakota and on July 4 in Washington. For these occasions he provided a history lesson. But it was a lesson with a political edge: he was critical of those who were demanding the removal of offensive statues and he countered with his own plans for a statuary garden of heroes.

And his history lessons were based on what many would consider an ideological and partisan message rather than an affirmation of shared values.

At Mount Rushmore he argued, "Our nation is witnessing a merciless campaign to wipe out our history, defame our heroes, erase our values, and indoctrinate our children." He insisted that left-wing radicals seek "to tear down every statue, symbol, and memory of our national heritage." Recently he has defended the Confederate flag, statues honoring Confederate military and civilian leaders, and bases named after Confederate generals.

He has insisted that Americans need to be careful of radicals who seek to "rewrite" history. His comments notwithstanding, our understanding of history is not doctrinal and is fortunately being revised and expanded regularly. Being rewritten.

History is the study of the past—and "the past" is the totality of the human experience. As Arnold Toynbee is reputed to have said, many think that history "is just one damned thing after another." And it is, much of which we can never recover in sufficient detail to really study. The past holds the record of human actions and of human reactions to those natural and human forces that affect them.

Seeking to know and to understand better the past is a basic human instinct. We need to know better where we came from, who and what preceded us, in order better to understand ourselves. Our lives and institutions are the products of our history. Abraham Lincoln cautioned, "we cannot escape history."

The effort to "rewrite" history is not, as critics claim, an effort to alter the record of the past. We cannot do that. It stands—and challenges us to learn from it. Oliver Wendell Holmes Jr. wrote, "History has to be rewritten because history is the selection of those threads of causes or antecedents that we are interested in."

There is obviously an opportunity in this constant rewriting to seek a history that expands our understanding of our heritage, our origins, our antecedents. And to many there is also an opportunity to narrate what we want our past to be and to justify our lives and our interest. To glorify our past, to locate ancestors who are worthy of their descendants.

Perhaps one of the most egregious and successful rewrites of history was that of the late nineteenth century, which revised the history of the American South and of slavery and of the nature and causes and consequences of the Civil War. "The Lost Cause" celebrated the Old South, a land of happy folks, Black as well as white.

Advocates depicted an idyllic Old South destroyed by a Civil War in which Southerners fought gallantly to defend the states and their way of life, and further savaged by punitive Northerners in the Reconstruction period. This nostalgic revisionism defined what became the dominant Southern "history," along with the savage Jim Crow laws and racism it accommodated. And the North acceded to this.

Whether it is our view of the Confederacy or Christopher Columbus or Andrew Jackson, this tension underlines what is substantively and intellectually at issue today—it is not about the history that happened, it is not about the history that historians write and teach and revise and rethink, but about the history we celebrate.

A few years ago, when I was meeting a class and speaking at West Point, a senior officer pointed out that in the superintendent's office there was a wall with portraits of several of the exemplary leaders of the academy—Douglas MacArthur, Otis Howard, William Westmoreland, Sylvanus Thayer—and Robert E. Lee. He asked me what I thought of having General Lee there.

I replied that I understood that Lee had been an accomplished superintendent of the academy and had served admirably as an officer in the Mexican War, but that he had then taken up arms against the United

States, an act of treason that violated the oath that he and all U.S. Army officers had taken. I thought it was inconsistent to celebrate him at the academy. Was he really a good role model for what we hoped for in our officers today? ...

The past is fixed, a given. We cannot modify it even when it makes us very uncomfortable. The history by which we understand this past is something that needs to be written and rewritten, expanded and thought about. Being uncomfortable is part of this.

The history we celebrate too often has little relationship to what happened or to the understanding of that. But the history we celebrate does have consequences. There is much in the history of this country and its articulated values and ideals from which we can take pride. And much that is not a source of pride.

Confronting the racism of our past and its icons is critical to shaping a world that will provide a history about which those who follow can take genuine pride. It is time to take on that confrontation.

War Veterans and
American Democracy

February 2, 2010, at the University of California, Berkeley

THIS LECTURE affords me the occasion to share some of my reflections and understandings about our historical treatment of veterans. In this presentation I would like to describe some of the assumptions and conflicts that frame the history of veterans' affairs in the United States. I will summarize the historical record of support for veterans. And I will share some reflections about changes in the dominant public attitude toward war veterans, from those who served in Vietnam to the present veterans of Iraq and Afghanistan.

One point I would like to make at the outset—this lecture is not going to assess American foreign policy nor the causes and justifications for U.S. wars. Nor is this a military history—at least not in a conventional sense. And finally, my focus on American war veterans and their casualties is taken fully cognizant of the fact that there are non-U.S. casualties and that these, notably the civilian ones, need be acknowledged. War is a violent and cruel human exercise, and can often be indiscriminate in its reach.

My subject today is U.S. *war* veterans—those who have served as part of a mobilized force drafted or otherwise called up for a declared or an undeclared war. For most of our history the U.S. military has been in a peacetime state and those who have served in these forces have been volunteers. Military forces during wartime on the other hand have been conscripted, drafted, or called up to duty from militia or reserve units. These have been the much-celebrated "citizen soldiers."

Last August at the Veterans of Foreign Wars convention President Obama said of the legacy of support for veterans, "America's commitments to its veterans are not just lines in a budget. They are bonds that are sacrosanct—a sacred trust we are honor bound to uphold." In November the United States Supreme Court seemed to affirm this commitment when it ruled in *Porter v. McCollum* for a new hearing for a Korean War veteran who had been convicted of a 1987 murder. The Court held that the defense had not presented evidence of the psychological state of the veteran as a result of his war experiences. The justices noted, "Our nation has a long tradition of according leniency to veterans in recognition of their service, especially for those who fought on the front lines."

I would defer to others to debate sacred or legal obligation. But I would suggest that the history of our relations with veterans is more complicated— less generous and more ambiguous—than these observations imply.

From the beginning of this republic, in revolutionary rhetoric and in legislative provision, those who established the new nation expressed an aversion to the idea of professional or standing armies. This was one of the issues that led to the revolt against the Crown. The minutemen at Lexington and Concord ennobled the American ideal, the citizen soldier.

As it turned out, the widespread discomfort with the idea of a standing army also provided some practical budget advantages for the young nation—armies and navies were expensive. And the citizen soldier offered a political supplement to the constitutional checks on the declaration of war: it was a widely shared and enduring assumption that in a democracy no war fought by the citizens of that democracy can be sustained unless there is clear popular support for the commitment and for the cost. This was consistent with an abiding principle of American democracy: civilian control of the military.

The ideal of the citizen soldier was a crucial element in debating the decision in the 1970s to end the draft and move to an all-volunteer force. And in recent years most proposals for a reinstatement of the draft have focused less on military requirements and have been based on the assertion that such a system would provide a more significant popular check on military activities. The assumption was that if *all* of our sons and daughters faced the possibility of being engaged in armed conflict in Iraqi villages and in the Afghanistan mountains, perhaps no sons and daughters would face this exposure—or if they did, there would be a full discussion and acceptance of the national interest that required this service.

This debate about the composition of the military obviously informs broader views toward veterans, but my question is a simple one: What does a democracy owe to its veterans, following their wartime military service?

This simple question does not have a simple answer in practice. Prior to World War II, the prevailing view tended to be that the country owes little to those discharged war veterans who are physically fit: as citizen soldiers, as beneficiaries of the compact of the democracy, their service was not a contract for which further compensation was due, but rather was the necessary obligation of citizenship in a free society.

Clearly this view of no compensation for healthy veterans has not been the prevailing one for the last seventy-five years. The GIs of the Second World War were cultural heroes and came home to a grateful nation. This reframed the dominant view of veterans' benefits. Yet it is important to note that even prior to World War II there were major exceptions to the principle that there was no obligation to healthy veterans.

The passage of time has always been important in the development of public affection for—and even mythologizing of—wartime service. Surely a grateful republic embraced the Revolutionary War veterans. In the early years, however, it was but a quick embrace, as the new nation and its citizens had much to do. Within a few years, however, the celebration of the historic revolution and those heroes who fought it became an important ritual of national unity. The pattern of support for veterans that evolved following the Revolution would frame the fundamentals that would mark our policy down through the First World War: support for widows and orphans of those who died in combat action, some limited support for combat-related disability, selective land grants down through the 1850s, and, for Revolutionary War and Union Civil War veterans, pensions for aged survivors.

The First World War was a war of citizen soldiers—conscription drew broadly from the population as the military forces increased in eighteen months from approximately 125,000 to nearly four million serving by November 1918. President Woodrow Wilson and the Congress provided a war-risk insurance plan for active-duty military personnel, who paid their own premiums. There was an initial expectation that along with health care for combat injuries, this would be sufficient—but it proved not to be adequate in many cases to provide for transitions back to civilian life.

Even though World War I individual veteran benefits were limited, the magnitude of the numbers who served in the armed forces and who required medical support was consequential. In the 1920s about 20 percent of the federal budget went to veterans. And in 1921, in response to the need Congress institutionalized veterans' support with the creation of the federal Veterans Bureau. This was the source of some of the embarrassing corruption during the Warren Harding presidency and in 1930 the agency was reorganized as the Veterans Administration (VA).

Within a few years of the end of the war, many of its veterans who had not required any of the medical treatment or disability-related support were increasingly of the view that they should receive some benefit in compensation for their service. Economic problems encouraged this position. In 1924 the veterans achieved, over President Calvin Coolidge's veto, passage of a bonus to be paid in 1945. By the early 1930s many sought early payment of this bonus as a result of the Great Depression, and a group organized as the Bonus Expeditionary Force or Bonus Army marched on Washington to lobby and to protest. In the summer of 1932 President Herbert Hoover ordered General Douglas MacArthur to remove them physically. He did this by using tanks and tear gas to expel them from their Washington encampment. This entire experience was an embarrassing one for many in the United States. The government's desire to avoid a repeat of any such confrontation was an important part of the policy consideration for the comprehensive veterans' programs provided to veterans of the Second World War.

The Servicemen's Readjustment Act of 1944—known simply as the "GI Bill"—was a program that fundamentally shifted the nation's treatment of war veterans. The comprehensive legislation provided for all veterans, including the able bodied, and was passed by Congress prior to the conclusion of the war. It expanded traditional medical and disability programs but also provided for a significant investment in the transition of all veterans back into American society. The legislation provided for up to fifty-two weeks of unemployment benefits, established an interest-free loan program for the purchase of homes, farms, or businesses, and offered a comprehensive and generous plan to support education or training for veterans.

As with earlier veterans' legislation, the 1944 GI Bill provided medical support, but this legislation set a new standard with an investment in healthy veterans. The GI Bill was not without flaws, however. There were political calculations involved in passage of the legislation and there were instances of fraud in the administration of benefits, as pointed out by

Berkeley historian Kathleen Frydl in her thorough analysis of the political context and full consequences of the law.

Nevertheless, it seems clear that the provisions of the GI Bill encouraged and helped underwrite much of the creative energy that American society experienced following the war. The education provisions of the GI Bill stand with the civil rights and women's rights movements in expanding the system of American higher education so that it became a model for access and democratization. Within a few years, veterans comprised nearly half of the students enrolled in American colleges and universities.

The GI Bill was more than a compensatory handshake, a gratuity, for the citizen soldiers of the global war. It built upon New Deal programs and one of the goals of the GI Bill was to ease the demobilization of a military force of nearly 16 million men and women. The GI Bill was the largest entitlement program up to this point in American history (Social Security would shortly surpass it but it had not yet done that). In the several years following the war the Veterans Administration had the largest number of employees of any government agency. In 1950, 71 percent of federal payments to individuals went to veterans through the various veterans' programs.

The public generosity toward war veterans in the 1940s would not be sustained at the same level even into the next decade. In the Cold War years and in the major postwar economic and social adjustments, there were a number of competing budget priorities. And there were concerns about some of the allegations of fraudulent claims under the GI Bill. In establishing programs for Korean War veterans and then Vietnam War veterans, the government increasingly scaled up military service requirements for eligibility and scaled down levels of support, including reduced unemployment benefits and loans. By the Vietnam period, the benefits simply did not cover full educational costs.

It is revealing that no one really questioned the basic assumptions of the GI Bill, even as they scaled back its coverage. The educational benefit came to dominate: the principle had been established that a grateful nation owed to its *wartime* citizen soldiers compensatory support that would enable them to pursue an education in order to advance their lives and to pursue their ambitions. Future debates would be over details, not over the principle. Additionally, there was broad acceptance of policies and programs that provided for medical and other support for veterans from discharge to death, and the medical support was not restricted to service-connected disabilities. Other veterans could meet eligibility standards for VA health care.

Vietnam veterans faced a nation divided in its support for the war, which for some at least meant a lessened sense of gratitude to those who served in the war. Even though there had been unpopular wars historically, there really was no precedent for a significant public sentiment blaming those called to fight these wars. The nature and the unpopularity of the Vietnam War did not noticeably influence the traditional programs for veterans—other than the reduced coverage that followed the post–World War II pattern. On the other hand, there was at best a slow, even grudging, recognition and acceptance of responsibility for some newly identified and newly understood consequences of combat service.

The government denied for many years the medical effects of weapons such as Agent Orange—despite compelling and tangible evidence of this powerful herbicide-defoliant's residual malignancies. In 1991, following years of litigation and medical claims, the Department of Veterans Affairs agreed to consider Agent Orange a presumptive factor in a range of cancers and other conditions. And only in the last few years has there been any acknowledgment of responsibility for the hundreds of thousands of Vietnamese victims of Agent Orange.

Post-Traumatic Stress Disorder (PTSD), the psychological malignancy, was also rejected in the immediate postwar years as a medical condition. Traditional accounts of "battle fatigue" and of "shell shock" were as old as warfare—in the Civil War it was called "soldier's heart." There was resistance to recognizing this as a chronic illness—with even some of the older veterans dismissing complaints as a whine that the Vietnam veterans needed to move beyond.

Finally, in 1979 Congress authorized the Veterans Administration to provide counseling for those suffering from PTSD symptoms. It was the fifth time such legislation had been introduced. This followed shortly after the American Psychiatric Association recognized PTSD as a clinical condition. This was easier and faster than the Agent Orange ruling because of the tremendous liability issues associated with the latter.

The post-Vietnam programs of support for veterans were comprehensive—and they were expensive. Neither of which presumes their adequacy in meeting the needs of veterans. In 2000, the department, at cabinet level since 1988, was the largest federal agency outside of the Defense Department. Over 20 percent of the federal nondefense personnel worked for the VA. And this expense was largely politically protected from cost cutters and critics. In the spring of 2001, the Pew Research Center learned that only 3 percent of respondents to a survey favored a reduction in spending on veterans' programs.

The Gulf War in 1990–91, Operation Desert Storm, had further enhanced this climate of public support for the military and veterans. The military effectiveness of the troops who had served in that operation strengthened the image. The 9/11 attacks underlined this climate of support for the military with an emotional jolt. Few events in American history have elicited such widespread fear, resolve, and national unity. If the U.S. military had little role to play on that fast-moving morning, it emphatically would soon. It quickly became apparent that these attacks were initiated by the militant Islamic fundamentalist group, Al Qaeda, led by Osama bin Laden. This group had been provided sanctuary and training sites by the Taliban government in Afghanistan. There was strong public support for the Americans to strike back militarily.

The U.S.-led NATO attack in late 2001 easily toppled the Taliban in Afghanistan. The rapid defeat in the early spring of 2003 of Saddam Hussein in Iraq, considered a co-conspirator in international terrorism, one who allegedly was emboldened by "weapons of mass destruction" in his arsenal, only increased the popular acclaim for the professionalism and the courage of the American military. This acclaim never really lessened— despite serious opposition to the rationale for the war at the outset, opposition that increased in the following months as there turned out to be no weapons of mass destruction. Support for those serving in the military and the veterans of the wars never wavered. Surely there were political calculations involved in this—many learned from the Vietnam experience that it was not only unfair to blame the warriors for the war, but it was also politically inexpedient to do so in this era of acclaim for those who served. There have been few public sports or cultural events in the last several years where servicemen and -women have not been saluted. Magnetic ribbons and bumper stickers on automobiles, lapel pins and refrigerator stickers all attest to this. Businesses, corporations, and not-for-profit groups elbow with each other to pay homage to this generation's armed forces. Communities across the United States have bonded in celebration of local units departing for the Middle East and have waited on the tarmac to embrace their return. And too often the routines of life have been altered as entire communities pause to thank and to mourn those whose sacrifice was forever.

But national celebration and individual grief do not necessarily result in the delivery of support: as these wars proved more complicated than they appeared when they began, it should not be surprising that some needs of those who served have gone unmet. There was a national wake-up call to this situation when two reporters for the *Washington Post* broke a story in February 2007 regarding deplorable conditions for outpatients at Walter Reed Army Medical Center.

Ten days ago I visited Bethesda Naval Hospital. It was my twentieth visit to one of the major military hospitals. On all of these occasions I have never met anyone with responsibility for serving patients at these medical centers, military or civilian, medical or support personnel, who was not fully committed to doing all that they could to comfort and to heal the patients and to support their families. But the record affirms that they have not always had the capacity or the facilities to meet their goals.

The wars in Afghanistan and Iraq have gone on much longer than anyone predicted in 2001 or 2003. The resistance in these countries has proved more durable, effective, and deadly than nearly any official projections made at the outset. As a result of this our forces have been pressed with multiple tours in the hostile areas, and as their equipment has been pushed too hard and sometimes proved inadequate to the demands of the theater, so too have the support systems domestically been strained. Hospitals and medical support facilities and VA transitional and ongoing services have faced unexpected demands and numbers. As no one in 2001 or 2003 had predicted wars of this length, nor had they planned for casualties of this magnitude and medical needs of this complexity.

In addition to the duration of the wars, the unanticipated need for medical support for wounded veterans has resulted from two other factors, both positive developments, but with consequences. One has to do with the efficiency and effectiveness of modern battlefield medicine and the other has to do with the quality of combat protective gear and its proven effectiveness in preventing some fatal wounds.

IN ALL U.S. WARS prior to this century, the ratio of surviving wounded to fatalities was 2.1 to one. This actually was pretty constant—in World War II it was 2.3 to 1 and in Vietnam it was 2.6 to 1. In Iraq, over the period from the invasion in March of 2003 down through mid-December of last year, the ratio of wounded to killed was 7.25 to 1. In Afghanistan from October 2001 to December 2009 it was slightly better than 5 to 1. Clearly battle-field medicine has advanced significantly from the Vietnam era. Speed and quality of treatment are critical. Military medicine is saving young men and women who would have died in previous wars.

Modern medicine has a companion piece in modern military technology. Even with its shortcomings, the body armor used in the field serves to protect vital organs from fatal damage. Modern body armor has helped prevent fatalities but it has not protected troops from loss of limbs, from horrible burns, or from head injuries, often resulting in significant cognitive brain damage.

Often enclosed in protective steel vehicles, our troops have been subject to major explosions, resulting often in serious burn injuries and major concussions. As of one year ago, there were 1,286 combat veterans with amputations. And down through 2007 there were 43,779 traumatic brain injuries. Their hospital stays are lengthy with requirements for sophisticated treatment, state-of-the-art prostheses, multiple surgeries, and extended physical and occupational therapy, all of which has often exceeded the capacity of the hospitals.

Let me add a brief personal observation. In my hospital visits over the last four and a half years I go room to room, bed to bed, to talk to the wounded veterans. I always ask them what happened to them and they are always quite willing to talk about it. Of the 150–200 patients with whom I have spoken, they describe snipers, mines, mortars from the back of a pickup speeding away behind a berm, but most commonly they talk about an improvised explosive device—hidden under the road or a bridge, sitting in road trash, perhaps a suicide bomber in a car or in a crowd. At most a half dozen have told me that they saw the person who attacked them. The Iraq war has not been marked by many conventional firefights or battlefield engagements, where the U.S. military can dominate.

There generally has been a strong political commitment to address the issues of the wounded veterans. For several years this clear resolve was absent in another of the major post–World War II veterans' programs, the GI Bill for education. In 1984 Congress approved the Montgomery GI Bill. This peacetime program was restricted in terms of eligibility and the benefits were often inadequate. Remedies proved politically complicated.

The sharp divisions that marked discussions about remedying shortcomings in the Montgomery program were somewhat surprising. The GI Bill after all was the celebrated symbol of a successful veterans' program. The surprise is lessened, however, when we consider the immediate context—both the nature of the all-volunteer military and the nature of the wars in Iraq and Afghanistan. With a force that was pushed hard by frequent deployments, with a mission that had become complicated and nuanced, and with technology that was increasingly sophisticated, the military needed trained, experienced personnel. If too many men and women left the service following their initial enlistment in order to enroll in school or a training program, there could be major personnel problems.

The tension between veterans' benefits and military requirements was largely unprecedented. Previous wartime benefits were either part of a demobilization process (World War II and Korea) or of an engagement such as Vietnam that was sustained by the draft and draft-induced enlistments to maintain personnel goals. Reenlistments had always been critical to maintain experienced non-commissioned officers, but in the All-Volunteer Force they became even more critical. In the wars in Iraq and Afghanistan, the Pentagon had no draft to increase the pipeline of recruits. Within a few years after the 9/11 surge in enlistments, enlistment and reenlistment goals were challenged by the nature of the war and the optional opportunities in a growing economy. The Army especially was straining to meet its goals.

Senator James Webb of Virginia, a decorated Vietnam Marine officer, former assistant secretary of defense, secretary of the Navy, and accomplished novelist on the Vietnam War and on the military, introduced legislation in January 2007 to provide current veterans with educational benefits roughly equivalent to those of the Second World War. Officials in the Pentagon projected some significant reenlistment problems that would result from this expanded GI Bill.

During debate over the proposed legislation, the Defense Department and the White House publicly opposed the bill and they were joined by a number of congressmen and senators. Secretary of Defense Robert

Gates insisted that any enhanced benefits program contain the option of "transferability"—so that military personnel who reenlisted and served a minimum number of years could transfer the benefit to a spouse or child. Advocates believed that such a provision would provide a means to stay in the service and still utilize the benefit—it might even make reenlistment more attractive.

The Webb bill, with the transferability amendment, was approved by Congress and signed by President Bush in June 2008. In the fall of 2009 over 180,000 veterans enrolled under the provisions of the new GI Bill. But the entire debate over the legislation signaled a major shift in the way many policymakers and government officials regarded veterans' benefits. In addition to being a service bonus from a grateful nation, this now was considered a personnel tool in the task of managing the modern military.

With this overview of official veteran policy historically, let me turn to an intriguing question that is unresolved. As I engaged in researching the history of veterans' benefits, one thing stood out particularly: The difference in attitudes toward the current generation of veterans as compared with the reception of the Vietnam War veterans in the late 1960s and 1970s. Clearly the war in Vietnam and the war in Iraq—and more recently Afghanistan—have not had sustained popular support. Yet the servicemen and -women who have served in our current wars have been warmly welcomed and thanked for their service—and the Vietnam veterans largely came home to neither welcome nor thanks.

As Max Cleland, Vietnam triple amputee and head of the Veterans Administration and one-term U.S. senator from Georgia wryly observed, he and the veterans never had a ticker tape parade and instead were treated as "co-conspirators in some escapade with sinister overtones." Tim O'Brien, a Vietnam veteran, wrote in *Going After Cacciato*: "They did not know even the simple things: a sense of victory, or satisfaction, or necessary sacrifice. They did not know the feeling of taking a place and keeping it, securing a village and then raising a flag and calling it a victory" (270).

Those who have served in wars other than Vietnam generally recognized that if their fellow citizens did not always consider what they had done as heroic, neither did they reject it as criminal. In the case of Vietnam, the opposition to the war was often expressed in pretty sharp rhetoric. This was about more than a mistaken policy. Daniel Berrigan's sense of being "morally outraged...ashamed" had a resonance. And when a distinguished journalist such as Anthony Lewis referred to the 1972 bombings of Hanoi as "a crime against humanity" it was hard not to include the airmen as among the criminals.

The culture of the 1960s was marked of course by young people, of military age, revolting against the conventional and affirming values of love, brotherhood, and sisterhood. Surely Bob Dylan and Joan Baez assuring that "The Times They Are A-Changin'," Country Joe and the Fish's "I-Feel-Like-I'm-Fixin'-to Die" challenge, and John Lennon's "Give Peace a Chance" plea mirrored as they also shaped a generation's and an era's sense of revolution—and resolution.

Demonstrations at the 1968 Democratic Convention in Chicago and the acoustic cultural manifesto at the Woodstock festival in 1969 stood as symbols of the time—symbols that were in sharp counterpoint to all that the military in Vietnam seemed to represent in terms of culture, values, and goals. In his compendium of accounts of returning veterans, Bob Greene included many reports of veterans being spat upon at airports and of being called "baby killers" on the street. Some have challenged the veracity of these reported incidents, but as one veteran wrote, "If the number of 'spitting' incidents are inflated, it doesn't change for a minute the feelings of rejection and scorn that a bunch of depressed and confused young men experienced when they returned home from doing what their country told them to do."

The Defense Department has estimated that over 2.7 million Americans served in the military in Vietnam. There were 47,424 battle deaths in Vietnam and 10,785 other deaths in the country. There were over 150,000 wounded who did not require hospitalization and 153,303 hospitalized. This was a major and costly war, but as the purposes and origins came under question, so did those who were fighting it—as did their sacrifices and those of their comrades. The anger and emotions, the defensiveness and moral judgments of this volatile mix should never be minimized.

Public perceptions of the war in Vietnam had been influenced by events during the war and by coverage of them—by disclosure of the horror of My Lai, the photo of Vietnamese General Loan executing a Viet Cong officer, the small Vietnamese girl and others, clothes burned from their bodies, fleeing from napalm. In 1971 Gallup reported that 50 percent of

Americans polled believed that incidents such as the atrocity at My Lai were "common occurrences" in Vietnam. Louis Harris learned that 81 percent of his respondents believed that there were "other incidents" like My Lai that had been unreported. Of course, we now know there were other incidents. But the incidents became the commonplace in the minds of many. And Lieutenant Calley of the Americal Division, rather than "the boy next door" of World War II, became to many critics the symbol of the military in Vietnam.

The war in Vietnam was in America's living rooms. Television footage was far more timely and graphic than were World War II newsreels, and correspondents in Vietnam had far more independence than did their predecessors (or, indeed, their successors in Iraq and Afghanistan).

In February 1968 there were 636 accredited correspondents in Vietnam. They had pretty free movement throughout the theater. The tragic images of war and accounts of its complexities became part of daily American life. Some veterans of the war confirmed incidents they observed or even participated in, that were morally indefensible—or at best morally ambiguous. In the minds of many there was a heavy burden of guilt, or at least doubt, placed—unfairly—on all of those who served. Who were the "baby killers"?

In a comparison filled with ironies, perhaps the greatest one is that those who have served in Iraq and Afghanistan have volunteered for military duty—yet they have been celebrated for serving in unpopular wars. In Vietnam the draft served to fill enlisted ranks and the threat of the draft encouraged enlistments. The unwilling—or at least the unenthused—found themselves criticized for answering the call to military duty. Draftees paid a high price for this—in 1965 28 percent of the soldiers killed in Vietnam were draftees and by 1969 it was 62 percent. But the draft was not the great leveler that it promised to be.

The historian Christian Appy studied the casualties in Vietnam and determined that the combat forces there were perhaps the youngest in U.S. history. As he noted, "Thus most of the Americans who fought in Vietnam were powerless, working-class teenagers sent to fight an undeclared war by presidents for whom they were not even eligible to vote." If this led to some sense of unfairness and injustice on the part of the combat troops, it did not necessarily lead to a bonding with antiwar protestors—with the Vietnam Veterans against the War being an obvious counterexample. In fact, many veterans came home from Vietnam with mixed feelings about the war and its conduct. Some significant numbers of them were openly critical. But they did not easily make common cause with the antiwar movement.

Nonetheless, reconciliation did come—even as for many veterans the scars remained. President Jimmy Carter's decision to extend amnesty to all draft resisters helped to move beyond that divisive issue—although in the short term it served to harden the views of those who viewed this group as heroic on the one hand and those who considered them traitors on the other. By the late 1970s President Carter was reminding Americans that it was crucial to separate the warriors from the war and to honor the patriotism and courage of those who had served in Vietnam. He insisted that they deserved better than to be treated "as an unfortunate or embarrassing reminder of the divisiveness of the war itself." President Ronald Reagan rekindled some divisions when he described the Vietnam War as a "noble cause"—but he backed off from that somewhat by focusing subsequently upon the need to honor the veterans.

By the late 1970s public opinion polls affirmed a far more positive public attitude toward the Vietnam veterans. President Reagan played an important role in restoring the credibility of the military—this was important to him strategically, politically, and personally. He and Defense Secretary Caspar Weinberger oversaw significant new investments into the defense infrastructure, including better compensation for active-duty military personnel. And the Reagan rhetoric consistently evoked gratitude for those who served. This found a responsive audience and a bipartisan chorus—few Democrats were eager to challenge the president on this ground.

The Vietnam Memorial in Washington would prove to be an important symbol of remembering, honoring, and reconciling—even if in its formative years it too got caught up in significant and emotional debates over the design and the message. The focus and discipline and commitment of Jan Scruggs, who had been wounded while serving in the Army in Vietnam, were critical for this process. He never once lost his focus on the need to have the memorial. He and a group of committed veterans and supporters navigated through the political divisions that Vietnam still engendered. Scruggs believed that reconciliation could only follow remembering. He quoted from Archibald MacLeish: "We were young. We have died. Remember us."

The Veterans Day 1982 "homecoming" celebration welcoming, belatedly, Vietnam veterans and a ceremony formally dedicating the Vietnam Wall provide examples of the ongoing divisions from the war. Those who sought a more "heroic" memorial continued to be frustrated that the Wall did not have any traditional statuary—the Frederick Hart statue "Three Infantrymen" had not yet joined Maya Lin's wall. There was also concern from some groups that the antiwar veterans' movement had too much influence over the celebrations. This apprehension caused President Reagan finally to decline to appear at the dedication ceremony. It nonetheless proved to be an occasion when reconciliation truly began. But as often seemed to be the case regarding Vietnam veterans, the process was different. Columnist Mary McGrory wrote of the Vietnam veterans' celebration, "Naturally they had to organize [the "homecoming" parade] themselves, just as they had to raise money for their wall, just as they had to counsel each other in their rap centers, just as they had to raise the cry about 'Agent Orange.'"

The contrast with today is sharp. As was the case with Vietnam, many Americans have believed that the wars in Iraq and Afghanistan are mistakes and have challenged these engagements and their advocates. But unlike forty years ago, the troops who have engaged in these current wars have avoided being drawn into the controversy—except as positive references and allies, as both supporters and critics of the wars affirm their interest in protecting the safety and the honor of those who serve.

It is intriguing that the dominant image and rhetoric today invests in the All-Volunteer Force all of the imagery of the celebrated citizen soldiers who were called up to fight our wars historically. In fact, in today's military only the National Guard and Reserve units mobilized for combat tours really fit this historic model. Last year's Jefferson lecturer, the distinguished historian David Kennedy, called the current military a "mercenary" force. He insisted this was not pejorative but he was concerned about the consequences of not having some form of draft that would make the military more representative of our society.

There is a professionalism that marks the armed forces today, partially a deliberate and disciplined military leadership response to the perception of the state of the military during the Vietnam era. The high level of training, the focus on accomplishing goals and minimizing casualties, the sophistication of modern military technology, all serve to advance more professional armed forces.

The demographics of the armed forces have changed from those of the Vietnam era. Active-duty personnel as compared to 1973 have an older mean age, are more female (2.2 percent of those serving in 1973 and 20 percent in 2007), are significantly more likely to be married, to have a high school diploma, and are less likely to come from the northeastern states. They are less likely to be white—with the change in this profile coming from increases in Hispanic and Asian members of the military.

A recent study determined that 75 percent of those killed in Iraq were white. In Vietnam the figure had been 86 percent. The median age of the Iraq dead was twenty-four years—and in Vietnam it was twenty-one years. The troops killed in Iraq tend to be more middle class or lower middle class in background than representative of the poorest income areas. This may largely be a reflection of the medical standards and education minimums required for enlistment today and the fact that the poorest families have the lowest health profile and the poorest record of completing a high school education.

Public opinion polls affirm support for the military. In the early 1970s, 27 percent of the public had "a great deal" of confidence in the military—lagging behind confidence in institutions such as medicine, universities, organized religion, and major companies. By the turn of the century 44 percent of the public had great confidence in the military—more than any other institution in the country.

The professional image of the modern All-Volunteer Force does influence current public attitudes toward the military. It also reinforces a somewhat abstracted, even video game, perspective on combat activities. Scholars such as Richard Kohn and Andrew Bacevich have commented that military action has become nearly the equivalent of a spectator sport. As Professor Kohn has suggested, "war" has become an all-purpose metaphor for any proposed initiative. It is a trivialization of something that should never be thought of as trivial.

The United States may have many political divisions today, but President Obama had no challenges when in his State of the Union message last week he said to those in uniform: "Americans are united in sending one message: we honor your service, we are inspired by your sacrifice, and you have our unyielding support."

We have come a long way from the revolutionary generation's belief that the nation owed nothing to healthy veterans and from the Bonus Army protest encampment. And we have come a long way from Vietnam veterans being marginalized or worse. We need remember always: in our democracy, under our Constitution, the military does not start wars. They fight them. On our behalf and at the direction of our political leadership.

Wars are not pretty things. This past December Secretary of Defense Gates spoke to U.S. troops stationed near Kirkuk in Iraq. He said, "One of the myths in the international community is that the United States likes war. And the reality is, other than the first two or three years of World War II there has never been a popular war in America."

One could debate some elements of the secretary's assertion, but in fact I think it is largely accurate. And I would further observe that this is a good thing. While wars may sometimes be necessary and surely need to be supported in order to be sustained, it can be a dangerous thing if they are "popular." But this leads us to a different subject, a terribly important one, and I shall not ask us to take that on now. It is relevant, though, to this concluding thought: those who serve at risk on our behalf should never again feel that the gratitude of the republic for their sacrifice is dependent upon the popularity of the war we have asked them to fight.

Veterans Day in America: The Place of the Korean War in a National Day of Memory

*November 11, 2010, at Yonsei University
in Seoul, Republic of Korea*

Today is "Veterans Day" in the United States, an official national holiday. This holiday had its origins in the wake of World War I as the Western Allies commemorated the conclusion of that devastating war on November 11, 1918. The day was celebrated as Armistice Day in the U.S. and Remembrance Day in the Commonwealth countries.

Such national commemorations are ways for societies to share, to remember, to mourn, and to teach. They affirm national pride and they honor individual sacrifice on behalf of a nation. In the United States, Armistice Day was renamed Veterans Day in 1954, recognizing all veterans and including specifically those who had served in World War II and in the war in Korea.

Today I want to share with you some observations on the way American society has thought of war and of those who fight our wars. Specifically, I will discuss the way in which Americans have remembered those who served in the brutal war on this peninsula from June 1950 to July 1953. This year marks the sixtieth anniversary of the start of that war, which was defining for the two political entities that are Korea.

I will not presume to use an American holiday to comment on Korean memory. But I will use the occasion to share with you some observations more broadly about the way that societies remember wars and their warriors. These are not trivial modes of cultural celebration, nor are they simply exercises in academic history. The memories and the rituals and the symbols associated with war may be charged with politics. Popular wartime histories for the victors can become a source of patriotic boasting and manipulation. And for the losers, the memories of war can be a source of pain that can lead to regret or humiliation—and, again, to manipulation.

The significance of official memory can be illustrated by the ongoing controversy over the way in which Japan remembers World War II. Especially in China and Korea, memories of harsh occupation and atrocities, as well as brutalities such as "comfort women," are very real and relevant legacies of that war. As recently as 2001 President Kim Dae-jung said of Japan, "How can we make good friends with people who try to forget and ignore the many pains they inflicted on us? How can we deal with them in the future with any degree of trust?"

My interest is not in stoking this controversy but rather to illustrate that memories and understandings of war can stir emotions long after the wars are ended.

The ways in which Adolph Hitler manipulated emotional and distorted memories of World War I was a crucial part of the Nazi political narrative. The distinguished historian George Mosse referred to the "cult of the fallen soldier" and the "Myth of the War Experience" as building blocks in Hitler's themes of treachery and humiliation that cried for Aryan revenge.

An example from the United States was when, following the American Civil War, some Southerners began to romanticize their defeat as "the Lost Cause." By the 1870s and well into the twentieth century—and in some quarters perhaps the twenty-first century—Southerners developed an image filled with nostalgia and pride, and one that often greatly distorted the causes and the conduct of the war.

There are universal examples of the memory of war. From the remains of statuary in Athens and Rome to the Victorious Fatherland Liberation War Museum in Pyongyang, from the *Iliad* to the Lost Cause to Tolstoy's *War and Peace* to Hwang Sunwon's "Cranes," individuals and cultures have remembered and defined war and its purposes. But finally, for the survivors, memories are of individual sacrifices that wars cruelly impose upon those who are asked to fight them.

Abraham Lincoln dedicated the cemetery at Gettysburg battlefield after the bloody Civil War battle there by reflecting on the debt of the nation—and the inadequacy of citizens ever to honor properly such sacrifice: "The brave men, living and dead, who struggled here, have consecrated it far above our poor power to add or detract. The world will little note, nor long remember what we say here, but can never forget what they did here."

President Harry Truman's promise to "never forget their sacrifices" is engraved on the World War II Memorial in Washington. It is this commitment to "never forget" that has moved most cultures over the last century and a half to establish cemeteries for the war dead—be it at Arlington Cemetery in Virginia, the Punchbowl Cemetery in Hawaii, the Yasukuni shrine in Tokyo, the Seoul National Cemetery in Dongjak-gu, or the U.N. Memorial cemetery at Busan.

A good example of the way that even cemeteries remember differently can be seen at Normandy in France. This was the scene of the massive Allied landing in June of 1944 that finally led to the defeat of Nazi Germany. Following an extremely difficult battle on the coast and the bluffs the Allies established a beachhead. Tens of thousands were killed within sound of the sea.

The United States provided several cemeteries for Americans killed in these battles, with the major one being at Colleville-sur-Mer, above Omaha Beach. In this immaculate cemetery marked by white crosses and Stars of David rest 9,387 American military dead. Another 1,557 names are inscribed on the Wall of the Missing. It is a place of peace and tranquility, with reflecting pools, grand open structures of limestone and granite and marble, bound by the green grounds and the slope to the beach below. It is marked with a bronze statue, not of a warrior but of a soaring figure evoking memory of those who died too young, "The Spirit of American Youth Rising from the Waves." Colleville-sur-Mer is a solemn place of memory, one that whispers of sacrifice more than it shouts of heroism—but the sacrifices are indelibly marked by a proud and grateful nation.

Just a few miles from Colleville is the German cemetery at La Cambe. The victorious allies did not permit the Germans to construct any war memorials until 1952—and indeed at the end of World War II had ordered the destruction of all German monuments that glorified the military and German memory.

The cemetery at La Cambe is heavy, Wagnerian, melancholy. It evokes the tragedy of war—the unnecessary loss of those who, as the inscription reads, rest there in a "graveyard for soldiers not all of whom had chosen either the cause or the fight." With its dark horizontal marker stones embedded in the ground and its funereal Celtic crosses, La Cambe remembers over 21,000 Germans, tragic figures buried with no symbol or sense of patriotism or pride. The tumulus in the center, a mass grave for identified as well as unidentified remains, is topped by a dark cross. This space hovers and does not soar.

Americans were still constructing the cemetery at Colleville when on June 25, 1950, the forces of North Korea crossed over the temporary dividing line and invaded South Korea. The United States and the United Nations saw this attack on a free people as an assault upon the world order by international communism. And so within a few days President Harry Truman authorized General Douglas MacArthur to use whatever military units were necessary to meet the U.N. goal of "restoring peace in Korea."

The South Korean government and military were totally unprepared for the ferocity and the discipline of the North Korean attack. And the American military units first dispatched to Korea were equally unprepared. President Truman, seeking language to confine the engagement legally and politically, in the absence of a congressional declaration of war, described it as a "police action."

It would finally involve quite a police force: over the three years of engagement, nearly 1.8 million U.S. military would serve in Korea, 33,667 died or were missing in action (another 3,249 died in the Korean theater of operations), and 103,284 were wounded in action. Other U.N. forces lost 3,960 in action and 11,528 wounded. And the Republic of Korea (ROK) had as many as 250,000 military killed in action. South Korean civilian casualties were well over a quarter of a million—some estimates of Republic of Korea deaths from all causes are as high as 900,000. North Korean and Chinese figures, not surprisingly, are hard to come by—ROK estimates are that the Korean People's Army had some 300,000 killed in action and the Chinese People's Liberation Army may have lost half a million. By any estimate, this was a costly war—and no more so than for those who lived here on this peninsula.

American engagement was ideological and geopolitical. The U.S. joined with the United Nations to stop aggression and to cry halt to communism, understanding Kim Il-sung to be an accomplice if not a puppet of Josef Stalin and Soviet strategy. Americans in 1950 took very seriously the threat posed by Stalin and by Soviet communism.

American confidence—indeed, overconfidence if not outright arrogance—was high. The military historian S. L. A. Marshall wrote in July 1950 that in the U.S. there was "an air of excessive expectation based upon estimates which were inspired by wishful optimism." A young American soldier dispatched to Korea in those first weeks wrote, "Everyone thought the enemy would turn around and go back when they found out who was fighting." The first six months of the Korean War provided a roller coaster of emotions for the U.S. public several thousand miles away.

The summer of 1950, when the allies were pushed back to the Pusan Perimeter, was followed by General MacArthur's audacious landing at Inchon in September and then his drive to the Yalu River. With the sometimes uncomfortable approval of the U.S. government and the even more uneasy U.N. participants, the war had shifted markedly by fall.

General MacArthur and his command in Tokyo basically ignored threats that the Chinese would enter the war if we approached the Yalu River border with Manchuria. Even more troubling, they dismissed the capacity of the Chinese to be of any real military consequence if they did enter the war. They promised U.N. troops that they would be "home for Christmas."

When the Chinese entered the fight in force in late November 1950, the war took on an altogether different face. U.N. forces were overwhelmed by sheer numbers and several days of bitter fighting up in the cold and snow led to a difficult withdrawal, with the Eighth U.S. Army and the ROK II Corps decimated along the Chongchon River on the western side of the mountains. The U.S. Army 2nd Infantry Division took terrible casualties near Yangpyon, where they had three thousand killed or wounded in a few hours. As General Paik Sun-yup wrote of their trial on the road to Sunchon, "The God of Death himself hovered with heavy, beating wings over that road."

To the east, the 1st Marine Division and two Army battalions of the U.S. 7th Infantry Division were surrounded and forced to fight their way out of the area around the Changjin (Chosin) Reservoir. They suffered remarkably heavy casualties as they finally withdrew to the Port of Hungnam, from which they and upwards of 90,000 civilians were evacuated. Within weeks the U.N. forces were again fighting along the Han.

General MacArthur, whose miscalculations about Chinese intent had enabled the entrapment, now began insisting publicly that he wished to take the war against the Chinese into China. Quite inappropriately, he told the

U.S. News and World Report that failure to do this burdened his forces with "An enormous handicap, without precedent in military history." When the general continued his public statements, President Truman removed him from command in the spring.

News accounts from Korea to the U.S. were always spotty and the initial American confidence was replaced by a sense of confusion, which was followed by concern; the elation of early autumn yielded by the end of the year to puzzled pessimism. In the first days of the war, only 20 percent of Americans thought our engagement in this war was a mistake. By January of 1951, 49 percent believed it was a mistake.

By the summer of 1951 fighting had stabilized—not that losses had lessened significantly—along the 38th parallel and the two sides agreed to commence truce talks. This brought the war into a new phase, one in which American public support would prove to be harder to sustain. The strategic objectives, murky enough at the outset, became less clear. Places such as "Pork Chop" Hill and "Heartbreak" Ridge became symbols for bravery, resolve, and heavy losses on all sides. And the outcome of these operations probably had little impact on the truce.

In January 1951, *Time* magazine named "G.I. Joe" as its "Man of the Year" for 1950. *Time* introduced its honoree in this ambivalent way: "As the year ended, 1950's man seemed to be an American in the bitterly unwelcome role of the fighting-man. It was not a role the American had sought, either as an individual or as a nation. The U.S. fighting-man was not civilization's crusader, but destiny's draftee." By the first anniversary of the beginning of the war, many of those on the ground in Korea moved their focus from military pursuit of victory and of geographical objectives to survival.

One young officer recalled, "For the GIs the general idea was to stay alive. The army wasn't going anywhere, and everyone knew it. There would be no big push to end the war. The name of the game was to hang in there and survive until something happens at the peace talks in Panmunjom. To get killed was to be wasted, and no one wants to be wasted."

Another remembered, "It wasn't like World War II; you knew there was no big push coming, no fighting until the enemy surrendered. This was a war that was going nowhere." In his book on the Korean War, David Halberstam described the sentiment on the front simply: no one wanted to "die for a tie."

But this stalemated phase was not a time of peace. One mother whose son was killed wrote a scathing note to President Truman: "It is murder to send boys to fight with their hands tied by your 'limited police action,'" she said. She asked the president: "Have you forgotten how America fights?" Young men continued to die—in large numbers. The established lines evoked the tragedy of trench warfare in World War I. Finally on July 27, 1953, the parties signed an armistice agreement at Panmunjom. The fighting ended, although there has not yet been a full peace treaty and the division between North and South continues along the 38th parallel.

My question on this Veterans Day is how Americans have remembered this war and the young men we sent to fight it. Have we recalled Abraham Lincoln's advice at Gettysburg to "never forget" those who have represented us in battle? The simple answer is no. If Korea is often described in the United States as the "forgotten war," then it follows that those who served in this war have been and remain the "forgotten veterans."

David Halberstam described it this way: "Korea would not prove a great national war of unifying singular purpose, as World War II had been, nor would it, like Vietnam a generation later, divide and thus haunt the nation. It was simply a puzzling, gray, very distant conflict, a war that went on and on and on, seemingly without hope or resolution, about which most Americans, save the men who fought there and their immediate families, preferred to know as little as possible."

A veteran remembers a Marine band greeting the troops when they disembarked in San Francisco, but he later observed, "The Korean War is called the Forgotten War because no one cared about it except the boys or men fighting there. Then we say we won the battle, but lost the war. When we got home, there was no big blowout. Everyone kept quiet. None of the veterans complained. People never knew where Korea was on the map." Most of the veterans quietly went back to their civilian lives—but their memories would not allow them to forget this war.

One Marine veteran of the Chosin Reservoir campaign returned home on leave and was told he really was not eligible to enter the local Veterans of Foreign Wars club since he was not the veteran of a recognized war. There was no victory parade for the Korean War veterans—at least not for forty years.

In 1991, New York City hosted a parade for Korean War veterans. Nine thousand veterans marched and an estimated 250,000 watched—just months after millions had turned out for the parade for returning Gulf War veterans. And forty years after millions had feted General MacArthur, who had been relieved of his command. One of the 1991 participants noted simply, "We're finally being recognized. This was long overdue." Another said, "I guess it was an unpopular war. It wasn't considered a war, just a police action. But to the fellows who were there it was a war, and we're here not for us but for the guys we left in Korea."

It was only in 1998 that the Congress of the United States designated the Korean deployment as a "War"—it had earlier evolved from "police action" to "conflict." But for the fiftieth anniversary of its beginning, what had always been a war now officially became one.

In Korea, of course, the war has been a powerful part of the memory of the people. The North Korean government taunts the U.S. for seeming to ignore this history. The message from the North Korean Travel Bureau about the Victorious Fatherland Liberation Museum advises: "In the West the Korean War is sometimes referred to as the 'Forgotten War' as it is one of the major armed conflicts of the twentieth century but gets much less attention than other wars. In North Korea it is referred to as the 'Victorious Fatherland Liberation War' and seen as a great national accomplishment against 'US aggressors.'"

The museum in Pyongyang recalls the heroism of the North Koreans resisting the "invaders" and displays military hardware, including substantial war trophies. Here in South Korea the War Memorial symbolizes the themes of heroism and of reconciliation. The June 25th Tower signals military strength and the promise of peace. And if this was too abstract, the statuary near it, "The Statues Defending the Nation" and the "Statue of Brothers," make the theme clear. Older messages reminding of North Korean brutality and atrocity and the general horror of war have little place in this memorial. But memories fade even in South Korea. General Paik Sun-yup, a genuine hero of the war, wrote his memoirs in 1992 and said he was "saddened to consider that so many of my countrymen know so very little about the Korean War or about the role their army played in defense of their homeland."

The Republic of Korea has remembered and thanked the Americans who sacrificed here in the war. This government has done far better than the U.S. government has done. South Korea erected the MacArthur statue at Inchon in 1957; in 1975 the government established a memorial at the Ministry of Defense at Paju; and the Republic of Korea made certain to establish a U.S. memorial at the U.N. Memorial Cemetery at Pusan, even though there are few Americans resting there.

One scholar has noted that there are in the United States far fewer memorials to the Korean War than to any of the other twentieth-century wars—and, I would add, far fewer than those for the Civil War and the American Revolution, and likely for the Spanish-American War. The Congress authorized a Korean War Memorial in 1986 and it was dedicated in 1995, forty-two years after the truce—and thirteen years after the Vietnam Veterans Memorial was dedicated.

The Korean War Veterans Memorial is situated in an honored place on the National Mall in Washington, located in an area bounded by the Lincoln Memorial, the Vietnam Veterans Memorial, and the World War II Memorial. The World War II Memorial is traditional and magisterial. It has a theme engraved in marble: "Americans came to liberate, not to conquer, to restore freedom and to end tyranny." One could argue that this theme was consistent with public understanding of all wars since World War II. The wall with 4,048 gold stars symbolizing the over 400,000 Americans killed in the war, reads, "Here we mark the price of freedom." The Korean War Veterans Memorial makes the same point: "Freedom is not free."

The Vietnam Veterans Memorial designed by Maya Lin is simple—and painful. Here on a polished black granite wall seventy-five meters long are engraved the names of the (now) 58,267 who died as a result of the Vietnam War. There was substantial controversy at the time the wall was constructed about the absence of any traditional acknowledgment of heroism. The "Three Soldiers" statue was added in response to this and then later the Vietnam Women's Memorial joined these monuments.

The Korean War Veterans Memorial fits in this triangle of memory on the mall. The long delay in this recognition can partially be explained by the fact that veterans of that war did not organize or seek public acknowledgment. The Korean War Veterans Association was not founded until 1982. When I asked one of the early organizers why this had been so long delayed, the answer was that the veterans had been part of the "forgotten" war so they also tried to forget. The group that first met to associate with others was primarily moved by what one called "nostalgia"—a desire to see some friends from a faraway war.

The Korean War Memorial Advisory Board was composed of veterans of that war, veterans still moved by powerful emotions but a few years removed from the immediate and raw pain of their war. Under their influence, the Korean War Veterans Memorial is about a sharing of experience. Nineteen figures, seven feet tall, imposing but not monumental, human rather than statuesque, move across a field. They are caught in the cautious, alert motions of patrol, representing the range of those who served in Korea. They are reflected on a black wall that has images taken from photos that display the range of military service in Korea. A reflecting pool with a wall and an imposing flag mark the point for the patrol. It is not a memorial only to those who died but to all who served there.

It was the hope of the Korean War Memorial Advisory Board that with this permanent memorial, Korea would be "No more the forgotten war." A prime mover in this effort, Colonel William Weber, said that the "Memorial does not attempt to glorify war." The inscription at the memorial describes the sentiment:

Our Nation Honors
Her Uniformed Sons and Daughters
Who Answered Their Country's Call
To Defend A Country They Did Not Know
And a People They Had Never Met

I visited the memorial recently on an early morning at the end of September. It was very quiet and peaceful. There were three stands of flowers at the far point of the figures. All were from Korean organizations, remembering and thanking. At the wall behind the flag and the Pool of Remembrance, there were a few other flower stands, one from the Korean War Veterans Association and one marked simply, "Beloved Dad." There was no one at the memorial until just before I left, when a tour group arrived on a bus. They were quiet, even reverential. I went over to one young woman who was with this group to ask her where they were from. She said they were from a place outside of Shanghai, China.

When the Korean War Memorial was dedicated, one veteran said, "A lot is said about the Vietnam Memorial and how it has helped the nation heal wounds. Well, many Korean War vets have healing to do, too. This will help. This will let some of the feelings out—not just feelings of fear in combat long repressed, or resentment at a lack of recognition, but also great feelings of pride in what they'd done."

This week some veterans of the 1st Marine Division who fought at the Chosin Reservoir sixty years ago are in Seoul to gather and to remember. The South Korean government has worked hard to arrange and to enable this reunion and it is a privilege for me to be on this peninsula with them. When I joined the Marines in 1957 they were already part of Marine Corps legend.

Dispatched to far North Korea in October and November of 1950, they found themselves in the mountainous area around the Changjin Reservoir, surrounded by 60,000 Chinese who had crossed the Yalu River. Sixty years ago, on the night of November 9–10, the latter marking the Marine Corps birthday, the mountains around the reservoir received the first snow of the season. Overnight the temperature dropped forty degrees in a few hours, and a harsh wind from the north made it worse.

Over the next several weeks these Marines engaged in some of the heaviest fighting in the storied history of the Corps. A young Korean, Yi Jong Yun, joined the Marines at Pusan and served throughout the campaign as their interpreter and liaison. He wrote: "Chosin was the coldest place in Korea, the only place where no rice grows because of the weather. Hagaru was on a plateau, with the Chinese watching us during daytime, to attack at night. Hagaru was like an island in a Chinese sea, and we were like fishes in a fishbowl. All the Korean civilians I met wondered how the Marines would escape the trap. They thought this was impossible."

When Peking Radio announced that "The annihilation of the 1st Marine Division is only a matter of time," correspondent Marguerite Higgins was at Hagaru-ri with the Marines. She would call the fight through snow and cold out of Yudam-ni "the Korean Valley Forge." The Commanding General of the 1st Marine Division, General Oliver P. Smith, noted simply of this fight, "War leaves no soft options."

Some 15,000 Marines had gone into the Chosin mountains. When they were evacuated at Hungnam in mid-December, they reported 718 killed, 3,502 wounded, and 192 missing in action. There were another 7,313 casualties—mostly frostbite. It was estimated that they killed 25,000 Chinese and had wounded another 12,500.

The Chosin Reservoir was but one of many places where young Americans fought bravely and died cruelly. Korean War veterans insist that theirs was a "forgotten victory"—they halted the North Korean takeover and they take pride today in the strength of South Korea. We can debate the terms of "victory," but those who served here deserve better than to be in their country the forgotten veterans of a forgotten war.

A year ago on Veterans Day I was a speaker at the Vietnam Veterans Memorial in Washington. I observed that those of us who personally knew and remember the individuals whose names are on the wall are fewer every year, and that memories fade—therefore we must make certain that those names never become simply letters on granite but are always remembered as vital people with unfulfilled dreams who made the ultimate sacrifice.

One Marine veteran of the Chosin campaign, who never discussed his experience and often woke up screaming from nightmares of remembrance, described visiting the Korean War Veterans Memorial in 1996: "As I stood by one of the statues for my wife to take a picture of me, I placed my hand on the shoulder of the statue and looked into its face and I saw the expression that I saw forty-five years ago on the faces of fellow comrades. Tears came into my eyes and my hand and arm began to tremble; for a few seconds I was back in Korea on the front line, a scared young man twenty-one years old, letting myself remember for the first time since the war what it was all about. I had shut out of my life most of the events that occurred during my war days."

In so many ways, so had his country shut out these events. Now, sixty years later, it is time to place hands on those who served and to say thanks—and that we too remember.

What We Learned from the Korean War

July 2013

THIS WEEK IN JULY 2013 marks an important anniversary. Sixty years ago, on July 27, 1953, representatives of the United Nations, led by U.S. Army Lieutenant General William Harrison, met their North Korean counterparts in Panmunjom, Korea, to sign an armistice agreement ending the thirty-seven-month-long war. Negotiators had been discussing the agreement for nearly twenty-five of those months in 158 separate meetings.

The document was not a peace treaty. It provided for a truce. The historic occasion had no mark of formality and no sense of finality. The representatives signed the agreement without speaking a single word to each other, and no one offered handshakes. The South Korean representatives refused to sign and did not join in the meeting. There surely was no ceremony comparable to the one on the battleship *Missouri* in Tokyo Bay in September 1945. The *New York Times* reported from the treaty site, "Outside the thin wooden walls there was the mutter of artillery fire—a grim reminder that even as the truce was being signed men were still dying on near-by hills and the fight would continue for twelve more hours."

Americans at home were similarly restrained. There were no celebrations in Times Square—or anywhere else. The *Washington Post* noted, "Washington greeted news of the Korean truce yesterday with a matter-of-fact attitude—quietly, without evident jubilation." It was peace without a clear victory.

Is Korea still, as it was called then, the Forgotten War? Unfortunately, it is. But it shouldn't be. The objectives, the conduct, and the conclusion of that war are significant in too many ways. This anniversary provides an occasion to remember them, and to honor those who served in that war.

Those who fought there have said that, at a heavy cost, they accomplished their objective. This had been described by the United Nations declaration of June 1950 and President Harry Truman's statements at the time he authorized American troops to participate in the action: securing "a withdrawal of the invading forces to positions north of the 38th parallel."

The 1953 agreement provided that Korea would be divided along that line and specified that there should be a follow-up conference within three months to conclude a comprehensive peace treaty. That conference never convened. Even if permanent peace remains a work in progress, the strong democratic government in South Korea today affirms to those who fought that they did their job.

We have much to learn from the Korean War—and this is relevant as we face decisions about the pending drawdown from Afghanistan. History is not a blueprint or a lesson plan, but it surely does provide a real-life insight into the problems we face. There are stunning examples of the consequences of wars with shifting military goals—and absent realistic public discussion about the likely means and the costs of achieving these goals. Without these shared commitments and understandings, we should not send men and women to die.

The Korean War veterans who claim that they accomplished what they were sent to do are absolutely correct. This assessment requires a sharply defined assignment focusing on the original goal. In fact, the Korean command had accomplished that objective by late September 1950. Those who fought in Korea demonstrated courage and sacrifice that is the equal of any American forces in any war. They did not have a victory parade—at least not until New York City belatedly held one in 1991. In fact, their "police action" was not congressionally recognized as a "war" until 1998. Nearly 1.8 million Americans served in Korea from 1950 to 1953, and 36,574 died there.

The U.N. forces—largely from the U.S.—had some extremely difficult early months in the summer of 1950 with heavy casualties. By August they were defending a last enclave around Pusan, with some even fearing the need for a full withdrawal. Finally sufficient forces arrived that enabled General Douglas MacArthur to order a landing at Inchon on September 15, 1950. This fractured the already stretched North Korean supply line. Within days the North Korean invaders were routed and U.N. troops had recaptured Seoul.

On September 29, MacArthur accompanied Republic of Korea (South Korea) President Syngman Rhee back into the National Assembly Hall in

Seoul. By the end of September, U.N. forces were moving into North Korea. Country singer Jimmie Osborne wrote and recorded a song on October 2, "Thank God for Victory in Korea."

Despite all of the euphoria of an objective reached, this had not been an easy victory. In three months, 8,182 American troops were killed in Korea. To underline the magnitude of this sacrifice, that number is nearly 1,400 more than have been killed in Iraq and Afghanistan in the past twelve years.

This costly victory in three months only previewed the compounded tragedy that followed. General MacArthur insisted that the total defeat of North Korea was certain and the peninsula could be reunified, as the World War II Russian–United States agreement for a "temporary" division had promised. Confident of an easy victory, the American Joint Chiefs and the Truman administration urged the United Nations to expand the war goal to accomplish the reunification of Korea. The U.N. did.

Some worried in October 1950 about Chinese statements that they would enter the war if the U.N. forces approached their border on the Yalu River. Ignoring his own intelligence reports of Chinese troop movements and consumed with his own confidence, MacArthur assured Washington that China would not enter the war—and if they did, he was certain they did not have the means to mount a significant threat. One of his top generals dismissed them as Chinese "laundrymen." MacArthur boasted that he would bring "the boys home by Christmas."

The only American boys who got home for Christmas in 1950 came on hospital ships or in coffins. The Chinese entered the war as they had promised they would, and they did it in far greater numbers and with greater military capacity than MacArthur had predicted. By late November the 1st Marine Division faced annihilation at the Chosin Reservoir and fought their way out in what some have described as one of the great military actions of American history.

The Army's 31st Regimental Combat Team was nearly annihilated northeast of the reservoir. And units of the Eighth Army that had advanced far to the north on the western side of the peninsula retreated under heavy Chinese assault. South Korean general Paik Sun-yup said the "God of Death himself hovered" over them. Correspondent Homer Bigart reported that it was "the worst licking Americans had suffered since Bataan." The largely American U.N. force was pushed back south of the 38th parallel and 5,964 Americans died in November and December 1950.

The war would continue for thirty more months, pushing and pulling a little north and a little south of the 38th parallel. And nearly 22,000 more Americans would die from 1951 to 1953.

In the last months before the 1953 truce, the U.S. Army fought the Chinese for Pork Chop Hill in a brutal battle. Everyone knew the treaty was coming but the fight continued over a piece of real estate whose ownership would finally be resolved at the Panmunjom talks rather than on the battlefield. In July 1953, as all recognized the agreement was near conclusion, 1,160 more Americans died. As some of the troops in Korea described it, they "died for a tie."

Thirty Americans died on July 27th. A recent special Veterans of Foreign Wars publication described the last American killed that day, a young Marine from Illinois who stepped on a land mine and died the next morning.

As we note the anniversary of the end of this war, we need to do two things: resolve that it is long past time to honor those who served and sacrificed in this brutal war, a war that many of their fellow citizens ignored. We might also pause now to reflect on the nature and consequences of this war. We can learn much from the Korean War experience.

Korea established a pattern that has been unfortunately followed in American wars in Vietnam, Iraq, and Afghanistan. These are wars without declaration and without the political consensus and the resolve to meet specific and changing goals. They are improvisational wars. They are dangerous.

The wars of the past sixty-three years, ranging from Korea to Vietnam to Afghanistan to Iraq (but excepting Operation Desert Storm, which is an outlier from this pattern), have been marked by:

- Inconsistent or unclear military goals with no congressional declaration of war.
- Early presumptions on the part of the civilian leadership and some top military officials that this would be an easy operation. An exaggerated view of American military strength, a dismissal of the ability of the opposing forces, and little recognition of the need for innovation.

- Military action that, except during the first year in Korea, largely lacked geographical objectives of seize and hold.
- Military action with restricted rules of engagement and political constraints on the use of a full arsenal of firepower.
- Military action against enemy forces that have sanctuaries which are largely off-limits.
- Military action that is rhetorically in defense of democracy—ignoring the reality of the undemocratic nature of regimes in Seoul, Saigon, Baghdad, and Kabul.
- With the exception of some of the South Korean and South Vietnamese military units, these have been wars with in-country allies that were not dependable.
- Military action that civilian leaders modulate, often clumsily, between domestic political reassurance and international muscle flexing. Downplaying the scale of deployment and length of commitment for the domestic audience and threatening expansion of these for the international community.
- Wars fought by increasingly less representative sectors of American society, which further encourages most Americans to pay little attention to the details of these encounters.
- Military action that is costly in lives and treasure and yet does not enjoy the support that wars require in a democracy.

Some of the restraints and restrictions on the conduct of these wars have been politically and even morally necessary. But it is neither politically nor morally defensible to send the young to war without a public consensus that the goals are understood and essential, and the restraints and the costs are acceptable.

On June 27, some veterans of the Korean War and their survivors will gather at the Korean War Veterans Memorial on the National Mall. This is a powerful memorial that every American needs to visit. And it is a memorial that lacks a record of the names of the 36,574 Americans who died in Korea.

The veterans of the Korean War want those comrades they still mourn to be recorded as individuals who served and who sacrificed when their nation asked them to. Retired U.S. Army Colonel William Weber, the chair of the Korean War Veterans Memorial Foundation, possesses three Purple

Hearts and two prosthetic limbs from his service in Korea. He recently wrote to Speaker of the House of Representatives John Boehner, "The surviving comrades of the 36,000+ fallen have been ravaged by time and illness and their numbers dwindle, but they cry out in their last plea to their countrymen and the Congress to honor their fallen comrades by recording their names for posterity."

This recognition needs to be considered as honoring the implicit contract that a nation presents to those who serve. Those who died on our behalf and at our request in Korea deserve a public accounting and a permanent record equivalent to that powerful reminder provided across the National Mall to those who fell in Vietnam. Wars marked by unknown casualties mourned quietly by anonymous families and largely unnoticed by a preoccupied nation—forgotten wars—are profoundly dangerous.

In addition to remembering those who served, we need to reflect on the lessons of Korea. In fact, it is three other wars with over 65,000 dead—and counting—past the time for us to do this. And it is tragically past time to quit repeating the experience while expecting a different outcome.

If the agreement signed at Panmunjom sixty years ago remains temporary and tentative, it nonetheless ended a cruel war. As President Dwight Eisenhower said when announcing the agreement, the conference table had worked: he hoped that "all nations may come to see the wisdom of composing differences in this fashion before, rather than after, there is resort to brutal and futile battle."

The Baby Boomer War

April 2017

O F ALL THE TROPES about the Vietnam War, one stands out far above the rest in American memory: It was the Baby Boomers' war. By the spring of 1967, most American soldiers being killed in combat had been born in 1946 or after.

To understand the war, we have to understand what motivated that generation of Americans not only to protest but also to fight, and later to seek some sort of closure. Wars are far easier to initiate than to conclude. And for those who serve, the memories endure long after the fighting stops.

At his inauguration in January 1961, President John Kennedy said, "Let every nation know, whether it wishes us well or ill, that we will pay any price, bear any burden, meet any hardship, support any friend, oppose any foe to assure the survival and the success of liberty."

Those born after the Boomers may find it quaint to read about a president asking citizens to sacrifice, to "pay any price." Nonetheless, their parents or grandparents, the Baby Boomers, will most likely remember a brief shining moment of energized promise and of unfulfilled dreams. It was the echo of that call, just a few years later, that motivated hundreds of thousands of young men to enlist for Vietnam, for the chance to ensure "the success of liberty"—and many others back home, at least at the outset, to support the fighting.

In popular memory, the Boomers quickly turned against the war. Many did, but many also served. Over ten million Boomers served in the military, some 40 percent of the males of their generation. Many of them served in Vietnam. More Baby Boomers died in Vietnam than went to Canada or to prison for refusing to serve. Those Boomers in uniform were more blue-collar and minority than their generational median, but they were not some marginal part of it, nor were they the only ones to fight. So did college dropouts and graduates—and not only as officers.

The profile of those who served was more complicated than their stereotype—the men and women in Vietnam were not defined by peace symbols and love beads, although some displayed them. They were not a group of mutinous draftees, although many were drafted, and if they did not begin their tour disillusioned by their war, they most likely concluded it with that view. They were not a band of rebellious "fraggers" assassinating their officers, or marauding killers piling up body counts of the innocent in a haze of marijuana smoke.

They were soldiers and Marines, sailors and airmen, doctors and nurses, who learned about survival, about protecting buddies, about cruel death. They witnessed the suffering of the Vietnamese and they served even when an ending to their war and a clear meaning for it seemed increasingly elusive. Their favorite song was the Animals' recording of "We Gotta Get Out of This Place." But when they did get out, their homecoming was often difficult and lonely. The impact of their indifferent, if not hostile, reception was all the greater because they had assumed the responsibility of citizenship they understood was theirs.

The Baby Boomer generation grew up in the world of the 1950s, a world of "duck-and-cover" drills in schools in preparation for a nuclear attack, of reminders of the threat posed by Soviet and Chinese Communism, of the fear of the near-inevitability of war, and of their obligation to serve in this war. It was a time of fear, but also an era of national confidence and of individual obligation. These children of World War II veterans learned their responsibility to serve when called—or to volunteer before being called.

The journalist Philip Caputo was a young Marine officer who went ashore with the first American combat units in Vietnam, in 1965. He recalled, "For Americans who did not come of age in the early 1960s, it may be hard to grasp what those years were like—the pride and overpowering self-assurance that prevailed." When they marched across rice paddies, he said, they carried, "along with our packs and rifles, the implicit convictions that the Vietcong would be quickly beaten and that we were doing something altogether noble and good."

Few could have anticipated the duration and cost of this commitment. Their leaders did not, although they were seldom honest about this. So when President Kennedy proclaimed at his inauguration that the torch had passed to a new generation, his World War II generation, it was a torch that few held very long. Within a few years, they quickly passed it along to their children.

In 1965, when President Lyndon Johnson sent in ground combat troops, there was criticism and dissent, but the dominant image was of young Americans taking a stand in the jungle, a heady sense of Americans defending the "free world."

This changed as the numbers of troops grew, their casualties increased, as draftees made up more of the units, and as the rationale for the war and its conduct were more broadly challenged and unpersuasively defended. As Americans became disillusioned by the war, some of their sons and daughters, siblings and friends, continued to go to Vietnam. To the protesters and critics, by 1967 the troops had become objects of pity for serving on a dangerous assignment in a cruel and unjust war.

In 1968, the chant from protesters was "Hey, hey, LBJ. How many kids did you kill today?" But by late 1969, when Americans learned of the atrocities committed against an estimated 600 civilians at the village of My Lai, some protesters focused on those who were serving in Vietnam, not as victims but as willing participants in their cruel and unjust war. Johnson was back in Texas, and the young men serving now were the baby killers. Pity became contempt. More people probably knew Lieutenant William Calley, the man in charge at My Lai, than knew the name of any other combat officer who served in Vietnam. This left little room in the Vietnam narrative for stories of courage and sacrifice.

My Lai framed the image that for too many retrospectively described the Vietnam generation. Theirs was the *Apocalypse Now* war. That movie bore as little relation to the conduct and experience of the Vietnam War as *South Pacific* did to World War II—except the latter was kinder to those serving. An overwhelming majority of Vietnam veterans served honorably and bravely.

As Americans turned against the war, as political leaders danced around the subject, these young men and women slogged through it. Out in the field, Vietnam was a cauldron of heat and humidity. It was about walking through jungles and rice paddies and elephant grass, and about being wet, infected, and dirty. It was searching for elusive enemy forces while encountering Vietnamese civilians who just wished the Americans would leave and the war would end.

We cannot come to terms with the Vietnam War until we acknowledge the story of the generation who served there and understand the emotional complexity they confronted. In the years after the war, as civilians they have continued to serve their country and their world and to make a difference. Powerful, often unshared memories remain.

Understanding this is essential: those with responsibility to send the young to war need always to consider the enduring consequences of war and the human cost of undertaking this action. Winston Churchill, reflecting on the Boer War, understood it a century ago, and the Vietnam generation experienced it a half century ago. As Churchill wrote, "The Statesman who yields to war fever must realize that once the signal is given, he is no longer the master of policy but the slave of unforeseeable and uncontrollable events." He argued, "Let us learn our lessons."

The Real Lessons of Vietnam— and Afghanistan

October 2017

As the Trump administration reshapes American strategy, they should look to history for guidance, yet understand that it offers no blueprint.

For some fifty years, politicians and pundits have shouted out "lessons of Vietnam" to clinch any number of policy arguments. Yet the actual lessons offered are seldom unambiguous, and can even be contradictory. Such "lessons" have been deployed, for example, to support and oppose the whole range of approaches to Afghanistan and Iraq. Ironically, one of the most compelling lessons of Vietnam—and of history in general—is to be wary of those who claim that history has informed them how to proceed.

President Lyndon Johnson and others of his World War II generation insisted that they had learned from history not to ignore aggression, not to concede to a bully—the Munich lesson. So they developed rationales from what they considered the mistakes of World War II—and devised their own mistakes. Their "lessons" were untouched by an understanding of nuance and difference—and by the recognition that leadership requires more than assuming roles prescribed by history.

In his September 19 speech to the United Nations, President Donald Trump promised "a new strategy for victory" in Afghanistan. As he and Congress shape this strategy, hopefully they will look to history for guidance. And hopefully they will appreciate that history is not a blueprint.

Afghanistan in 2017 is not Vietnam in 1954 or 1965. Despite some Chinese and Russian and Iranian mischief, these nations do not have the role in Afghanistan that China and the Soviet Union had in Vietnam. Afghanistan has no equivalent of the large, well-trained and modestly well-equipped North Vietnamese Army. Indeed, it has no equivalent of North Vietnam. Pakistan is far more consequential diplomatically and militarily than were the staging and storage areas along the Ho Chi Minh Trail in Laos and Cambodia. And the Taliban are assuredly not the National Liberation Front in size, organization, or capacity. Afghanistan remains a dangerous nurturing ground for international terrorist groups; it is not part of a broader Cold War contest.

Nonetheless, we can learn some things from Vietnam (and from sixteen years in Afghanistan):

- Among the great tragedies of Vietnam was that American leaders, including Presidents Kennedy, Johnson, and Nixon, had serious private reservations about their commitments even as their public statements promised success. The difference in Afghanistan is that President Trump's reservations, like those of President Obama, have been publicly expressed.
- War is more than a weapon in a diplomatic game. And it is not as flexible to reorient as diplomatic initiatives are. Wars are easier to start than to end, to escalate than to draw down. The human consequences endure.
- The goals set for the military must be unambiguous and they should be military in nature. Remember, U.S. armed forces had accomplished their original goals in Afghanistan by November 2001 and in Iraq by May 2003 ("Mission Accomplished"). But then the military goals evolved into important civic ones: we would modernize the government, education, and the economy, especially agriculture.
- Congressional and public support is essential—and it is mercurial. It is far easier to elicit this at the outset of a military engagement than it is to sustain it. Clear statements of purpose, candid assessments of likely costs, and as much transparency as is militarily possible are crucial. If these are insufficient to sustain support, then our democracy makes the next step clear.
- In a democracy, all citizens should have a stake in the war—as George Washington said, either through their service or their treasure. Or both.
- Make certain the local government we are defending is defensible, morally as well as politically. And that it is capable of playing a major role in its own defense.

- Be cautious when generalizing about the inhabitants of a country, of fitting them or their own conflicts into presumptive Western ideological or cultural categories. They have their own histories and cultures, their own memories and ambitions.
- Seeking to win hearts and minds may be hyperbolic overreach, but securing the trust of local population is critical. Excessive military force can be counterproductive in this effort. When liberators or benefactors become occupiers, relationships change markedly. It is not good to be perceived—or to enable your opponents to identify you—as another colonial or occupying power, especially in places that have had much experience being colonized or occupied.
- War is a tragic human enterprise. It requires a commitment of a country's most treasured resource. The modern "boots on the ground" slogan abstracts the enterprise and substitutes shoe leather for the flesh-and-blood cost of war. Especially in rural, nonindustrial countries, fighting requires combat troops on the ground, which means casualties.
- Making certain our young did not die in vain usually results in more of our young dying. Potentially in vain.
- Handing the war fighting over to the indigenous allies ("Vietnamization") is a complicated transaction that requires patience and understanding—and loss of control. If it is a cover for an exit strategy, its failure is pretty much inevitable.
- Never confuse the war fighters for the war. Honor and care for them.

President Trump promised victory in Afghanistan just as Lyndon Johnson pledged to "hang the coonskin on the wall." But there is no conventional victory in wars marked by negotiations, by strategies to outlast rather than traditionally defeat an enemy. Repetitious small-unit skirmishes, patrols, and ambushes are not concluded by epic flag raisings. They are, in fact, generally repeated more than concluded. Such wars will likely end with political compromise and unmet goals, with weary relief more than symbolic coonskins or real victory parades. And the relief—the "peace with honor" of Vietnam, the "armistice" in Korea—may well prove temporary.

Remembering Vietnam

November 15, 2017, in Boston, Massachusetts

Tonight I would like to share some reflections on how I think Americans have remembered Vietnam—how they have remembered those who have served and sacrificed. This is largely about our collective memory, our formal national memory—not the agonizing grief of personal loss.

During the intense political debate in the United States over the Vietnam War prior to the 1972 election, Senator Edmund Muskie described the war as a "mistake."

Muskie was a distinguished public servant from the state of Maine who had served as Hubert Humphrey's running mate in the 1968 presidential election. He was the odds-on favorite for the 1972 Democratic nomination until George McGovern secured this in the primaries with an aggressive antiwar campaign. Antiwar was the popular position in those years, with "mistake" being among the more gentle criticisms, and President Richard Nixon won reelection on a platform that assured he was ending the Vietnam War, promising "peace with honor."

One young Georgian responded passionately to Senator Muskie's description. A Vietnam veteran who had attained the rank of captain, the thirty-year-old Max Cleland had been awarded a Bronze Star and a Silver Star for bravery. And he held a Purple Heart—awarded when he lost both legs above the knee and part of an arm in a grenade explosion.

Cleland asked, "What do you mean, a mistake? Where's the meaning? Where's the purpose? What does that do to a guy like me, who lost so much? What does it do to all those who lost so much in Vietnam? Those are questions I'll be trying to answer for the rest of my life."

And Max Cleland has wrestled with these questions—as director of the Veterans Administration during the presidency of fellow-Georgian Jimmy Carter, and as United States senator from Georgia from 1997 to 2003, ironically losing in the latter year to Saxby Chambliss, who questioned his patriotism.

Other veterans have wrestled with these questions. Bobby Muller, a Marine veteran, suffered injuries that left him a paraplegic. He said at a public gathering in New York in 1979 that Americans considered the Vietnam veterans to be "Lieutenant Calley types, junkies, crazed psychos or dummies that couldn't find their way to Canada." He said that the veterans quietly remembered those years: "We fought hard and we fought well." Muller founded Vietnam Veterans of America and has spent his life working with peace organizations.

Most Americans have still not determined how to recognize those who served and sacrificed while at the same time holding the view that Vietnam was a "mistake." It is a complicated emotional and intellectual juggling act: we hated your war, thought it was a mistake, and by the way, thank you for your service.

More profoundly, more emotionally, the prior question is how do those who served and sacrificed, those who lost friends or loved ones, reconcile these things. Vietnam was a war with remarkable acts of heroism and courage—as much surely as any war—but there really are no *publicly acclaimed* heroes. References to the war almost always are negative—many argue it was a mistake to become involved, others point out it was poorly if not immorally executed, and finally there is the reminder that its conclusion was an embarrassment. And it is a consensus among many that all of these criticisms are correct. *No more Vietnams.* What does this leave for those who served?

By the early 1970s Americans were tired of the war. They wanted it to end. And the news in December of 1969 of the massacre at My Lai nearly two years earlier compounded the resistance with a sense of moral outrage. Those who served were now more commonly implicated in this outrage.

Over 2.5 million American servicemen and -women served in Vietnam and 58,318 died there or later as a direct result of combat wounds. Over 300,000 were wounded—physically and medically. There is no accounting of the psychological wounds.

Estimates of Vietnamese deaths have gone as high as three million. Many innocent civilians. We need to never allow this larger picture to slip away— even as we look at the American experience.

For the Americans, the inability to reconcile acknowledgment of service along with the negative views of the war happened early.

In my research and interviews I was struck by how veterans of Vietnam described their homecoming. Getting "Out of This Place" and going home was the major goal, but it was not without apprehension about the reception they would receive. Their grapevine warned them of protestors and provocations and the evidence is clear that some of them did encounter hostility and attack, although I do believe that the incidences of these were exaggerated. Surely the Nixon and Agnew administration tried to link the peace activists with an un-American and antiveteran ideology. But for the Vietnam veterans, if the outright acts of hostility were not so common, what was common was a tortured silence.

Fred Downs told of walking across the campus of the University of Denver with his prosthetic hand with a hook. A student came up to him and asked if he lost his hand in Vietnam. When Downs said "yes," the student replied, "serves you right" as he walked away. The veteran just stood there, "too confused with hurt, shame, and anger to react."

Most encountered debilitating indifference. They spoke of the "Sound of Silence." Families greeted them warmly—and never asked them about Vietnam.

One returnee acknowledged that he did not experience hostility, "but nobody ever said, 'Welcome home,' or 'Thank you for your service and time and what you did for us in Vietnam.'"

For one army nurse, it was only when she returned home that she had "problems dealing with my having been in Vietnam" because she had no warning about the attitudes of most people. She didn't encounter hostility but rather people who were "absolutely, totally indifferent."

One came home just before Thanksgiving, and at a large family celebration he expected to "be bombarded by questions and stuff," but no one mentioned Vietnam to him. So he never talked about it to them—for the next forty years.

Those experiences and emotions have continued for many Vietnam War veterans and their families, as has the process of remembering and healing. And we surely need to understand the Americans who served there, who they were and what they experienced.

An important step toward recognition and that healing took place on July 1, 1980, when Congress authorized the Vietnam Veterans Memorial Fund to proceed with fundraising for a memorial to those American servicemen and -women who had lost their lives in the Vietnam War. No public money was appropriated but there was a priceless contribution: the allocation of a site on three acres of land on the National Mall near the Lincoln Memorial.

The Vietnam Veterans Memorial Fund worked hard to raise the money for a memorial and initiated a competition for a design. Despite skeptics, they succeeded in raising over $8 million with the support of the major veterans' groups, corporations, and labor organizations—and nearly 300,000 individual contributors. Accomplishing this proved easier than proceeding with a design that garnered widespread support. Expectations differed. How to remember?

When the design review committee chose the design submitted by Yale University architecture student Maya Lin, there was wide approval—and also significant pushback. Some of the negative reaction to the design was condescending, occasionally racist and misogynist, challenging a memorial developed by a young Asian woman. Some of it was political and aesthetic—Tom Wolfe described it as a tribute to Jane Fonda.

Some Vietnam veterans such as Jim Webb, an early and significant leader in the initiative, were troubled by the plan for a memorial that did not acknowledge the honor and courage of those who served in Vietnam. And the patriotic commitment of those who sacrificed.

Many critics looked wistfully across the Potomac to the Marine Corps Memorial. This was a dramatic, iconic reminder of courage. The Felix de Weldon statue based on the Joe Rosenthal photo of the six Marines raising the flag on Mount Suribachi on Iwo Jima in February 1945 was a stirring tribute to the Marine Corps. It came more broadly to serve as a tribute to the World War II generation who served and prevailed. There was no touch of equivalent heroism in the Maya Lin design.

The Vietnam Veterans Memorial leadership, headed by the indomitable Jan Scruggs, worked out an accommodation with many of the critics. They agreed that there would be an American flag prominently displayed at the apex of the memorial wall. And they commissioned Frederick Hart to design a statue representing those who served that would stand nearby.

With these plans in place, President Ronald Reagan's Secretary of the Interior James Watt finally approved the plan. Not everyone was satisfied—

some of the critics of the original design continued to be troubled by it and some of the supporters were not happy at the expanded representational art. Maya Lin was displeased with this modification.

The memorial was dedicated on Veterans Day 1982. The veterans organized a parade and a program.

The statue, "Three Soldiers," was dedicated two years later. President Reagan spoke at the latter occasion—he had avoided the 1982 event because of the controversy then associated with the memorial. And in 1993 the Vietnam Women's Memorial was dedicated, recognizing the thousands of women who served courageously in Vietnam.

The tension between a memorial, a place to remember sacrifice and to grieve lives lost, and a monument that inspires, is neither semantic nor recent. Monuments celebrate the purpose, the accomplishments, the heroic. They remember and remind of the cause. They inspire the living. This national act of remembering and celebrating is at least as old as the world of Pericles.

In Thucydides's telling, Pericles eulogized the Athenians who died in the Peloponnesian War, men "who preferred death to survival at the cost of surrender." He judged them as the valiant dead who *proved worthy of their city.*

In the address that is considered among the most eloquent in American history, Abraham Lincoln stood at Gettysburg in 1863 and eulogized the dead in the most general terms. No numbers. No names. No individual heroes. All of the Union dead were patriotic heroes.

The Marine Corps Memorial in Arlington is highly inspirational—I have a treasured photo of myself at age seventeen with four high school friends posing beside it a month before we all joined the Marines. It is a monument to heroes.

I have looked at Marine Corps photographs from Iwo Jima in the late winter of 1945—row after row of shallow graves in the sand, bodies waiting to be transported home. We remember their courage, their accomplishments, and say less about the cost, the sacrifice.

The Vietnam Memorial stands as a symbol of the effort to reconcile private grief with public recognition. If some of the veterans were initially unsure of the proposed memorial, they moved on to pretty universally embrace it. Literally. They came to consider it their holy ground. One

Marine who had seen seven men in his platoon die when they were hit by friendly fire shared with me a poem he wrote after visiting the wall:

I cried, but not enough, nowhere near enough.
I carried on.
We moved out an hour later. First Platoon on point.
I passed the night dug in next to a 4-deuce mortar,
My insides jerking each time it blasted out another load of what
Blew you to bits.
Now I live here and you live on this wall.
You live in my life, too.

The Vietnam Memorial remembers the sacrifice of war—in its scale, tablet after tablet marked by line after line of names after names. The magnitude of loss is overwhelming. But its personal memorial is as well. Each and every name reminds of a life lost, someone with dreams and plans and grieving survivors. Each name encourages its own private memorial. Over 400,000 photos, notes, personal items such as medals and combat boots, have been left at the base of the wall. And many tears. Each item, each tear, a deeply personal reminder of a person, more than a name etched in stone.

Let me close with a story I shared with you a year ago. One of the men I interviewed recounted for me his time serving on a swift boat on the delta. They dealt with regular ambushes and firefights and had lost a few men so they were always on edge. One morning on a canal they took fire from a position in the brush along the shore. They fired back quickly with massive firepower.

They obviously hit an ammunition store because there was a major explosion. They saw the bodies of two men, the ambushers, fly into the air. He said they all cheered at the sight. A great victory. And he said that for several years after that he would talk with pride about seeing those two bodies flying through the air.

Then, about a decade after this, he was on a church retreat in the Shenandoah Valley. Part of the program was to walk alone through a maze and reflect on how to live a richer life. He remembered his Vietnam experience and started weeping. He ended up running from the maze up into the woods where he cried and cried.

He said that he knew that killing people was a terrible part of war. But he should not celebrate killing another human being. These men had families at home, perhaps pictures of children in their uniforms that were then incinerated. These soldiers were also god's children.

These are poignant reminders of the personal memories of war. And if the rest of us can never experience them, we can make certain that these stories are shared and remain part of the national narrative of war and of the costs of war.

Enduring Vietnam:
An American Generation and Its War

May 16, 2018, in Arlington, Virginia

WE ALL JOIN in thanking and applauding you, the Vietnam veterans who are here. And what I am seeking to do tonight—and sought to do in my book *Enduring Vietnam*—is contribute to understanding the story of your generation and then telling that story.

It is time. It is long past time. We have much to learn from your experience, from your story. Last fall we confronted the Vietnam War through the searing lens, the remarkable research, and the well-tuned presentation of Ken Burns's and Lynn Novick's films. Of course, there were critical reactions to parts of the series—this was about the Vietnam War, after all! But it forced us all to think again about this war and those who served. That war continues to hover over so many of our deliberations today. "No More Vietnams" is a defensible position, but it is a slogan rather than a policy. Most Americans don't know the Vietnam experience. Few did in the 1960s either.

. . . CERTAINLY TODAY the vast majority of American citizens have no idea what servicemen and -women go through when they are trained to fight, sent into battle, and return home. Over 60 percent of Americans were born after the last U.S. combat units left Vietnam in 1973. Over 75 percent of our citizens today never had to face the possibility of a military draft.

Framed somewhat differently, some 50 percent of American men over seventy-five, my age group, are veterans. About 36 percent of men aged 65–74, the Vietnam generation, are veterans. And about 1.5 percent of men and women aged 18–34 are veterans. War and the threat of war continues today even as a smaller percent of the population understands what this means. I wanted to try to contribute to understanding what this experience was for the Vietnam generation.

A few years ago, when my wife Susan and I attended a performance of *Hamilton*, many of the lines struck me. But one kept running through my head. Eliza Hamilton, the widow of Alexander Hamilton, sang, with a chorus of Founding Fathers, "Who Lives, Who Dies, Who Tells Your Story." I thought of this simple set of questions a lot. My book then was essentially finished but I realized that Mrs. Hamilton summarized well some of the very questions with which I had been wrestling.

In any armed confrontation, whether Athenians outside the gates of Troy or the troops from the 61st Cavalry Regiment at Combat Outpost Keating at Kamdesh, Afghanistan, in 2009, the first questions are the determinative ones: Who Lives and Who Dies? Apart from all other descriptions, this is the fundamental question, the tragic consequence, indeed—and we must never forget this: killing or being killed is the cruel purpose of war.

That is why I have such trouble with the "boots on the ground" metaphor that politicians and pundits have used in recent years. With 99 percent of the population having no personal engagement or stake in the wars, it is easy to abstract these distant conflicts to drones fighting video games or cute little memetic boots marching around. When we talk of war, we are not talking about shoe leather. We are talking about our young who serve. And we are asking them to confront, to participate in answering the most basic question, Who lives and who dies?

But then the burden that continues after the shooting stops is the lingering question: Who Tells Your Story? The shared narrative of battles and wars fought, of those who served and those who sacrificed, this is the story that must be heard.

The story of war must include accounts of lives lost, remind us of who they were, for their fate marks forever the lives of the survivors who knew them and who carry the memories. And carry their own experiences. Without these human faces and without confronting the human costs, it is far too easy to narrate war as a dramatic and bloodless tale.

We all need to assist in the responsibility of carrying these stories. And to make certain that these become embedded in the national narrative. That is an important part of what I have tried to do with my Vietnam book—to remind readers of the human face of war. The human cost of war.

The shadow of the Vietnam War still hangs over us; the human consequences endure, as does the debate over the decision for war, the conduct of the war, and the results of the war.

But the story of the war, the experience of the war—this often becomes abstracted and shuffled aside in the great debate over the war. And the debate points are pretty consistently negative ones. Those who served there deserve better.

I set out to learn about the American experience of Vietnam from those who were there. I interviewed 160 people for my book—I call them my collaborators and sent each of them a personally inscribed copy of the book.

They shared many powerful stories, personal stories, largely of combat experiences. They affirmed my belief that in so many cruel and perverse ways, there is nothing more human than war. Testing our fundamental values and our courage.

. . . I DO PROVIDE a history of the war—I am a historian. It is important to set context and frame the world of the Vietnam generation. I am not very kind to those who sent them to war. They seldom shared their own doubts. They allowed politics and ego to dominate too often. And candor and honesty were set aside.

But in this book I am less interested in critiquing the nation's leaders than I am in assessing the view of the world they stressed—and the Baby Boomers learned. Theirs was a world of expanding opportunity—and of constant threats of doomsday, underlined by duck-and-cover drills in schools.

They grew up in the world in which John Kennedy reminded them of obligation. . . . President Kennedy's generation, their parents' generation, talked of accepting the torch of liberty—and they quickly passed it along to their children.

I have long been haunted by a copy of *Life* magazine that I have in my office—on June 27, 1969, *Life* published a cover story, "The Faces of the American Dead in Vietnam: One Week's Toll." The magazine included the names, hometowns, and ages of 242 young men killed in Vietnam whose deaths were announced by the Pentagon in the last week of May 1969. (Almost twice that many were actually killed in that week.)

Most of the 242 had photos—eleven pages of photographs, of young faces, smiling, confident, most high school graduation pictures or boot camp or basic training pictures. They looked so young. And they were.

Many were nineteen or twenty. Those remarkable photos and the brief profile of each made the war real and its costs very human.

I came back to this magazine again in 2012–13 and thought that I wanted to close the circle here. My own life, my own experiences, merged with the historian I was. I knew I had something more to learn. I knew I had something I had to say—I had to convince myself that I could say it.

In 1965, when the American ground war began, the dominant public image of those serving in Vietnam was of young heroes fighting communists someplace in the jungles of Southeast Asia.

Within a few years, as casualties increased significantly and the draft picked up, many came to consider them objects of sympathy fighting a cruel and ill-advised war.

The protests were directed at the nation's leaders and the chant was "Hey, Hey, LBJ. How many kids did *you* kill today?"

After the story of My Lai became public in late 1969, in the minds of some these young Americans became instead the perpetrators of that cruel war, drug-addled psychotics.

I think it is tragic that in the 1970s more people likely knew the name of Lieutenant William Calley, who led the unit that massacred the civilians at My Lai, than knew any others who fought in Vietnam. There certainly was heroism in Vietnam. But there were no publicly embraced heroes.

It is hard perhaps to provide popular heroic accounts for a war that was not embraced. But I would argue that service—and heroism—are even more compelling in such a war.

Let me take this occasion to share with you a few examples of my effort to reflect on the days of that war, now ended for many years, to reflect upon the very human experience of the Americans who served in Vietnam.

In my interviews I found some compelling stories—of those on the ground. And I tried to introduce those who died on that ground.

. . . Let me share with you a few of the accounts of those stories:

I learned so much from my interview with Donald Sullivan, a veteran of the battle for Hamburger Hill. He was one of the few young platoon leaders to still be on that hill when the top was secured after ten days of fighting. It was a costly fight, with the men day after day trying to assault the entrenched enemy and move up the hill. On the tenth day, when Sullivan told them they had orders to move up again, he faced a revolt. The men said they had had enough of this. He admitted that he had no training to deal with such a situation, so he finally picked up his rifle and started to move up. Someone asked where he was going. Sullivan said, "We have orders to move up the hill and I am moving up the hill." A few rolled their eyes and sighed and picked up their weapons. Just then a mortar round struck near the men, not injuring any of them but exploding on some of their equipment and belongings. One man ran over and picked up his pack. It had a tear and was soaking wet. He looked and saw that a piece of shrapnel had pierced a C-ration fruit cocktail can he had been saving, planning to enjoy the sweet liquid and fruit at a good moment. The soldier shouted out in anger, "We're going to go up there and get those fuckers! I'm going to kill those bastards!" So was this platoon inspired for the final assault of the battle.

The platoon had already had serious casualties. On the fourth day of the battle a grenade wounded several members of the platoon. Staff Sergeant Willard Dufresne Jr., an athletic and popular leader, organized a party to carry one of the seriously wounded down to a medevac landing area. As they were starting down, a rocket propelled grenade struck the group, killing some including the soldier on the stretcher. Dufresne was seriously wounded and told the men he was not going to make it. They assured him that he would and that a helicopter was coming to get him to a medical station. He said, "No, a chariot is coming to get me" and started to sing "Sing low, sweet chariot, comin' for to carry me home." He died on the stretcher. His son was born back in Minnesota a few months later.

One young man told me he had dropped out of school because he just was not doing well, was partying and not studying. He knew what would happen and it did: losing his student deferment, he was drafted. He had opposed the war but thought that maybe this was a good move for him. And he went all in and volunteered to serve as an Army Ranger. He said then he might "grow up a little bit." This growing up occurred quickly in Vietnam. He told me about his first hostile fight near their base camp out in the jungle. He recalled that he found it "exhilarating" to have engaged in "life-and-death combat."

But once the adrenaline stopped pulsing, he started thinking about this and moved to a feeling of deep dread. Then when he had to help carry the remains of one of the men in his unit, killed in this firefight, to a landing zone to be evacuated, he realized he had nearly a year left to serve and to face these situations. "I went from exhilaration to utter despair."

One woman I interviewed told me that she and her husband had married while in college and both opposed the war. When he graduated and received his draft notice, she wanted to move to Canada, but he said that if they did that someone else would just have to go in his place. He would go, and if he went to Vietnam, he assured her that he would never kill anyone. He went to Vietnam and was killed in a nighttime attack. When the army returned his remains to their Iowa home, she made two decisions. First, contrary to standard policy, she wanted an open casket at the wake so that people could see his mutilated body, could see what war does. Secondly, she asked the army honor guard not to fire a salute at the cemetery: "my husband has had enough gunfire."

I interviewed the sister and the niece of Lenny Hickson, a Navajo paratrooper who had been killed. He along with two sisters were the first recorded triplets on the Navajo reservation. Lenny Hickson was buried at Fort Defiance Cemetery on the reservation. Following a Catholic funeral mass, the Navajo elders performed a ceremony for a dead warrior. One of his triplet sisters threw herself on the coffin and begged to be buried with her brother.

One man who served as a Marine platoon leader told me that when he arrived in Vietnam, he was surprised when during orientation a senior officer told these young lieutenants, "Whatever you do, don't let your men see you cry." Shortly thereafter he found this tested when the young Marine walking point was killed and he struggled to control his emotions. And he struggled again, especially when he saw seven men in his platoon die when they were hit by friendly fire. He told me that in the years since Vietnam he has done his crying.

I interviewed soldiers who served with Bruce Saunders. He was by every account a remarkable young man. And as a Black soldier, despite being an officer in the U.S. Army, he and his wife Deborah encountered "white only" signs in the South—including outside their Fort Benning, Georgia, base. He persisted. Men considered him a natural leader, a "benchmark." Within a year after being told he could not enter some doors in Georgia, he was leading a unit in the 2nd Battalion of the 501st Infantry on Firebase Airborne. In May 1969 they suffered a massive nighttime assault from the North Vietnamese. He died that night with twenty-six others, and in the course of the heavy fighting displayed the leadership and bravery for which he had always been known. The Bronze Star he received only touches on his courage.

I interviewed James Milliken, an infantryman who served in the Mekong Delta and was wounded in a nighttime raid by the North Vietnamese Army. Milliken wrote of his Vietnam experience, "The hot weather, mud, and constant wetness from sweeping filthy rice paddies are reducing my stamina. I am tormented daily by the native pests, including mosquitoes, rats, red ants, and leeches. The mosquitoes are terrible. At night the repellant lasts less than twenty minutes before the pests fly in your ears, nose, and mouth.... My body is covered with infections from cuts incurred in the field. They won't heal because I'm in water each day for hours at a time. The bottoms of my feet are full of small holes, and I develop a mild case of immersion foot. The ringworm around my waist and ankles is unmanageable because my belt and boots remain wet most of the day. I get very little rest and sometimes suffer from battle fatigue when I deal with booby traps, firefights, suicide missions, and the trauma associated with friends getting wounded or killed."[1]

This is the face of war. The heart of war. The memories—and the tears—of war. We need always to remember and recognize what this generation did. They are not asking for sympathy, to be remembered as suffering. But they do need to be remembered as serving at a difficult time and with little recognition.

This generation has in fact gone on to continue to do remarkable things for our country. Even if they say little about it, as you can all attest, they do remember their service. And so should we. So must we.

... IN THE PLAY *Hamilton*, George Washington, the old soldier, sings along with Eliza Hamilton. "Let me tell you what I wish I'd known / When I was young and dreamed of glory / You have no control: Who Lives / Who Dies / Who tells your story."

My book represents my attempt to contribute to the effort, to the obligation, to make certain the stories are told.

My regards to all of the veterans here. Thank you for your service and your sacrifice. All of us, veterans and nonveterans, need to join to tell the stories—and even more importantly, to listen to the stories. And, most important of all, to learn from the stories.

NOTE

1. James W. Milliken, *Enter and Die* (Bloomington, IN: Xlibris, 2009), 82.

How Modern Wars Are Changing
the Definition of Heroism

September 2018

L ABOR DAY WEEKEND in 2018 was marked by the memorial services for Senator John McCain of Arizona.

Eulogists described him as a patriot and a maverick, a generous man, and a hero.

Few challenged these salutes—although President Donald Trump famously suggested in 2015 that McCain was not a hero for being captured. While most disputed Trump's remarks, candidate Dr. Ben Carson said, "It depends on your definition of a war hero."

By any definition with which I am familiar, John McCain, a Vietnam War prisoner of war, was a hero. McCain deserves the honor not simply because he served. Not even just because he was captured—although he and the other Vietnam War POWs demonstrated remarkable courage and endurance and deserve the praise they have received.

But McCain was a hero because of his conduct as a pilot and as a captive. The descriptions of his captivity and the citation of his Silver Star award make this clear.

Today, approximately 1 percent of the U.S. population serves in the military. They are not from a demographic or geographic cross section of the country. Most Americans do not know anyone who currently or recently served. No one under the age of sixty-three has ever faced being drafted.

One consequence of this distance from the military is less public understanding of what serving means. Perhaps, ironically, this has resulted in greater public approval of those who do serve, describing all in uniform as "heroes."

There is ample evidence that most troops are not comfortable with the general label of hero: if all are heroes, what remains to describe the truly heroic?

Achilles and Henry II may not have recognized twentieth-century weaponry or fortifications, but they would have understood and saluted Sergeant Alvin York in World War I and Audie Murphy in World War II—widely recognized heroes, Medal of Honor recipients who attacked, engaged, and defeated the enemy.

In all of the American wars after World War II, political objectives shaped military strategy. Korea was marked by changing political goals, as was Vietnam.

Vietnam was a war of tactical maneuvers and small unit actions, with approximately 80 percent of ground combat engagements initiated by the enemy, a pattern accelerated in the post-9/11 wars.

In Vietnam, "winning" battles often became more a tactical goal of engaging the enemy and killing them, or at least deterring them—and then returning for another skirmish the next day or the next week. At or near the same ground. Winning was surviving. The wars in Vietnam, Afghanistan, and Iraq have been essentially wars of attrition, wars without crisp military objectives, and operations that, for the American forces, involved strict rules of engagement.

Assaulting enemy positions, streaming ashore in the face of hostile fire in places like Normandy or Iwo Jima, securing enemy defeat or surrender, raising a victory flag—these actions were far easier for noncombatants to understand and to celebrate. They fit comfortably into a public narrative in ways that the wars since then have not.

In World War II, more than 60 percent of the 472 Medals of Honor went to those engaged in an assault on an enemy position. In Vietnam, a war of small-unit actions, only 21 percent of the 260 men recognized with the nation's highest medal were involved in offensive actions.

In World War II, 17 percent of the medals went to those who exposed themselves to enemy fire in order to protect or retrieve wounded comrades. In Vietnam, 44 percent of the awardees were cited for such heroic conduct. This trend has continued in our twenty-first–century wars.

Just two days before Senator McCain's death, President Donald Trump awarded the Medal of Honor, posthumously, to the widow of John Chapman, an Air Force enlisted man who led a team into enemy fire on a snowy peak at Takur Ghar in Afghanistan in March 2002 and individually fought the enemy until his own death. He went there in an effort to retrieve a wounded colleague.

President Trump said of him, "He gave his life for his fellow warriors."

In Afghanistan, 50 percent of the Medal of Honor awardees, like Technical Sergeant Chapman, were recognized for putting their lives at risk to save comrades.

For all of the combatants, these twenty-first–century wars involve the daily courage of driving or marching off a base, or even existing on a base when presumed allies sometimes kill Americans, of patrols warily approaching a piece of trash or an animal carcass on the road, of encountering groups of civilians at a crossroads where fear, if not hostility, is present.

In these wars, firefights are with enemy combatants who are not wearing uniforms and can fade easily back into the civilian population.

There has been no ceremonial raising of victory flags in Afghanistan or Iraq—nor were there in Korea or Vietnam. Political protocol required that these not appear to be "American wars."

But they were, and are, and yet because of their nature, they have been wars without traditional victory narratives.

The heroic victor, draped in laurel and hoisting a banner, enters folklore more readily than the young heroes who threw themselves on a grenade to protect others. And perhaps more readily than the young Navy prisoner of war who refused an opportunity to be released because others had been there longer than he had been.

Nonetheless, however heroism is defined, they are heroes all.

As We Remember Normandy, Let's Not Forget Hamburger Hill

May 2019

O N Memorial Day 2019, Americans will consider some significant anniversaries that relate directly to this time of national reflection. On June 6 the United States and its World War II allies will mark the seventy-fifth anniversary of D-Day, the massive military landing on the beaches of Normandy that would result eleven months later in the end of the European war.

On the evening of June 6, 1944, President Franklin Roosevelt gave a radio address in which he framed a prayer for those who fought: "They will be sore tried, by night and by day, without rest, until the victory is won. The darkness will be rent by noise and flame. Men's souls will be shaken with the violences of war."

He had predicted on June 5 that the road ahead "will be tough and it will be costly."

It would be tough and it would prove very costly. But by the end of August the American 28th Infantry Division marched down the Champs-Élysées. Allied forces were greeted there and in the French countryside by cheering, newly liberated French citizens. It was a heady time even though Bastogne and the Rhine and Berlin lay ahead. And of course, to the east the foreboding home islands of Japan.

There will surely and appropriately be many programs and speakers that remind us of this historic D-Day battle. As Americans in 2019 remember Normandy and celebrate that step to victory, it will be important to also pause to consider another anniversary, one that has little place in our national memory. It was a battle that engaged the sons of the World War II generation, a battle won but not celebrated.

This May marks the fiftieth anniversary of the major extended Vietnam battle for the mountain named Dong Ap Bia and recalled as Hamburger

Hill. When units from the 101st Airborne landed at this desolate place in the A Shau Valley on May 10, 1969, no one recognized that they were about to engage in one of the few sustained battles of the Vietnam War. Following a vicious, eleven-day fight, only 30 percent of the force that landed there on May 10 would reach the top on May 20.

Their accomplishment, their victory, was greeted at home by silence—or by criticism directed at those who ordered the assault. It was hard to celebrate a victory in a controversial, unpopular, war. There were no presidential statements about the battle, no national prayers, no celebration. No flags were raised. And on June 5, two weeks after the conclusion of the battle, the army abandoned the hill.

The next day Americans celebrated the twenty-fifth anniversary of D-Day. President Richard Nixon proclaimed: "Twenty-five years have not diminished but have, rather, enhanced the profound importance of that day." He made no statement about Hamburger Hill. He quietly ordered the Pentagon not to initiate any more sustained offensive operations like that assault. A few days later he would announce the "Vietnamization" of the war and the beginning of the drawdown of American forces.

Each battle in its own way marked an important step in the ending of their wars.

On this seventy-fifth anniversary of the Normandy landing, there will be a gathering at Colleville-sur-Mer above Omaha Beach. Some veterans will be there and will be recognized warmly, as they should be. To mark the fiftieth anniversary of the battle of Hamburger Hill this month some 187th Infantry Regiment veterans of that battle will climb the hill, accompanied by some current 187th soldiers. It will be a gathering filled with memories but no memorials.

Above Omaha Beach in Normandy there is the peaceful, well-maintained Normandy American Cemetery with the elegiac statue "Spirit of American Youth Rising from the Waves." It looks over the immaculate rolling grounds with row after row of white markers at the graves of 9,380 Americans.

On the top of Dong Ap Bia there is a small memorial placed by the Vietnamese government celebrating "the anti-American resistance to save the country." Despite the language, there was no Vietnamese victory there in the spring of 1969. And despite the outcome fifty years ago, there was no American celebration of their victory. The American War in Vietnam was

a war without the markers of time-honored claims of conquest, of liberation, of the consequential "fall" or "capture" of strategic geographic places.

The D-Day landing on the Normandy beaches, along with the paratrooper landings nearby, was a long-planned strategic operation, a means
to liberate France and unconditionally defeat Germany. 160,000 U.S. and
allied forces came in as part of a massive operation involving tactical and
strategic air and naval assaults. It was an essential part of a military strategy.
Operation Overlord had taken a year of careful intelligence gathering and
planning. With the Italian campaign nearing completion, this foothold in
France was essential.

On the first day the Allies, landing on five different Normandy beaches,
had over 10,000 casualties including over 4,400 killed. By the end of the
operation on August 20, 1944, 20,668 Americans had died. Paris was liberated. But as the president predicted, it was costly.

The American War in Vietnam never sought a traditional military victory but a satisfactory political resolution. Military operations in Vietnam
were generally platoon sized and involved patrols and ambushes and more
patrols and ambushes. The battalion-sized attack on Dong Ap Bia was a
large operation.

Operation Apache Snow aimed to force a withdrawal of the North Vietnamese Army forces that had occupied areas in the A Shau Valley, in the
northwestern part of South Vietnam, just a few miles from Laos and the Ho
Chi Minh Trail. They sought to destroy what some called the "warehouse"
area for enemy ordnance and supplies. The 3rd Battalion of the 187th landed
on Dong Ap Bia and they were joined in the operation at nearby sites by
other battalions from the 501st and 506th regiments of the 101st Airborne
Division, two battalions of the Army of the Republic of Vietnam, and units
from the 9th Marines at the northern end of the valley.

There was never a plan to occupy and hold these areas but only to punish
the North Vietnamese, destroy their supplies, and hopefully convince them
that they could not secure a military victory and would have to engage in
serious political discussions to end the war. It was a tactical operation and
one that was not based on good intelligence and planning. As Lieutenant
Colonel Weldon Honeycutt, who led the 3rd Battalion of the 187th into the
valley, said later, the division headquarters and the Military Assistance
Command, Vietnam, "had no idea" what to expect on the mountain.

There were 102 Americans and thirty-one South Vietnamese army soldiers killed in Operation Apache Snow. Seventy-two members of the 101st died in capturing Dong Ap Bia. If these figures do not compare with those of Normandy, it would be a cruel way to measure cost and consequence.

In the fall of 1969, Neil Sheehan, a distinguished *New York Times* Vietnam correspondent, wrote, "Perhaps there is no difference, but it ought to be one thing to perish on the beaches of Normandy or Iwo Jima in a great cause and another to fall in a rejected and unsung war."

Sheehan raises a fundamental question of modern wars that is worth contemplating. The sacrifices are no less final but the acknowledgment, the recognition, the sense of accomplishment that to some seems to justify the sacrifice, is far more muted, more easily ignored. Battlegrounds like Fallujah in Iraq and Combat Outpost Keating in Afghanistan have joined Hamburger Hill and Khe Sanh and other places, many nameless and few known, where we have posted young Americans. Perhaps the best response to Neil Sheehan's question actually preceded his asking it. The *Washington Post* editorialized on the Vietnam War on Memorial Day 1969: "Those who fight this war are very properly heroes—because they fight to no applause, because the cause is not supported, because all of it is so unequal. It is as if all the injustices of life have been concentrated in one unlucky place, where the burden is borne by a brave few whose stake in its outcome is very small. A man's death is no less because it occurs at Danang rather than Remagen, and an exploit like Hamburger Hill is no less gallant than Iwo Jima. But it is not common now to speak of gallantry, any more than it is to speak of heroes."

This echoes today. And as we quite properly applaud those who scaled Pointe Du Hoc on Normandy on June 6, 1944, it is important to recall those who clambered onto the peak of Dong Ap Bia on May 20, 1969. Those heroes.

We need to acknowledge that the difference in our reactions to their battles has nothing to do with their commitment, courage, and sacrifice. It has to do with the national purpose of and the national support for their deployment to these places. Those things are relevant today, for this is a story that has no end.

The Capture of Hamburger Hill

June 2019

IN MAY 1969, U.S. soldiers paid a heavy price in America's last great combat assault of the Vietnam War. Was it worth it?

The 3rd Battalion of the 187th Infantry Regiment, 101st Airborne Division, came onto Dong Ap Bia, a mountain in northern South Vietnam, the morning of May 10, 1969. Most of the men were veterans of other assaults and this one, in the A Shau Valley near the Laotian border, seemed no different at first—except for its scale. John Snyder of Bravo Company recalled that this was "the biggest movement of troops I had ever experienced and the most helicopters I'd ever seen in one spot.... you knew something big was happening but you didn't know exactly what you were getting into—other than we already knew the A Shau was bad." That suggested the approaching battle was not likely to be a "normal" engagement.

At least this was not a hot landing—no enemy fire met the Americans jumping off the helicopters. But that did not mean there was no enemy presence, as combat veterans well knew. As the men set up camp for the night, one officer looked at the forested hill above them and said, "I think we're heading toward some pretty big shit."

On the morning of May 11, the 187th Infantry prepared to move to the top of Dong Ap Bia, designated Hill 937 on military maps, about 3,000 feet above sea level. Bravo Company was assigned the lead, and company commander Captain Charles Littnan told the men: "Go up that hill there and see what you can find, and then after that there's a ridge that seems to lead in the direction we want. If all goes right, we should be on top of Dong Ap Bia by 1400," or 2 p.m.

Littnan knew from experience that in Vietnam things did not always "go right." They would be on the top by 1400 hours—but 1400 hours, ten days later. By then Dong Ap Bia had become a slaughterhouse better known to Americans as Hamburger Hill.

The assault on Dong Ap Bia was a major part of Operation Apache

Snow, conducted by the 101st Airborne, under the command of Major General Melvin Zais, to break the North Vietnamese Army's (NVA) control in the A Shau Valley. The valley, especially the western Laotian side of it, served as a major logistics center—a "warehouse" some Americans called it—for NVA forces. Tunnels and underground facilities harbored enemy units that could quickly infiltrate the surrounding areas and engage in attacks on coastal regions, as they had dramatically done during the 1968 Tet Offensive.

Joining the 3rd Battalion, 187th Infantry in the operation were the 101st Airborne's 2nd Battalion, 501st Infantry Regiment, and the 1st and 2nd Battalions, 506th Infantry Regiment. These units, along with two battalions of the 3rd Infantry Regiment, 1st Infantry Division of the Army of the Republic of Vietnam (ARVN) were ordered to assault different locations between the A Shau Valley and Laos, then converge at or near Dong Ap Bia. Meanwhile, the 9th Marine Regiment, 3rd Marine Division would block the northern end of the valley.

Ever since the November 1965 battle in the Ia Drang Valley—the war's first big battle pitting U.S. and NVA forces against each other—the North Vietnamese and Viet Cong had recognized the danger of sustained, conventional engagements with the Americans. U.S. firepower, including artillery and air, was too overwhelming, so communist units engaged in close-range firefights to negate or complicate the Americans' ability to use their most powerful weapons. Communist forces usually resorted to surprise attacks, ambushes of small American patrols and units. They then withdrew before heavy firepower was directed on them. When Americans attacked, the North Vietnamese would defend their position for a short time, then pull back.

The experience at Dong Ap Bia would not follow the usual pattern of combat in Vietnam. The North Vietnamese had decided this would be a good place to fight. Their supply sources and reinforcements were only about a mile away in Laos, and Ap Bia was honeycombed with tunnels and peppered with formidable bunkers. An Air Force intelligence report had even predicted that for the North Vietnamese, Hill 937 "was a better place than most to defend." However, it is clear that U.S. commanders did not have good intelligence about enemy numbers and fortifications on the mountain.

The 3rd Battalion, 187th Infantry's commanding officer, Lieutenant Colonel Weldon Honeycutt, recalled that no one in the high command knew what to expect, neither the division headquarters nor the organization that oversaw all U.S. operations in the country, Military Assistance Command, Vietnam (MACV). "They had no idea," he said. "They were just like us, going in raw."

According to First Lieutenant Frank Boccia, leader of 1st Platoon in the 3rd Battalion's Bravo Company, "We just knew we were going into the A Shau and that we would be seeking out the enemy, wherever he was." Another platoon leader agreed: "Somebody should have known what we were going into. For whatever reason, they didn't."

Colonel J. B. Conmy, commander of 101st Airborne's 3rd Brigade Combat Team, said later, "This is my third war, and I haven't bumped into a fight like this since World War II in Europe. The enemy has stood up and fought and refused to retreat."

On May 11, when the 3rd Battalion's lead platoon, 4th Platoon, Bravo Company, moved out of the tree line and began to cross a meadow beneath the heavily wooded mountaintop, it faced heavy fire from well-fortified bunkers. The platoon struggled to inch forward and then withdrew—a pattern of engagement that continued throughout the battle.

Three days later Honeycutt maneuvered the 3rd Battalion's Charlie Company around to the north for a flank assault. Its troops were decimated by machine-gun fire and rocket-propelled grenades. The battalion sent Bravo Company to support Charlie. As Bravo platoon leader Boccia moved up to the ambush site, he saw bodies everywhere. "For that first mind-freezing moment it had seemed as if the ground was literally covered with them," he said. Boccia discovered that many of the American bodies were wounded, not dead. The advancing units thus had to stop and get the casualties down to a clearing where medevac helicopters could pick them up. These evacuations were a continuing problem as the Americans pressed up the steep slope in the face of heavy machine-gun, mortar, and rocket fire from the bunkers above.

The 101st Airborne had run into the 29th NVA Regiment, a seasoned combat unit. The fighting was sustained and ferocious. The 2nd Battalion, 501st Infantry and 1st Battalion, 506th Infantry, along with the ARVN 2nd Battalion, 3rd Infantry, moved to support the 187th, but struggled to get up adjacent hills.

The 101st Airborne sustained heavy losses, including the twenty-seven men killed on May 13 when North Vietnamese sappers assaulted Charlie Battery at Fire Base Airborne, an artillery base on Dong Ngai, a mountain just a few miles from Dong Ap Bia.

Critics later asked why the U.S. did not use B-52 bombers to destroy the enemy's tunnels and bunkers. One reason was the intelligence failure that provided an inaccurate assessment of the defensive fortifications and the number of enemy troops, which became clear only after the 101st Airborne was on the hill in force. B-52 bombs could not be dropped with precision on a small specific target, a problem when friendly troops were nearby. American troops' close proximity to the enemy also complicated the use of other air and artillery support.

Nonetheless, the U.S. still hit the hill with a massive amount of fire-power: 1,088.5 tons of bombs, 142.5 tons of napalm, and 31,000 rounds of 20-mm shells. Mac Campbell, a Marine F-4 Phantom II pilot who flew air support missions, recalls that American aircraft "just pounded that hill. I still visualize that hill. We cleared that place." But even with careful strikes, Americans inevitably suffered "friendly fire" casualties.

Despite the 3rd Battalion's significant losses, Honeycutt insisted the men were capable of making the final assault, planned for May 20. The colonel's battalion, reinforced by Company A of the 2nd Battalion, 506th Infantry, once again headed for the top. They were supported by other battalions, which attacked from different sides of the mountain. This time Honeycutt's men reached the summit and stepped onto a devastated moonscape of smoldering fires. The remaining NVA forces had slipped away into Laos.

Veterans of the battle vividly recalled the ferocity of the fighting and the courage of the men who repeatedly pushed through a torrent of enemy fire. They talked about the smell of death and the body parts ripped off by rocket-propelled grenades or land mines that sprayed metal fragments. "It's just unimaginable," one infantryman said. "Bullets were just trimming the bark off the trees and the leaves were falling down like it was fall." A medic remembered, "It was just absolute confusion and mayhem."

Another soldier put the days of battle in perspective: "We went up that day . . . we got ambushed. We withdrew. We went back up again that same day, probably just within 20 or 30 minutes—got hit again. Withdrew. Spent the night, went up there the next night to recover the dead bodies. The next afternoon, we started going up again around 1:30 in the afternoon. We got hit again. At this time, we're going, 'What the hell is going on?'"

Another said, "You'd go up, you'd battle, see people get killed, see people get wounded. After so many dead, we'd pull back and chow down and reorganize and take care of the wounded and evacuate them, and the next time, the exact same thing."

After getting orders to go back up again, one platoon leader thought, "This is the way that the guys at D-Day must have felt." He also recalled thinking, "Oh no, we can't go back up there." But he did. There were a few instances when men said they weren't going back, and one officer recalled being "scared to death of mutiny." But after men griped and vented their frustration, they always picked up their weapons and moved back up the mountain.

Dong Ap Bia was called "the mountain of the crouching beast" by the Montagnards, a group of tribes that had lived in the region since ancient times, and by the end of the battle some American soldiers felt that the beast had spit them out like the ground meat of a hamburger. John Wilhelm, a *Time* magazine correspondent, went to the top of Ap Bia after the fighting and spotted a 101st Airborne neckerchief, pinned to a tree with a piece of cardboard that had two hand-scrawled words: "Hamburger Hill."

The tally of Americans killed in this battle is somewhat complicated because casualties from other parts of Operation Apache Snow may or may not have been included in the figure for the battle for Dong Ap Bia. But recent counts indicate seventy-one or seventy-two, with some 400 wounded. The American body count of North Vietnamese dead is 630.

Only four of the twenty platoon leaders in the 187th Infantry who went to Ap Bia on May 10 made it to the top of the hill on May 20. The sixteen others were dead or wounded. As their leaders fell, junior enlisted men assumed greater responsibility. "A lot of them had not been out of high school and in the Army for a year before they came to Vietnam," noted one soldier. "And here they were taking over tactical operations in the jungle in Vietnam."

Among the first men to reach the top of the hill on May 20 was 2nd Lieutenant Don Sullivan from Winthrop, Massachusetts. He was accompanied by just eighteen of the forty-two men originally in his 2nd Platoon, Charlie Company. Sullivan said that when they reached the top one of the men crawled over to him and said, "You know, sir, when you took over your platoon, we all thought you looked about fifteen years old. Now you look really old, and you'll never look young again."

After the battle, the survivors had an R&R break at Eagle Beach, on the South China Sea northeast of Hue. Sullivan remembered the showers, clean uniforms, plenty of hot food and cold beer. While there he received a letter from his mother, Helen, who wrote: "The News this week is all bad. They are constantly talking about the 3/187th taking horrible casualties attacking a hill. I certainly hope you had more sense than to go up there."

The constant talking back home about Hamburger Hill was quite unusual for a specific battle in Vietnam. By 1969, the war itself was a subject of constant debate and criticism, but specific battles were largely unnoticed in the States. Unlike many past wars with large-scale engagements involving thousands of troops, combat in Vietnam was marked by intense and brief skirmishes, ambushes, and small-unit actions. Those fights were over quickly and seldom had the drama for news coverage back home. By 1969, the Vietnam War had just a handful of sustained battles: Ia Drang in 1965, Dak To in 1967, Hue and Khe Sanh in 1968, and now Hamburger Hill.

Five days after the battle began, Walter Cronkite in his May 15 broadcast on the *CBS Evening News* made a brief, vague reference to it: "Tonight American paratroopers are battling for control of a key mountain in the area."

In the following days the battle was mentioned in other news reports, including a detailed story on May 19 by Jay Sharbutt of the Associated Press. Sharbutt, attached to the 187th Infantry, quoted a soldier who said, "That damn Blackjack [the call sign for Honeycutt] won't stop until he kills every damn one of us." Another told the AP reporter: "I've lost a lot of buddies up there. Not many guys can take it much longer."

By the next day the moniker "Hamburger Hill" had made it into news stories. A *New York Times* front-page headline read: "G.I.'s in 10th Try, Fail to Rout Foe on Peak at Ashau." Ironically, that was the day the 187th Infantry secured the hill. It was also the day Democratic Senator Edward Kennedy of Massachusetts criticized the Nixon administration on the Senate floor for talking about peace while engaging in a "senseless and irresponsible" battle that sent "our young men to their deaths to capture hills and positions that have no relation to ending this conflict." He insisted that "American boys are too valuable to be sacrificed for a false sense of military pride."

Criticism of the war, although present virtually from the beginning, picked up significantly as the fighting continued with heavy casualties and no clear resolution in sight. In the 1968 election Richard Nixon promised that he had a secret plan to end the war, and public opinion polls indicated that most Americans wanted it to be over. Nonetheless Kennedy's argument marked a new turn: He questioned the tactics and military decisions on the ground.

This led to a great debate about the battle, a debate that intensified in early June when Major General John Wright, who had succeeded Zais as the 101st Airborne's commander through a scheduled rotation, announced that the division was going to withdraw from the contested hill.

That departure made the purpose of the battle even more controversial, reflecting the military's difficulty in explaining tactical operations to Congress and the American public. Zais had earlier pointed out that the operation had not been designed to seize and control ground. This was a war of attrition, and the goal was to kill enemy soldiers and disrupt their supply system.

There is no evidence that the U.S. military command ever intended to occupy Dong Ap Bia for the long term. Occupying ground near Laos without secure supply routes over land was not a good military option. "We didn't retreat from that hill," Zais said. "We left it because we had defeated the enemy."

Some of the soldiers complained later about abandoning the hill. One said, "We felt like we owned that damned property and needed to keep it." But most shared the view that this was the nature of war. As one said, "We went up a lot of hills and a lot of ridgelines and we didn't keep 'em. You just went up, and if you had a fight, you had a fight, and then you went off."

On the cardboard sign that bestowed the name Hamburger Hill, someone had written at the bottom: "Was it worth it?"

Neil Sheehan, who had served in the Army in Korea and was a distinguished correspondent in Vietnam, wondered if the men who fought and died there had questioned their purpose. "Perhaps there is no difference, but it ought to be one thing to perish on the beaches of Normandy or Iwo Jima in a great cause and another to fall in a rejected and unsung war," he wrote in *Harper's Magazine*.

Perhaps. But there is little evidence that most of those who were in combat gave much thought to whether they were fighting for a "great cause" or engaged in a war that many Americans rejected. They fought for the day, for their buddies, for their own sense of purpose, and for staying alive. Indeed, the men who fought at Normandy and Iwo Jima framed their encounter in a similar manner. As a weary Marine fighting at Korea's Chosin Reservoir in 1950 said when asked by a correspondent what he most wanted: "Give me tomorrow."

Another Vietnam War correspondent, Ward Just of the *Washington Post*, said it is not useful to wrestle with questions of whether a battle was "worth" the losses. "An army is fielded, and if it is a good army, it fights. If it must fight against an entrenched enemy on a hill, then that is what it does. The war does not take place in a classroom or on the pages of a newspaper, and it is not fought by … men who read headlines."

One Hamburger Hill veteran said the battle was of a greater magnitude, but not much different from others in Vietnam. The men who survived moved on, "and then you were back in the jungle doing what you got the big bucks to do," he said.

The Battle of Hamburger Hill was consequential, not just for those who fought there so valiantly, but also for the publicity and controversy it generated, which influenced the country's war strategy.

Nixon, looking for time and a means to secure a "peace with honor," indicated during the battle that the United States was not seeking a "military victory" in Vietnam—something that had always been the case, but now he made it explicit.

After an early June meeting at Midway Island with South Vietnamese President Nguyen Van Thieu, Nixon announced a plan dubbed "Vietnamization"—handing more of the fighting to South Vietnamese forces and beginning a drawdown of American troops starting that summer. The nature of tactical operations also began to shift that summer as the Pentagon informed MACV that it did not want any more extended engagements. There would be no more Hamburger Hills.

IV

RESPONSIBILITIES

Bearing the Cost of War:
Why the U.S. Should Raise Taxes—
Just As It Has in Previous Conflicts

August 2011

Aᶠᵗᵉʳ ᵗʰᵉ Uɴɪᴛᴇᴅ Sᴛᴀᴛᴇs invaded Afghanistan in 2001 and Iraq in 2003, the costs of these wars ballooned. In 2010, the United States spent $167 billion on "overseas contingency operations" in these theaters—a figure that includes expenditures by the Defense and State Departments and the U.S. Agency for International Development but excludes spending on the Department of Veterans Affairs. The economists Joseph Stiglitz and Linda Bilmes estimated in 2008 that the wars in Iraq and Afghanistan will eventually cost $3 trillion, and they now acknowledge that the number may be even greater. Much of the expense for these wars has been financed by debt or represents future obligations.

Now in the summer of 2012, with U.S. forces mostly out of Iraq, the debate in Washington's foreign policy circles has focused primarily on the war in Afghanistan, with some critics, concerned in large part about the war's costs, advocating an accelerated withdrawal strategy. The biggest controversy in Washington this summer, however, has been over the federal budget and debt limit. It is no secret that the wars in Afghanistan and Iraq have contributed to the debt and to budget deficits. Yet other than some symbolic antiwar suggestions, no political figures have proposed actually paying the cost of these military actions today. It is time for this to change—Congress should consider enacting a wartime surtax, as it has done for nearly all past U.S. wars.

The current arrangement is unfortunate, since it means that the vast majority of Americans share none of the costs of war; instead, the burden is shouldered almost exclusively by the men and women fighting the wars and their families. American military personnel have suffered through multiple deployments and endured disabling casualties; their families and personal lives have been disrupted and sometimes permanently shattered. Over 6,100 Americans have died, and more than 44,000 have been wounded (a figure that only counts physical wounds). In mid-July, I visited the National Naval Medical Center, in Bethesda, Maryland. The numbers of patients in the wards were as high as I have seen them in recent years, and the injuries were severe; everyone I met had been in Afghanistan, where explosives are now the Taliban's weapon of choice. Americans insist that they "support the troops." But for most of them, it has been a cost-free form of support.

Part of the problem, as former Secretary of Defense Robert Gates and Chairman of the Joint Chiefs of Staff Mike Mullen, among others, have pointed out, is that the soldiers serving in today's military are not representative of the U.S. population. They are disproportionately from small towns and rural areas, from the South, the Midwest, and the Great Plains states. And they represent a sliver of the population. About one-half of 1 percent of the U.S. population is in the military today; during World War II, the proportion was over 10 percent. Back then, most families, neighborhoods, and communities in the United States watched their young men go to war. Today, few Americans know anyone on the front lines.

For the generation who established the United States, the assumption was that a democracy's wars would be fought and paid for by its citizens. This dual obligation was supposed to serve as a restraint on entering wars and a continuing reminder of their costs. George Washington insisted that every citizen owed a "proportion of his property" and his personal services to the nation's military in wartime. Today's wars, by contrast, are fought by other citizens' sons and daughters, husbands and wives, and they will be paid for by the children and grandchildren of today's generation. This is out of line with tradition. Beginning with the War of 1812 and up through the Vietnam War, Congress levied special taxes to pay for its wars.

Without a central government, the colonists who fought the Revolutionary War had to fund their efforts through debt, which was later assumed by the new government. During the War of 1812, the antitax Jeffersonian Democrats insisted they could carry on the conflict without levying any new taxes, but they had to back down from that position as the war's costs exceeded wartime revenues. The government imposed higher tariffs, a national property tax, and new excise taxes on the sale of certain goods. For the Mexican War of 1846–48, surplus tariff income covered the costs.

During the Civil War, both the Union and the Confederacy had to resort to income taxes. Some Southerners, concerned about a government with such strong confiscatory power, were especially resistant to the Confederate tax, but the necessity of collecting revenue prevailed. In the North, the Revenue Act of 1861 marked the first instance of a federal income tax (of 3 percent), but the tax affected only a very small high-income group. During the war, that tax was expanded somewhat, and Congress also levied an estate tax. The Spanish-American War of 1898 was financed by, among other things, a renewed estate tax and a telephone tax.

War taxation expanded in the twentieth century as major wars became even more expensive. The bill for World War I totaled some $32 billion. With a "pay as you go" philosophy, Congress raised a significant amount of revenue by expanding income taxes (establishing very high rates for the wealthiest Americans), inheritance taxes, and war profits taxes on businesses. Debt, however, still covered most of the war's costs.

World War II witnessed the most massive mobilization in U.S. history—military and fiscal. The U.S. government spent some $200 billion on the war; by 1945, military expenses equaled over 37 percent of Gross Domestic Product and nearly 90 percent of federal spending. The government held large public bond drives, and the number of Americans paying income taxes grew dramatically as the threshold for income taxes was lowered and as the implementation of the withholding tax assured payment.

During the Korean War, House Speaker Sam Rayburn, a Democrat from Texas, insisted that the United States should not finance the war with debt. "I think the boys in Korea would appreciate it more if we in this country were to pay our own way instead of leaving it for them to pay when they get back," he said. Republican leaders such as Senator Robert Taft and Congressman Richard Nixon agreed, and Congress approved President Harry Truman's war tax. In 1968, a bipartisan congressional vote also supported a surtax when President Lyndon Johnson belatedly asked for taxes to pay for the war in Vietnam. Johnson's aversion to this tax was part of his reluctance to ask for any sacrifices for the Vietnam War—except from the disproportionately blue-collar army that was fighting it.

Since 9/11, no national leaders have proposed that the country actually pay for the current wars. In fact, the theme from the outset has been to reduce taxes—a response without a wartime precedent in American history. And for the last two years or so, the mantra in Congress has been to not impose any additional or restored taxes on anyone. Only recently has the financial cost of the wars even been part of a public discussion.

It is long past time for Americans to affirm their common responsibility and share in some way in the sacrifice of war. Congress should consider enacting a surcharge on individual and corporate taxes that would retire the debt accumulated by these wars, pay their current operating costs, and establish a fund that would provide for veterans. This new tax could be deferred until the still fragile U.S. economic recovery gains strength. It would conclude when the wars have ended and the debt and obligations have been met.

A surtax would spread this cost over multiple years, and the rate could be applied progressively. Soldiers and their families should be exempted for some number of years for every year served, and families with casualties who had been principal taxpayers or dependents should receive a permanent exemption. A war tax would not mean that all Americans were sharing the full burden of war, but it would be a start.

President Woodrow Wilson's Treasury Secretary, William Gibbs McAdoo, took issue with those who resisted special taxes to pay for World War I. "Should we be more partial and tender to those who are protected in safety at home," he asked, "than we are to those who make the supreme sacrifices for us in the field of battle?" Who has asked for sacrifice today? The country's political leaders might be surprised at the willingness of Americans to share, in some clear way, in the burden of war. After all, this is the United States' historic legacy.

The Forgotten 1%

October 2012

ONE MONTH BEFORE the 2012 election we are marking an important calendar milestone: on October 7 we will have been engaged in the war in Afghanistan for eleven years. The 2,000th American was killed in Afghanistan this past weekend. We fought this war while we also carried on a costly seven-year war in Iraq. As of late September, 6,474 Americans have died in these wars and 49,871 have been officially designated as wounded.

It is long past time for us to consider these matters in a substantive manner in our election campaigns.

In mid-September many noted the first anniversary of the "Occupy" movement. These protestors raised the 1 percent argument, insisting that the top 1 percent of the U.S. population has a disproportionate share of the nation's wealth.

The current campaign reflects this issue of economic fairness. Candidates for offices ranging from state assembly to the presidency will sharply dispute whether the wealthiest Americans should pay more in taxes. This was underlined in the first presidential debate.

Less noticed, this same ratio of privilege also describes, although reversed, those who fight our wars. Ninety-nine percent of us, the privileged 99 percent, have been untouched by these wars. Historically an election during wartime has debated the issues of that war. There is little political debate in 2012 over the war in Afghanistan. Candidates will chest-thump about new engagements in Iran or even Syria more than they will discuss the status and remaining objectives of the war in Afghanistan. They will not acknowledge the disproportionate burden of this war and that in Iraq.

Fewer than 1 percent of our sons and daughters have served during these wars. About one half of one percent have actually been deployed. While the Obamas and the Bidens have reached out to the newest veterans and their families, this needs to become part of the broader culture. We cannot continue to ignore the real medical and other support needs of this generation of veterans. We cannot continue to ignore the embarrassing fact that veterans of the current wars have higher levels of unemployment and homelessness than do others in our society.

Assuredly, political candidates from both parties for all offices will "support the troops." Many will illustrate their support by opposing Department of Defense sequestration cuts on defense contractors. Even those who supported the legislation that provided for these reductions will now oppose them. They will describe defense contracts as jobs bills—with little sense of the irony of the Congress recently killing a jobs bill for unemployed veterans.

Americans applaud the "troops" but few really know them. These men and women come disproportionately from rural areas and small towns, most commonly from the South and the Midwest and the plains and mountain states. They are both more white and more Black than the population as a whole. More of them have high school diplomas than their peers and fewer of them have any college education. They are older than those who served in previous wars. Some 56 percent of them are married, most with families. Many have served multiple deployments in the combat zones, with all of the tension this creates for them and their families.

Few Americans encounter the casualties of these wars—the terrible wounds veterans courageously bear with missing limbs, disfigured and scarred bodies. Even fewer know the hidden wounds that individuals and their loved ones bear silently.

Well over 99 percent of us have not experienced the fear of a knock on our door and the sorrow of escorting a flag-draped coffin. Few even know the names of those who have made the sacrifice that is forever. We abstract them as "heroes" without knowing how they lived, how they died, or what dreams died with them.

These wars have been the first sustained wars in American history not to be at least partially funded by designated taxes. No political candidate this fall will propose that we actually tax ourselves to pay for these wars. We will continue to issue debt to do that. No candidate will ask for any sacrifice. The 1 percent who have sacrificed can come home and then spend twenty years paying for our wars.

Over the next month we will continue to debate whether to renew tax cuts for the top 1 percent of the economic pyramid. And we will neglect to acknowledge, except in the most stereotyped slogans, the heavy, heavy taxes we have imposed on that 1 percent who have volunteered and who fight our wars. George Washington, who insisted that wars must demand sacrifice from all, would be ashamed. The most shameful thing today is the absence of any sense of shame about the forgotten 1 percent. Caring for them is a cost of war.

War in Afghanistan:
The Unseen Sacrifice

December 2012

NEAR THE END of Steven Spielberg's film *Lincoln*, the president rides slowly across the battlefield at Petersburg. The cannons are stilled and the landscape is filled with the swollen and grotesque and tragic faces of the dead. This reminds Mr. Lincoln of the tragedy of war—and contrasts sharply with the politics in Washington, just a few miles away.

This is a reminder that we all need to remember the costs in our current war in Afghanistan. I do not mean the financial cost—although these are considerable. More importantly, we need to confront those costs that have been even more hidden than the future bills for these deficit-financed wars. Wars mean service and sacrifice and the costs of young lives. Our recent wars have been more than a few miles away—and as a result much easier to ignore.

So far this year 302 American servicemen and -women have died in Afghanistan, 2,166 since the war began over eleven years ago. There have been 17,674 wounded. Plus countless others bearing silent wounds. Each of them freely volunteered and went to war on our behalf. They served and sacrificed out of a sense of patriotic duty. Now their families and friends and comrades grieve as they try to impose some sense on it all.

For the rest of us, the war is abstract and distant. Fewer journalists and photographers cover its details any longer and even fewer politicians publicly discuss its reality. Anonymous sacrifice in unseen wars is not healthy for a democracy.

Deaths and wars go together. And with a military that represents less than 1 percent of the population, few Americans need personally to confront the human cost. But some surely do. As one family who lost a son in Afghanistan in the spring of 2011 wrote to the parents of a soldier killed last month, "Our family knows the pain and heartache your family is going through." Most of us have no idea.

In November of 2012, sixteen American servicemen died in Afghanistan. They came from Booneville, Arkansas; Gardiner, Oregon; Gillette, New Jersey; Arcata, California; Shenandoah, Iowa; Rocky Mount, North Carolina; Running Springs, California; Grand Rapids, Michigan; Spokane, Washington; Greer, South Carolina; Island Heights, New Jersey; Glendora, California; and Jordan, Minnesota. Three were from upstate New York, reservists from the 178th Engineer Battalion, whose homes were in Alden, Campbell, and Port Henry. These soldiers died on November 3 as a result of an improvised explosive device.

Largely from small towns, these Americans died in distant places that few of us know: Helmand, Paktia, Kandahar, Ghazni, Faryab, and Uruzgan provinces. Their ages ranged from nineteen to thirty-two. Several of them had children and at least one left a pregnant wife. Their hometown and base newspapers and local television stations often had pictures of them smiling with their families. Most had served multiple tours in Afghanistan and/or Iraq.

If their nation was essentially unaware of these final sacrifices, their communities turned out to welcome them home for a final time. In a Minnesota town there were 1,300 American flags along the seven miles of the funeral procession. A friend who had been best man for this Marine's wedding said, "He's my best friend and he was supposed to come back." Sharing feelings that were repeated in several obituaries, the teacher of a dead soldier remembered that he was "quiet" and "sincere." He just wanted to serve and "to do what was right."

In Greer, South Carolina, the Army Honor Guard folded and presented the flag on the coffin to the dead soldier's grandmother, the woman who had raised him. A reporter observed, "She caressed the flag throughout the ceremony, holding it securely in her arms."

The mother of another dead soldier said that her son was due to come home in seventy-three days, but now, "Everything I pick up, everybody's eyes I look into, I see him. He is just everything, he is my heart." The grandmother of another young man said, "I miss him so much; it just breaks my heart that Junior will never come back." His young daughter would never know him.

Nor will the nation he served. It continues. Five Americans have been killed in the first ten days of December: a Navy Seal rescuing a doctor being held hostage, a soldier who left two children, a Marine who sent a Facebook message to his mother saying, "All is well … I'll call you in the morning" a few hours before he was shot, as well as two National Guardsmen with the 164th Engineer Battalion. One was a twenty-year-old North Dakotan and the other was a forty-one-year-old Montanan. They belonged to a North Dakota Guard unit. The Montanan's two daughters sang at his funeral service and his wife asked everyone to hug their family and friends tightly. The young North Dakotan was a musician and a boxer and loved sushi.

It is critical to know the human face of war. This means focusing our attention on the war our citizens are now fighting, to know what we want them to accomplish if we deploy them for two more years—or longer. Maybe we can even modestly share the sacrifice by actually paying the financial cost of our wars—including the long-term cost of caring for those who serve and sacrifice. These have been the first sustained wars in our history without a designated tax to pay for the war.

But finally, this is about more than finances. Americans need to confront, as Mr. Lincoln did, the necessary human cost of war. In the summer of 1864 President Lincoln watched wagons with dead and wounded returning from what would become the long, bloody siege of Petersburg, and he said, "I cannot bear it. This suffering, this loss of life is dreadful." It still is.

Have Americans Forgotten Afghanistan?

March 2013

O N JANUARY 20, 2013, men of the 1st Battalion, 38th Infantry Regiment gathered at their outpost in southern Afghanistan. At Combat Outpost Sperwan Ghar in southern Kandahar, they held a memorial service for Army Sergeant David J. Chambers. A native of Hampton, Virginia, Chambers had been killed on January 16 by an improvised explosive device while on patrol. His commander said of him, "His subordinates trusted him, his peers learned from the example he set, and his superiors counted on him to get the job done." He had been wounded on a previous deployment to Afghanistan but he hadn't talked about this much because, as his mother said, "he never tried to worry us."

The day that the soldiers saluted their fallen comrade at Combat Outpost Sperwan Ghar, Sergeant Mark Schoonhoven died at Brooke Army Medical Center at Fort Sam Houston, Texas, from wounds suffered in Afghanistan. Schoonhoven was from Plainwell, Michigan. His mother and oldest daughter had sat by his hospital bed for nearly six weeks hoping he would recover from the coma. His wife had returned to Michigan to look after the five children at home. He never recovered from the injuries suffered when insurgents detonated explosives as his vehicle passed. At his funeral his wife and his mother received folded flags and each of his children put a rose on his coffin.

Other than local coverage, little attention was paid to these deaths. Certainly there was little notice in Washington. In August 2012, Secretary of Defense Leon Panetta expressed his frustration over the absence of any discussion of the war in Afghanistan during the political campaigns. He explained at a Pentagon press briefing, "I thought it was important to remind the American people that there is a war going on."

This reminder takes on a great importance as Americans reflect on the ten-year anniversary of the beginning of the war in Iraq. As pundits and politicians debate the origins of that war, they will not dwell too long on the Afghanistan war that started a year and a half earlier—and still continues.

Afghanistan did not become an issue during the fall presidential election campaigns, and the war seldom was a substantive issue in congressional races. Candidates scarcely discussed the war other than in passing references. In fact, they focused more on the putative next war in Iran. Ignoring the current war may have been politically or even morally derelict, but it was not of electoral consequence. Voters did not seem to consider war strategy as relevant to their election choices. Afghanistan did not figure in public opinion polls as a major issue and had not for some time.

Nonetheless, we could hope that after the election political leaders would finally focus on the war in Afghanistan. If it did not seem relevant to swing-state campaign strategy, it surely was an important issue in developing national military strategy. After all, there was a need to consider the objectives for the troops who remained there as well as the terms of the drawdown of these troops scheduled for the end of 2014.

Of course, fiscal cliffs, sequestered funds, the ongoing effects of the recession, the shocked reaction to the tragedy at Sandy Hook School, as well as the new political urgency to address immigration policy all took over the postelection debate and positioning. All of these were clearly important matters and genuine urgency was associated with them. But Afghanistan also cried out for attention—attention with the sense of priority that war has traditionally received in American politics.

Early in 2013, President Obama nominated Senator Chuck Hagel to replace the retiring Panetta as secretary of defense. This cabinet post was critical in the management of the war effort. The Senate confirmation hearings might have finally provided an opportunity for the sort of debate that Washington has had far too infrequently during America's wars in recent years.

Unfortunately, in the Senate Armed Services Committee hearings on January 31, Afghanistan was hardly mentioned. Gayle Tzemach Lemmon of the Council on Foreign Relations observed that those who watched the hearings on television "could be forgiven for forgetting that America is at war." She noted that, "Apparently, so did their senators."

Most senators, especially the Hagel critics, as it turned out were focused beyond Afghanistan—not beyond in terms of addressing the critical strategic questions regarding the mission of the post-Afghanistan military. In this case "beyond Afghanistan" meant the senators paid far more attention to a potential engagement with Iran than they did to the current war with the Taliban. And in the minds of many senators, equally troubling was the corollary question of how U.S. Iranian policy would support that of Israel. This in fact became the primary focus of the opposition to Senator Hagel. When Afghanistan did come up, it largely involved critical statements by Republicans, or slow-pitch questions by Democrats, and Senator Hagel's responses.

Perhaps the most pointed exchange in the hearing occurred not over future plans or concern about what we are asking our servicemen and -women to do, but over views of recent history. Senator John McCain, who had been an aggressive advocate of the 2007 "surge" in Iraq, asked Hagel to answer "yes" or "no" to whether the surge had been successful. Hagel, who had been wounded and cited for bravery while serving as an enlisted man in Vietnam, would not.

When given the opportunity by Senator Bill Nelson to explain his position on the surge, it may not have received as much press coverage as the testy exchange with Senator McCain, but Hagel's reflections were revealing—and finally got to the basic question that should be asked whenever American troops are sent off to war.

> I had one fundamental question that I asked myself on every vote I took, every decision I made. Was the policy worthy of the men and women that we were sending into battle and surely to their deaths?
>
> I saw it from the bottom. I saw what happens. I saw the consequences and the suffering when we are at war.

The Senate hearing was not encouraging to those who hoped to have a real debate on future plans for the war in Afghanistan. Secretary Panetta's August inquiry seemed to still hang over the ongoing theater. It is hard to produce evidence that most Americans or their representatives do indeed know there is a war going on. Obviously, they do in a general, even an abstracted, way. And certainly they "care." But the war seldom intrudes into their world.

Wars do have costs. Human costs. It has become far too easy to ignore those when neither the wars nor those flesh-and-blood citizens who serve and sacrifice are acknowledged. Numbers on casualty reports do not bear human faces for most Americans.

The surge began in Iraq early in 2007. Between 2007 and 2011, 1,482 Americans died in Iraq, all but a few following the announcement of the new enhanced operation. Senator Hagel was correct. History will judge the final results of the surge. Andrew Bacevich recently observed of the surge, "avoiding defeat should not be confused with winning."

There still remain the unanswered questions of what the United States will do next in Afghanistan. Or in Iran. History will judge our record here as well. Our task, our political leadership's task, is not to preview that judgment but to frame the policies and goals that will be part of this record. What will be the rate of withdrawal of American troops from Afghanistan? What will be the objectives of troops in Afghanistan during this period? How many troops will remain, if any, after 2014? What goal do we have for the next twenty months—and for the period following that? What are the likely casualties in this period? Is this an acceptable cost?

Senator Hagel sought to remind his colleagues of the personal consequences of military policy. He had tried to do that in January 2007 as well, when he spoke in opposition to the Iraq surge: "This is a ping-pong game with American lives. These young men and women that we put in Anbar province, in Iraq, in Baghdad are not beans; they're real lives. And we better be damn sure we know what we're doing, all of us, before we put 22,000 more Americans into that grinder."

Surely six years later Americans are even more tired of hearing about the wars than they were during the Iraq surge debate. But as a military spouse once said, "I understand that the American public is war weary. I only wish they understood what war weary really meant." Well under 1 percent of Americans serve in the military today—a smaller fraction has actually served in Iraq and Afghanistan. Most American families have not been absorbed with worry and have not had to deal with grieving for the loss or serious injury of a loved one. They have not had to wait for the ring of the doorbell at night.

War and death do go together—and we have managed to put the current wars out of our lives sufficiently that grief from their sacrifices has seldom touched most of us. But it is there. Over 6,660 U.S. servicemen and -women have died in these wars—145 have been women. Over 1,000 of these men and women were under twenty years of age; more than 3,800 were twenty-five or younger (fatalities in Iraq were on average younger than those in Afghanistan). The survivor's organization TAPS has estimated that the wars in Iraq and Afghanistan have left 3,659 widows and widowers with 4,790 surviving children, 13,306 grieving parents, and 19,559 grandparents. Since 2001, 18,311 Americans have been wounded in Afghanistan. And 32,223 were wounded in Iraq between 2003 and 2011. These only count the visible wounds.

Of course, these wars have impacted people beyond our borders as well. There have been 619 casualties from the United Kingdom and 780 from other coalition countries—most of these have died in Afghanistan. And the United Nations has reported that in the last six years, 14,728 Afghan civilians have lost their lives as a result of the war (in the last year it is estimated that over 80 percent of these were due to antigovernment forces). A Reuters estimate places Iraqi civilian deaths at between 103,000 and 113,000.

But numbers can tally only; they cannot introduce us to the experience of war.

Wars with undefined purposes are dangerous things. Wars fought by men and women who are unknown to most citizens are more than dangerous—they strip war of the very human cost that is a necessary part of war. Americans need to assert ownership over the purposes of this war—and affirm responsibility for their costs and for those who pay these costs. Last August, just three days after Secretary Panetta reminded the American people, in frustration, that "there is a war going on," the 2,000th American victim of the Afghanistan war died in the Landstuhl U.S. Army/Department of Defense hospital in Germany. He had been in Afghanistan for a month when he was shot in the head while posted in Wardak Province. The twenty-one-year-old soldier from Grover, North Carolina, had played drums and guitar in his church and had always wanted to be a soldier. He left a wife and three stepchildren.

A few days later the New York Times published a lengthy story by James Dao and Andrew Lehren analyzing the casualties in Afghanistan. The first thousand were killed over nine years, from 2001 to 2010. The second thousand died in just twenty-seven months. The Times supplemented the

Dao/Lehren story with four full pages of photos of the thousand deaths since early in 2010, a period overlapping with the "surge" in Afghanistan announced by President Obama in December 2009. These small snapshots record the faces of dreams that ended—and scanning through them gives a sense of human tragedy that numbers can never convey. Other news sources, such as *Military Times*, the *Washington Post*, and *PBS NewsHour*, periodically present the photographs of the dead as well. *CNN* provides a comprehensive and interactive site. These are reminiscent of the striking *Life* magazine June 27, 1969, issue that had eleven pages of photos of the 242 Americans killed in one week in Vietnam. Today's presentations do not seem to have the political impact of the 1969 story.

In the months following the Panetta plea to remember the war, the human toll has continued. In this period Americans have conducted a national election and have confirmed a new secretary of defense without much mention of this loss of life. Accounts or photographs in hometown or base newspapers present the deceased with their families prior to deployment. Or they convey the grief of loved ones—clutching folded flags, weeping over coffins, hugging together. These news sources have local readership or viewers, and most Americans miss the moving and very human accounts of grief and loss.

A soldier from Coral Springs, Florida, killed on his fifth deployment, left behind a wife and three children. Before his final deployment he had arranged a sixtieth anniversary dinner for his grandparents. A family member said, "He really believed in celebrating marriage."

A Windsor, Colorado, soldier was on his third deployment when he and another soldier were killed by an Afghan ally. His mother said of her son, "There was just something about him that made him able to bring a smile to anyone's face." A Kentwood, Michigan, Navy Seal was killed when his Blackhawk helicopter crashed during a mission. Ten others died as well in the crash. His grandfather told a reporter that the young man and his girlfriend were going to get married before Christmas. "They were as happy as two kids in a candy store," he reported.

Most of us don't have to stay on alert. "The Marines are at war and America's at the mall," said the mother of Clay Hunt, a Marine who had served in Iraq and Afghanistan and had watched his friends die. He was wounded, and after three years of agonizing over his experiences, he committed suicide.

CNN correspondent Jake Tapper's book *The Outpost: An Untold Story of American Valor* puts a searing human face on the war in Afghanistan. It tells the story of American soldiers in an unknown place fighting a battle with little tactical meaning. Tapper introduces readers to the soldiers there, young men worrying about their situations, thinking about their families, planning for their futures. In October 2009 they repulsed a heavy attack by Taliban forces. Of the fifty-three outnumbered soldiers, eight were killed and twenty-two wounded. One of this band, Staff Sergeant Clinton Rome-sha, received the Medal of Honor from President Obama on February 11. Following brief applause, the nation went on about its business.

On February 13, President Obama announced in greater detail the plans for the drawing down of American troops in Afghanistan. With the Senate confirmation vote delayed, he did not have the opportunity to involve Senator Hagel in the discussion leading to the decision. United States senators on the Armed Services Committee did not avail themselves of the opportunity to discuss these options when they had it. None of his critics directly asked Hagel about his view on the drawdown plan.

On February 27, Chuck Hagel was sworn in as secretary of defense. He immediately faced the problem of sequestration of funds that would impact the department in two days. But first he met with some of his new colleagues, both civilian and military. He visited the Pentagon 9/11 Memorial, where he "reflected a bit on what had happened that day." The new secretary asked Army Sergeant First Class John Wirth, of Gordon, Nebraska, a veteran of the Iraq and Afghan wars, to introduce him to the Pentagon gathering. Wirth said that Secretary Hagel "knows the very real cost of war."

That same day in Window Rock, Arizona, the flag of the Navajo Nation was at half-staff. Marine Staff Sergeant Jonathan Davis had been killed in Helmand Province, the only American death in Afghanistan in February. A Marine since 1997, Davis had two previous deployments in Iraq and Afghanistan and had already been awarded a Purple Heart. He was married with a son and hundreds turned out in Flagstaff and along the highway home to honor him when his body was returned to the Navajo Nation. The tribal chairman announced that he was the fourteenth Navajo to die in Iraq or Afghanistan. On March 2 he was buried at Kayenta. That same day Marines and coalition troops who served with him held a memorial at Forward Operating Base Shir Ghazay in Afghanistan.

A week after assuming his new responsibilities, Secretary Hagel traveled to Afghanistan. He visited with the troops there and responded to President Hamid Karzai's allegation that the United States was working with the Taliban. During the Hagel visit, the Taliban detonated an explosive at the Defense Ministry in Kabul. On March 11 two American soldiers were killed by an individual wearing an Afghan army uniform, and five others died in a helicopter crash.

There is still a war going on.

Ten Years After "Mission Accomplished," the Risks of Another Intervention

May 2013

I n March 2013, many commentators reflected on the tenth anniversary of the invasion of Iraq by the United States and its coalition partners by recalling the alleged presence of weapons of mass destruction as a rationale for the war—and the discovery in the spring of 2003 that these weapons did not exist.

The absence of these threatening weapons provoked an important debate, one that still echoes. Critics accused President George W. Bush and his team of deceiving the country. Administration officials pointed to erroneous intelligence reports—reports that convinced many people in both political parties. Bush's Secretary of Defense, Donald Rumsfeld, would later insist that the administration leadership was not deceitful, but simply wrong. His deputy and a forceful advocate for the war, Paul Wolfowitz, recently made the same argument: "A mistake is one thing, a lie is something else." History will judge this distinction.

In a December 2003 interview with Bob Woodward, President Bush said he had no problem with waiting for history's assessment, since by then all of the principals will be dead—an observation that he repeated just recently in discussing the opening of his presidential library. Of course, the judgment of history will evolve, but it has already begun to take shape. So far it is not a favorable assessment of the rationale for war.

Even as this debate continues, it is important to expand the conversation from the case for the war to consideration of the military action itself. Kenneth Adelman, a leading neoconservative advocate of invading Iraq, had promised that invading Iraq would be a military "cakewalk" in 2002. Early in April 2003 he observed that he had been vindicated in this judgment. At that moment few challenged him. U.S. troops had occupied Baghdad, symbolically toppling the monumental statue of Saddam Hussein in Firdos Square on April 9. The city had fallen with less resistance than anticipated.

Now another tenth anniversary affords us an opportunity for reflection. On May 1, 2003, just six weeks after the invasion of Iraq began, President George W. Bush landed on the USS *Abraham Lincoln* and declared, "Major combat operations in Iraq have ended." When he spoke on the carrier someone had placed a banner behind him that read "Mission Accomplished." President Bush would later express his regret over this sign, describing it as "a big mistake," an inappropriate "victory dance."

Regardless of the banner, there was on May 1, 2003, a sense of victory, of a successful contest concluded. Most Americans, including the president's critics and opponents, gushed with him. Now of course, on this anniversary of the *Abraham Lincoln* speech, many will remind us that, alas, on that date it turned out the mission was far from accomplished.

At the risk of seeming to engage in sarcastic irony, let me suggest that in fact on May 1, 2003, President Bush and the banner makers may have been correct: the original U.S. military mission had been largely accomplished. American forces, with their coalition allies, had defeated the Iraqi regular Army units, had captured Baghdad and most provincial capitals, and had forced the Saddam Hussein regime to flee and to hide. These were the specific military objectives of the March invasion—along with securing petroleum production facilities, major transportation centers, and the presumed stockpiles of the weapons of mass destruction. These objectives had been met. The military had done its job, had largely accomplished its original mission.

To be sure, it had not been an altogether smooth military operation in those early weeks. American forces confronted inevitable startup costs involving the complexity of coordinating air, ground, cavalry, and armored units among the service branches. One air observer described the first days to me as "chaotic." The early days were marked by communication problems, equipment malfunctions, and difficult encounters with the reality of geography, terrain, and weather, all resulting in differential paces of movement. Intelligence had focused primarily on the Iraqi military and their potential chemical weapons and had not emphasized the likelihood of Fedayeen resistance.

The period prior to May 1 was marred by unfortunate U.S. and coalition casualties due to friendly fire episodes (nine deaths), air and vehicle crashes (thirty-two deaths in "non-hostile" situations), and the 507th Maintenance Company's mistaken, and tragic, turn into the narrow and hostile streets of An Nasiriyah. Eleven soldiers and eighteen Marines in the rescue group were killed there, and six soldiers were briefly taken prisoner, including Jessica Lynch.

Professional and well-trained troops, facilitated by hugely superior firepower and equipment, adapted to the situation in the field and worked through the initial confusion.

Predictions of an Iraqi welcome equivalent to the one extended in the 1944 liberation of Paris proved wrong. Most Iraqis were clearly pleased to see the Hussein regime routed. They were not looking to be occupied. Disorder and looting followed the breakdown of the old system and the American forces had no orders and little preparation to control this. Secretary of Defense Rumsfeld dismissed this situation as of little concern: "Stuff happens."

Tom Ricks observed that even though the president had not claimed in his remarks on the *Abraham Lincoln* that the mission was accomplished, what he did was "tear down the goalposts at halftime in the game." Once the tangible military goals of defeating organized military resistance, occupying major cities and transportation centers, and taking down the old regime had been achieved, the subsequent goals would be far more elusive and immeasurable. The goal lines went out with the goal posts.

The next assignments involved more than a military problem. A Marine officer recalled that when his command entered Baghdad in April, they had achieved their military objective, but learned there was "no real plan" to "get on top of the chaos that had been unleashed." In late April, the Army's 82nd Airborne ran into hostile fire in Fallujah and recognized that Sunni-dominated Anbar province was not secured. Organized insurgents fought back. An American officer there reported, "The war's not over."

Administration officials were initially reluctant to acknowledge that this new phase was indeed a new phase, to admit that the war continued. In June 2003 Secretary Rumsfeld described the remaining resistance fighters as inconsequential "dead enders" and Paul Wolfowitz called them the "last remnants of a dying cause."

When he spoke on the *Abraham Lincoln*, President Bush warmly praised the U.S. military for its accomplishments. He warned that the work in Iraq was incomplete. Few noted at the time that the unfinished agenda was a new and expanded agenda: "Now our coalition is engaged in securing and reconstructing that country." The next task would be "bringing order" to dangerous parts of the country, searching for the members of the Hussein regime and bringing them "to account for their crimes," and "helping to rebuild Iraq."

The president acknowledged that "The transition from dictatorship to democracy will take time," but he assured that the coalition would stay until this work was completed. Assuring peace and order, bringing the tyrants to justice, rebuilding a splintered country, and assisting in the establishment of democracy—these were complicated matters. They would prove far more elusive than defeating the Iraqi Republican Guard and pulling over a statue.

Secretary Rumsfeld would later note that he was surprised at the expanded commitment announced on the carrier. In his memoir, he insisted that no one had presented the objective of the United States overseeing the building of democracy in Iraq. He worried whether the American people would have patience for this sort of open-ended commitment.

And of course, in a few years Americans had wearied of Iraq. It would take until December 2011 before the last American troops withdrew from Iraq. When President Bush declared the end of combat operation in May, 2003, 139 Americans had died in Iraq and 552 were wounded. After May 1, 2003, 4,335 more American servicemen and -women would die in Iraq or as a result of injuries suffered there. An additional 31,671 servicemen and -women would be officially wounded—counting only physical wounds.

President Bush is correct that it will take time for history to judge the consequences for Iraq of the American military involvement. It is not too soon to acknowledge the costs of that involvement. Nor is it premature to recognize that wars with shifting objectives, wars that pursue values rather than tangible targets, are far harder to reconcile against the costs.

This experience should provide a lesson for the ongoing war in Afghanistan. In fact, the U.S., Coalition of the Willing, and Afghan Northern Alliance forces might also have warranted a "mission accomplished" salute in November or December of 2001. The Taliban government had fallen, Al Qaeda had fled the country, and all of their major training sites had been destroyed. These essentially were the American goals in October of 2001. Another mission accomplished.

As would be the case in Iraq, in Afghanistan the military took on an expanded mission. In the years since 2001 the effort in Afghanistan has focused on defeating insurgents and protecting the countryside, stabilizing the Karzai government, strengthening and training Afghan military and police units, and encouraging democratic institutions, a free society, civic responsibility, and economic growth. Each of these in the circumstances of Afghanistan requires a military presence and military actions; only the first of these is a true military objective. The counterinsurgency approach that is now a part of military operations is essential—but this is a strategy and should never be confused with purpose.

As we note the tenth anniversary of the May 1, 2003 speech proclaiming the end of combat operations in Iraq, we find ourselves engaged in a heated debate about whether the United States needs to become more involved militarily in Syria. The debate is energized by allegations that the Assad regime may have used chemical weapons against the rebels. The situation is different from that in Iraq in 2003, but the latter can inform policymakers about some questions—and provide lessons about military engagement without clear military objectives.

If the range of unintended consequences of potential military action in Syria is not sufficiently troubling, there is always Iran on the horizon. It may well be that the United States has interests and concerns in these places that will lead to military engagement. If so, let us hope someone describes convincingly these concerns and interests and frames clear military objectives before we decide upon any military commitment.

My interest for the last several years has been in reminding Americans of the human cost of war—the increasing burden on increasingly anonymous servicemen and -women. These costs are a consequence of military strategies and these in turn represent means to accomplish objectives defined by policymakers and political leaders. We cannot define the latter without confronting the final costs and those who will bear them. Over 99 percent of us will not.

In this era of drones and American air and naval superiority, no one should forget that finally securing places means troops in these places, "boots on the ground." We will not secure chemical weapon sites from the air. Recall the "shock and awe" campaign of March 2003. Fighting in wars means dying in wars. We have had that lesson underlined over the last twelve years in Afghanistan—and in the decade since combat operations in Iraq were declared over.

In his 2011 memoir, Donald Rumsfeld, with little apparent sense of irony, began his final chapter by quoting from Winston Churchill's reflections on the Boer War: "Never, never, never believe any war will be smooth and easy, or that anyone who embarks on the strange voyage can measure the tides and hurricanes he will encounter."

In the 1930 book from which Mr. Rumsfeld quoted, the young English politician had expanded upon this observation to present an emphatic reminder, "Let us learn our lessons."

Learning lessons requires studying lessons.

Remember: Those Who Fight Wars Die in Wars

July 2013

O N A WARM JUNE MORNING in 2011, two years ago—it was the week following Memorial Day—my wife Susan and I visited Gettysburg, stopping at peaceful places with pastoral names such as the Wheatfield, the Peach Orchard, Plum Run, and Rose Farm, and pausing at bucolic places like McPherson's Barn, Culp Farm, and Codori Farm.

We looked at a long line of Confederate cannons ironically resting on Seminary Ridge. Across a gentle valley Union cannons faced them. They sat on a peaceful Cemetery Ridge. The fields and hills in and around this community were filled with stilled and spiked cannons and with monuments: to individuals, battles, military units, and states. By one count there are 1,300 solid works of bronze or granite that silently memorialize.

The Southern states were reluctant in the early years after the Civil War to establish monuments at Gettysburg. In the twentieth century they did. The North Carolina Monument is striking. A bronze sculpture by Gutzon Borglum, who did the famous sculpting on Mount Rushmore, this monument has five figures in it. Each wears the look of a man engaged in a very emotional experience. One is downed with wounds and is urging his friends to advance; another is young and scared; others are resolute.

The sculpture is positioned on Seminary Ridge, near the fields where a North Carolina brigade went to join in Pickett's bloody and unsuccessful charge on the third and final day of the battle.

The 26th North Carolina Regiment had suffered heavy casualties on the first day of battle at McPherson's Ridge, and the remnants then joined with Major General George Pickett on day three. They suffered 82 percent casualties in these two days at Gettysburg, the highest of any regiment on either side in the battle. This included, by some accounts, four sets of twins, all of whom were killed or wounded.

Across from the North Carolina monument, we stood at the "Angle," that place where the old stone wall on Cemetery Ridge took a sharp perpendicular turn. Here was the high point of the Confederate charge, a high point touched but never held.

A small remnant of the 26th North Carolina planted its colors here briefly. A monument marks the spot where Brigadier General Lewis Armistead was mortally wounded while leading a charge into the Union lines. A few hundred yards away a few months later, Abraham Lincoln delivered his address inaugurating the cemetery.

Looking out from the Angle to the west and northwest you see a long, sloping field that was a major killing ground. Now a meadow, in the summer of 1863 it was corn, wheat, and clover. The Emmitsburg road, a country lane, meanders through, and its wooden fence evokes pastoral nostalgia.

On July 3, 1863, the fence that stood there was an obstacle that slowed the charging Confederates and made them even better targets for Union fire. Over three days in early July 1863, there were some 50,000 casualties in the fields around Gettysburg; about 7,900 men died.

David Smith was a thirty-nine-year-old blacksmith from Elmer, New Jersey, who served with the 12th New Jersey Volunteers. At Gettysburg he was near the Angle, and his unit was also involved in heavy fighting in the area down the hill where the Bliss farm was located. Smith would write to his wife, Elizabeth, in early August 1863, "I think you would not want to read the details of the fight as it was."

He said that on the afternoon of July 3, he sat by the stone wall at Cemetery Ridge and fired until he "had blisters on my hand as big as 10 cent pieces." His gun was too hot to touch. After the fight, he went down onto the field littered with Confederate dead and dying, "the hardest mission I had ever been on, the ground being nearly covered with the dead and wounded, the wounded crying for help & water & to be killed & so on."

Gettysburg is as good a place as any to reflect on the meaning of America's wars and the sacrifices they have required. Such reflections need to acknowledge that they cannot provide absolute answers or generalizable meanings. Each war and each battle in each war was different. Here, around this little Pennsylvania town, finally the momentum of this great and terrible war shifted; there would be more bloody battles, but the Union would be preserved, and it would be a Union without human slavery.

If these are causes worth fighting for, and I believe they are, it would require more providential judgment, or simple arrogance, than I care to inflict in order to proclaim that these causes worth fighting for were also worth someone else dying for.

But if we have learned anything, it is that the one always follows the other. The more abstractly the deaths are counted, perhaps the easier it is to rationalize their sacrifices. Among compilations of numbers on reports and then names chiseled in stone, there are very human stories to be told. Numbers obscure names, and in time even names fade away from signifying human beings doing difficult things and dying too soon. Or suffering for a lifetime the trauma of a single moment.

Harvard philosopher William James spoke in 1897 at the dedication of the Robert Gould Shaw Memorial in Boston. He was not comfortable with what he believed to be the romantic view of the Civil War. He said it was necessary to remember the horror, "the great earthworks and their thundering cannon, the commanders and their followers, the wild assault and repulse that for a brief space made night hideous on that far off evening, have all sunk into the blue gulf of the past, and for the majority of this generation are hardly more than an abstract name, a picture, a tale that is told." Soon, James said, the great war will be like the siege of Troy, "battles long ago."

Wars may sometimes be necessary, even unavoidable, but for those who must decide necessity, it needs always to be remembered that fighting in wars means dying in wars. It is perhaps even more essential in this era of different types of wars, less crisply defined engagements, fought by less representative American forces, that Congress and the president agree up front that this is a necessary engagement and that they agree upon the military goals.

And that they agree that the republic is willing financially to pay for them. If not, no one should ask others to pay, possibly with their lives. Wars will never be constant from declaration to conclusion; goals will change as circumstances do, but if there is not a clear consensus up front and sign-off along the way, these will become more undefined wars.

The heroic narratives of war and the abstract celebration of warriors do sanitize wars by stripping them of their personality. It is hard to take the personal stories of combat and fit them easily into the heroic narrative.

Moreover, if Lincoln would instruct us to remember our obligation to ensure that those who died on this "hallowed ground" did not die in vain, what about grounds less hallowed or even less remembered? Did those who died on Pork Chop Hill in Korea or Hamburger Hill in Vietnam or the Korengal Valley in Afghanistan, all places marked by fierce fighting that were later determined to be strategically unnecessary, then die in vain?

I hope not, but declaring these things is beyond my specialty. Nonetheless, each of these places is a reminder of what it is we ask young people to do.

SEBASTIAN JUNGER wrote the powerful book *War* and co-directed a companion documentary film, *Restrepo*, that focused on Battle Company of the 173rd Airborne Combat Team at Restrepo outpost in the Korengal Valley in Afghanistan in 2007 and 2008.

Mr. Junger was embedded with this company at that time of sometimes heavy fighting. In 2010, when the army announced it was withdrawing from this place where some forty soldiers had been killed, Mr. Junger wrote that the men with whom he lived "seemed to make 'sense' of combat in a completely personal way. They were not interested in the rest of the war and they were not much concerned with whether it was just, winnable or even well executed. For soldiers, the fight is what gives a place meaning, rather than the other way around."

As one man from Battle Company wrote, "They might have pulled out, but they can't take away what we accomplished and how hard we fought there."

It was just a base, but those who fought and those who died in this now forsaken valley were young soldiers who had answered the call. They deserve far more identity. They should not be reduced to the place where they fell. The soldier only asked, in words that might have echoed from every battlefield (including Gettysburg) on which Americans have ever fought, "Remember that."

Remembering Those Who Wore
the "Boots on the Ground"

May 2016

IN THIS ELECTION YEAR of 2016, Memorial Day comes amid debates
about how to respond to those who threaten the United States and its
allies. A military response or preventive action is a common suggestion to
deal with threats. The rhetoric from candidates, from political leaders, from
cheering sections, and from pundits has been aggressive. Recent months
have brought proposals for increased air strikes, carpet bombing, establishing
and enforcing no-fly zones, congressional declarations of war, authorizing
torture of suspects, and arming and aiding those whose weapons
now seem aimed in what America currently considers the right direction.

Some of these plans include the introduction of combat troops to
combat ISIS (Islamic State of Iraq and Syria)—calling for "boots on the
ground." This is unambiguously a muscular assertion. Foes beware and
friends take comfort—the American troops have landed.

But "boots on the ground" is about more than a figure of speech, a synonym
for combat deployment. The metaphor obscures and abstracts the
humanity of the young Americans dispatched on open-ended assignments.
Calling them "boots" substitutes leather for flesh and blood—flesh that
will be torn and blood that will be spilled. To advocate sending boots onto
hostile ground is easier than proposing to send young men and women
into a dangerous situation.

Calls for "boots on the ground" also evoke images of what is commonly
called the "battlefield cross." It is part of the unofficial military ceremony
that men and women often hold, either in the field or back at their home
base, to memorialize a deceased comrade.

This "cross" is not a cross but a field weapon, a rifle, with fixed bayonet
thrust into the ground. A helmet sits on the top of the butt of the rifle. This
inverted-rifle icon is at the center of a ceremony that enables comrades to

pause, to bend a knee, to remember, to grieve, to say farewell. There is often a final roll call, understanding that one—or more—of the names shouted out will elicit no response.

At least as far back as the Vietnam War, this memorial has been further enriched and humanized by a pair of field boots sitting next to the weapon, helmet, and bayonet. Many have seen this image or even just the empty combat boots placed in front of the Vietnam Veterans Memorial Wall and other sites to remember friends who served and died.

These boots are a forceful and personal reminder. The U.S. Army Manual describing the field ceremony notes that the boots symbolize the "final march of the last battle." Combat boots in the ceremony democratize a very old tradition in military funerals of leaders—the riderless horse with empty boots reversed in the stirrups, following the caisson with the body of the deceased. This rattling saber is silently sheathed.

Memorial Day is a single day, set aside for Americans to reflect upon and honor those whom they should reflect upon and honor every day. It provides a symbolic occasion to pause and consider those who serve in the military, and especially those whose sacrifice is forever—indelibly symbolized by the quiet markers in national cemeteries. But Americans need to make this act of reflection an enduring commitment rather than a perfunctory salute. If they have an obligation to remember these sacrifices when the shooting stops, they have a contract with those who serve to anticipate them before the shooting starts.

There unfortunately will be occasions when the United States needs to ask members of its military to take on an assignment on hostile ground. That can be a necessary action. And it can be an expected deployment for those who have volunteered to serve. They will go. But before such an order is issued, those who urge and authorize such an assignment should assess and explain it carefully, to make clear what the military's goal is and what the metric is for knowing this deployed force has achieved it.

Explaining these things has become far more complicated. Since World War II, American wars have been fought for often general, typically ambiguous, and always evolving political ends. Combat operations in Iraq and Afghanistan have been called "asymmetrical warfare," engagements in which there is seldom an enemy in uniform in the field. In these conflicts, American military forces need to follow stringent rules of engagement, to recognize protected areas, to respect and protect noncombatants, and to seek to win often-fickle and always-frightened hearts and minds among the civilian residents. They need to work as civic, economic, and cultural advisors, as well as a police force aiming to control carefully and seldom overtly. None of these are conventional military actions—and public debate has not kept pace.

One way to change that is to move from metaphor to reality. Those who urge this deployment must think not of robotic drones, of shock-and-awe video-game firepower, or of marching boots and of other bloodless euphemisms, but of the young countrymen and women involved. And to anticipate that these operations will inevitably result in real boots on the ground—empty boots sitting next to a rifle attached to a bayonet thrust in the earth. With loved ones grieving at home and comrades grieving in the field.

Think of these boots and those who wore them on Memorial Day. And every day.

The Human Face of War

June 2019

As the tempo of the drums of war accelerates in the Middle East, and two more U.S. troops are killed in Afghanistan, it is an occasion to pause and reflect on a previous conflict and the need always to consider the very human face and cost of war.

This summer of 2019 will mark a half century since the historic summer of 1969, the end if not the apogee of the '60s. In a few short months the nation was thrilled and startled by events such as Woodstock, the Apollo moon landing, the Stonewall riots, Senator Ted Kennedy at Chappaquiddick, the conviction of Muhammad Ali for draft evasion, and the Manson murders. Moviegoers were enthralled by *Midnight Cowboy* and Americans were reading *Slaughterhouse Five*. They listened to music from "The Age of Aquarius" and Creedence Clearwater Revival's "Bad Moon Rising."

Seldom far removed from any of these was the intense emotional debate over the American War in Vietnam. In the spring of 1969, there were major antiwar protests on a number of college campuses and in June President Richard Nixon announced the beginning of the drawdown of American troops from Vietnam. In early July, John Lennon and Yoko Ono released "Give Peace a Chance," recorded in a Montreal hotel room on Memorial Day weekend.

And, quietly, evocatively, in that noisy summer of acoustic protest and televised drama, *Life* magazine on June 27 published an issue with the cover story, "The Faces of the American Dead in Vietnam: One Week's Toll." It is hard to calculate today the impact of this issue, ironically coming at a moment when the great photo magazines of the previous half century were losing money and influence.

Television news footage of the war was often powerful, but due to the need to ship film back to the American networks it was often dated and quite transitory. The great enduring images of the war often came from photographers.

But even the prize-winning photographs of chaos, of combat, and of death seemed distant, surreal, compared to the photos that *Life* published in 1969. And more than newsreels could, these photos had an impact on American perceptions of the nature and the cost of the war. It was personal—and devastating.

The magazine had eleven pages of photographs, listing the 242 Americans whose deaths had been announced by the Department of Defense for the week of May 28–June 3. In yearbook style, the photos, provided by families of the dead, largely were high school graduation pictures or basic training/boot camp photos. So many looked so young.

By the end of May 1969, over 43,300 Americans had died in Vietnam. Over 6,300 died in the first five months of the year. The Pentagon provided weekly tallies of this growing cost. But tallies and numbers tend to abstract, to dehumanize the costs of war. Television broadcasts from the combat zones would touch on losses but were not able to name the dead. Local newspapers typically did include photographs with their obituaries, but this acted to isolate the impact, the grieving.

These photographs shocked in the aggregate. But even more, the individual images personalized and humanized the numbers. The photos reminded readers of sons, grandsons, siblings, classmates, boys from next door.

Ironically, cruelly, this feature story seriously understated the actual cost. The list included all of those announced by the Pentagon for the week—releases that only came after the families had been informed. And informing families was often a delayed process. So it is the case that many of those included in the story had died earlier. The true tally for those who died in the week spanning May and June was double the *Life* figure: 446 Americans actually died in that week.

The average age of those pictured in *Life* was twenty-one. Fifty-one of them were teenagers. There were also men in their thirties and forties, one of whom, the *Life* editors noted, had seven children. Nearly two-thirds of the junior Army enlisted men were draftees. Their hometowns were in forty-six different states, from cities and towns and farms from Seattle to Miami to the Navajo Reservation, from Maine to Honolulu to two who called Puerto Rico home. William Gearing Jr., a twenty-year-old soldier from Greece, New York, was on the cover of the magazine.

Twenty-seven were African American and two were Native American. The Pentagon did not compile data on Hispanic service members but surnames suggest that at least seven or eight of them were Hispanic. Indeed, the names on the list suggest a cross section of American national and ethnic groups.

One hundred ninety were in the Army and forty-nine were Marines. Three served in the Navy. Of the Army casualties, six of them were among the seventy-two who had died in the major and controversial May battle on "Hamburger Hill" in the A Shau Valley.

There was a national reaction to and conversation about this issue. Drew Pearson and Jack Anderson referred to it in their national columns. Newspapers from Canyon, Texas, to Charleston, South Carolina, wrote of the story. Some were critical, describing it as an antiwar ploy. Most were not. As the Sault Ste. Marie (Michigan) *Evening News* wrote, "One cannot fail to be profoundly moved by these photographs of men who, with only a few exceptions, died at an age that for most of us is but the threshold of adult life."

A Des Moines resident wrote to that city's *Register* that he did not know how any of the nation's leaders could look at the photos and "not see the utter waste of all these young men." Pearson, the columnist, observed that *Life* had its largest reader response in years. Some criticized the editors for, as one Texan wrote, supporting "the antiwar demonstrators who are traitors." An Indiana reader observed, "No peace demonstration, no dovish editorial, no antiwar speech could approach the mute eloquence of those young faces."

There is no way to assess the impact of the magazine on attitudes toward the war. Clearly it appeared at a time when the war had become the leading issue facing the nation and there was decreasing support for military involvement in Vietnam. In July 1965 Gallup reported that 24 percent of Americans thought the U.S. should withdraw or stop fighting in Vietnam. By July 1969, 55 percent thought there should be de-escalation/withdrawal.

In early July, the *New York Times* published an account of members of the 9th Marines preparing to ship out from Vandegrift Combat Base as part of the initial drawdown of American troops.

Several were looking at the *Life* issue, looking for pictures of friends.

As one officer noted, "The people just don't realize what these guys have been through."

Across the country some did realize. These photographs were of young men they knew. A mother in Utah met the soldiers who came to inform her of the death of her eighteen-year-old son by embracing his young brother and saying, "You are not going to get another one!" A young widow in Iowa asked that there be no firing squad at her husband's burial, saying he had already had enough gunfire. A young Marine from Quincy, Massachusetts, who had joined after a friend was killed, was mourned in the large Irish American community there. A soldier from Oregon was buried in the same grave as his brother, an earlier casualty of the war in Vietnam. A young Black Marine who had already been wounded three times and just wanted to be home with his mother in North Carolina, came home finally, with a Marine Corps honor guard after his death on May 29.

The *Life* editors prefaced this article by reminding readers that the weekly statistics and numbers of dead "were translated into direct anguish in hundreds of homes all over the country." They suggested it was time for the nation to "pause to look into the faces."

This advice remains true today, as the Pentagon just released the identities of the two latest casualties of war. It is too easy to abstract casualties into numbers or minimize deployment as "boots on the ground." We need to look into the faces to see who wore these boots, to always remember the very human cost of war.

Nixon's Leniency After My Lai
Hurt Veterans. Trump's May, Too

December 2019

THOSE WHO DISAGREE with President Donald Trump's 2019 pardons for two U.S. soldiers and a sailor who committed war-zone crimes have focused on how his actions undermine the military justice system, the code of conduct, military discipline, and the integrity of the chain of command. But there is another serious consequence, one that flows perhaps less from the pardons themselves than from the ways in which the president and others explained and justified them.

To understand this consequence, we must learn from our own history. In November 1969, the young journalist Seymour Hersh broke the story of a tragic atrocity in Vietnam. A few weeks later, Americans picked up *Life* magazine to find photos of a massacre in the Vietnamese village of My Lai. A U.S. Army platoon led by Lieutenant William Calley Jr. had swept into the town and, finding no enemy soldiers, proceeded to kill as many as six hundred villagers, largely women and children. Thirty soldiers were charged with crimes, including senior officers who allegedly ignored accounts of criminal action, but ultimately only Calley was convicted. In March 1971, an Army court-martial board in Fort Benning, Georgia, found him guilty of twenty-nine counts of premeditated murder and sentenced him to life imprisonment with hard labor.

There was considerable public support for Lt. Calley. In a Gallup poll taken the following month, 69 percent of the respondents said he was a scapegoat. Many of his defenders went farther, arguing that he was, in fact, a hero. Country music stations played "Set Lt. Calley Free" and "Battle Hymn of Lt. Calley," the latter of which eventually sold some two million records.

President Richard Nixon declined to publicly celebrate the disgraced Army officer, but he told Henry Kissinger that "most people don't give a shit" whether he had actually killed the Vietnamese civilians. As the court martial came to an end, Defense Secretary Melvin Laird privately urged Nixon not to extend any pardon to Calley. Military leaders, Laird explained, believed that making him a scapegoat or hero would poison the view of American policy and the public view of soldiers. Nixon rejected the argument, telling advisors that demanding accountability for the massacre reflected the "obsolete idea that war is a game with rules." The day after the verdict, Nixon ordered Calley released from the post stockade and placed under house arrest in the Fort Benning bachelor officer quarters. Appeals would eventually reduce his punishment to time served.

Public views of the war had been changing sharply. Though a kernel of opposition in early 1965 had grown to a much more widely held view, many Americans at home still viewed those serving in Vietnam sympathetically, as victims drafted to fight a cruel war. Few protesters faulted them for the war. President Lyndon Johnson was the perpetrator. The chant at antiwar rallies was, "Hey, Hey, LBJ, how many kids did you kill today?"

But after the My Lai story broke, opposition to the war increased. Many became critical of the troops who served. Rather than victims of a cruel war, they became its perpetrators. LBJ was back on his Texas ranch; in the minds of a vocal minority, those deployed to Vietnam were now the "baby killers." The My Lai atrocity framed this negative image; the Calley hearings and his defense, as well as some of the testimony in 1971 from the Vietnam Veterans against the War, deepened it. During the court martial, for the first time a majority of the country said that the war was morally wrong.

President Nixon's actions and statements in the Calley case seemed to validate the view that everyone did it and no one is guilty—or perhaps, as some argued, that we were all guilty. There was little recognition of individual responsibility and accountability, crucial elements in military justice. This had real consequences for the Vietnam generation.

Participating in this war and presumably in its atrocities was the burden that the Vietnam veterans carried, heavily in the 1970s, and in some respects they still carry. In the aftermath of the war, more Americans knew the name of Lt. William Calley than knew anyone who had served bravely and with integrity. The atrocity at My Lai claimed many innocent Vietnamese victims, and the rationales used to explain, criticize, or to exonerate Lt. Calley ultimately claimed many victims who served in American uniforms.

Pardoning or reducing sentences generally represents a determination that the process was prejudiced or unfair, that the accused was actually innocent, or that the sentence was excessive. Seldom does it represent a judgment that the pardonee actually committed the offense and moreover that doing it was a commendable thing. President Nixon was careful not to go quite that far in public statements regarding Lt. Calley. Others did.

President Trump also ignored Pentagon advice not to become involved—although his engagement was more vocal than that of the cautious Nixon. Defenders of the three men from the Iraq and Afghanistan wars, including Fox News hosts, insisted that in fact they were American fighting men doing their jobs, and doing them heroically and well. Lt. Calley's lawyer said his client was a "good boy" whom the Army had trained to "Kill, Kill, Kill"—and then punished him for doing his job. President Trump championed this defense. "We train our boys to be killing machines, and then prosecute them when they kill," he said. He insisted that in fact the men were "three great warriors," and, indeed, "heroes." The president invited the two pardoned soldiers to join him on the platform at a campaign fundraiser.

Engaging in combat is a cruel and nasty assignment. In Vietnam and in Iraq and Afghanistan it was often hard to distinguish combatants from noncombatants.

In the twenty-first–century wars, the military's rules of engagement became increasingly complex. And these needed to be followed in some remarkably intense, emotional, and frightening situations, and, in Iraq and Afghanistan, frequently by troops who had engaged in multiple deployments. These conditions made professional leadership and discipline even more important.

There have been instances of misconduct and, unfortunately, atrocity, in each of these wars. Offering clemency or pardon for those convicted of crimes can be debated. But by celebrating them and their actions, we make their conduct acceptable and the exemplary norm. If "everybody did it" becomes the defense, as it did in the Calley case, and if doing "it" results in ballads and television accolades and presidential cheers, the bar is lowered and the image of those who serve bravely and well suffers.

In the spring of 2014, I was at West Point, meeting with classes and with cadets and faculty. One session was with a senior class on military law. These young men and women would graduate and receive a commission in a few weeks. We talked about My Lai and the Army handling of the case—and the public handling of it. These cadets were thoughtful and impressive. I left with confidence that they and their Army would handle any such future situations better than the Calley generation did. And by all accounts, they have.

Of course, we could not predict then how civilian leaders and the public would respond to future infractions of Army regulations and the established conventions of war. We have just had an unsettling look at that. And history has provided some insight into the possible consequences.

We've Learned to Thank Those Who Serve, Whether It's in War or During a Pandemic

May 2020

In the waning days of April 2020, the number of people who died from Covid-19 in the United States surpassed the tally of those killed in the Vietnam War. The nation has been stunned by the many who have died in this pandemic.

We think of them today, Memorial Day, as we pause to remember and grieve for the nearly sixty thousand U.S. service members who died in Vietnam—and the hundreds of thousands of other Americans who gave their lives in other wars.

As the Covid-19 death count continues to mount, it has had a cumulative and numbing effect, much like the counting of war dead. Individual cases disappear into the whole. The focus is on the number, not our fellow citizens.

Many news outlets, including the *Los Angeles Times*, have sought to put a human face on the Covid-19 tragedy, publishing profiles of some of the deceased, reminding the world what they had done with their lives and what remained for them to do. The remembrances sometimes include heartrending stories of the many family members and friends who were unable to be with their loved ones at the end because of coronavirus-related restrictions.

Just as the Covid-19 dead have likely been undercounted, so have the U.S. military dead in Vietnam. The official number fails to include the many veterans who died after the war as a result of lingering medical and emotional conditions.

And such tallies often don't acknowledge that as many as three million Vietnamese died in that war.

Now, the American generation that suffered most in Vietnam is the most vulnerable to the coronavirus.

If Covid-19 disproportionately strikes the elderly and the vulnerable, the Vietnam War disproportionately killed the young and the vital. More than 60 percent of the names on the Vietnam Memorial belong to those who were twenty-two or younger when they died. Members of that once-young Baby Boomer generation are now senior citizens.

The day before Saigon fell on April 30, 1975, the last two U.S. servicemen died in the Vietnam War. Two Marines, Charles McMahon of Woburn, Massachusetts, and Darwin Judge of Marshalltown, Iowa, were killed in a rocket attack.

Darwin Judge was nineteen. He had been an Eagle Scout; a high school teacher described him as "rock stable." Judge had arrived in Vietnam the month before he died.

Charles McMahon had been active in the Boys Club in Woburn, where he excelled as a swimmer and taught and mentored young boys. In 1971, he was named the Woburn "Boy of the Year." He was twenty-one and died eleven days after arriving in Vietnam.

Twelve Marshalltown natives, from age nineteen to thirty-nine, died in Vietnam. Ten Woburn residents between the ages of eighteen and twenty-nine also died in the war. Had they lived, these twenty-two men would be among the most vulnerable to Covid-19.

The McMahon and Judge families had to delay saying farewell to their young sons. In the chaos of the U.S. withdrawal, the bodies of the two Marines were left behind. Their remains would not be repatriated for nearly a year.

Many observers have described the struggle against the pandemic as a "war." The Covid-19 fight is not a war but a public health crisis, striking randomly. The Vietnam War was not random; it was the result of calculated choices.

The Covid-19 and Vietnam eras do share unfortunate similarities, including officials ignoring reports and warnings, and confidently insisting on their capacity to control events. Leaders in the 1960s also assured that we could wage the war without economic sacrifice, and today many insist that we can remain safe while enjoying economic and social freedom.

That war and this pandemic have each been marked by a pronounced inequitable sharing of the burden and the cost by the poor and by racial minorities. And in neither was there official national recognition of this or a pause for national mourning.

In both crises, unspoken politics, personal ambition, and arrogance too often have framed public statements, as well as military and public health strategy.

Then and now we have seen official optimism and an absence of candor regarding projections of what was to come: "It is over; we have won" echoes from Vietnam to 2020. In April, President Donald Trump said there was "light at the end of the tunnel." General William Westmoreland reported seeing a similar light in Vietnam in 1967.

There is one lesson American citizens seem to have finally learned, between the Vietnam era and now: to thank in real time those who serve, whether it's in war or during a pandemic. We need to do that today. And every day.

The Election without
a Debate over War

November 2020

O N NOVEMBER 3, 2020, Americans will have an opportunity to vote and affirm their vision of the future. Eight days later, on Veterans Day, many will pause to honor those who have served. This is an occasion to reflect on some of the consequences of earlier elections for national security strategies and military engagement.

It is unfortunate that we have had little opportunity for such reflection during this campaign. In 2020, the presidential candidates have described and debated their views on Covid-19, economic recovery, confronting chronic racial inequities, and climate change. The campaign has seldom provided crisp answers, but at a minimum we have some sense of what to expect of the candidates on these critical matters. However, we lack any detail on the candidates' views on the American role in the world and the use of U.S. military force.

This could be a pivotal election in terms of America's global role. We can only infer from their records what Donald Trump and Joseph Biden might do with the next four years. The second debate had a section scheduled on "national security" that quickly deteriorated into conflicting allegations about bank accounts and Burisma. We learned virtually nothing about either candidate's worldviews.

Over the last four years, President Trump has demonstrated that he is driven by competitive instincts and a narcissistic ego. He has little sense of strategy or interest in or regard for history. He prefers transactional arrangements, bilateralism or unilateralism, to working with traditional allies and other international parties. He has ranged from sudden announcements of troop withdrawals to threatening war with Iran and North Korea.

Biden's record as U.S. senator and as vice president in the Obama administration is more traditional. He supports NATO and multilateral agreements and treaty commitments and recognizes American global obligations and responsibilities. But he has been inconsistent on his specific plans for American troop engagements in Iraq and Afghanistan.

Both candidates supported the Iraq war—before they didn't. Joe Biden has talked about maintaining some troop presence in Afghanistan. President Trump, in contrast, promised on October 7 to bring the troops in Afghanistan "home by Christmas." This tweet-as-policy-decision was later hedged by other administration officials.

As we consider the candidates' views and their records, this Veterans Day also provides us with an opportunity to confront our own history. It is relevant. Fewer than 3 percent of the living veterans we will honor this year served in World War II. Their war was fought with a clear military mission—unconditional surrender of the enemies—the achievement of which would mark the unambiguous conclusion of the war.

Our subsequent wars in Korea, Vietnam, Iraq, and Afghanistan have generally lacked clear and consistent military missions. With one outlier—1991's Operation Desert Storm—they devolved into repeated military tactical operations lacking any clear national strategy or specific goal. November provides a good marker to reflect on this record.

Seventy years ago, General Douglas MacArthur promised that American troops in Korea would "eat Christmas dinner at home." Tragically, the only ones home for Christmas in 1950 arrived on hospital ships or in coffins in the cargo holds. By October, the United States had expanded its goal, from defending South Korea against the invading North Korean army to defeating North Korea.

In that month, MacArthur had U.S. troops move toward the Yalu River, which divides the Korean peninsula from China. He dismissed Beijing's warnings that they would enter the war if we approached this border. Even as General MacArthur was declaring home-by-Christmas, the American Eighth Army was suffering heavy casualties in a battle in northwestern Korea and the Marine Corps 1st Division engaged in a major battle near the Chosin Reservoir and then fought their way back to the port at Hungnam.

The Christmas holiday found the American forces hounded from the north, enmeshed in a war with Chinese forces that would drag on nearly three more years. Five battles were fought just to control Seoul. Today,

American forces remain in South Korea and North Korean flags fly over the Chosin Reservoir.

Fifty-five years ago, in November 1965, the American 1st Cavalry Division fought the first large battle of the Vietnam War, at Ia Drang. President Lyndon Johnson had dispatched American ground forces to Vietnam the previous spring "to strengthen world order" and to "protect the people" of South Vietnam.

Each side claimed a victory at Ia Drang, but there was no change in control of the area—a pattern that would hold for seven years, until a truce was negotiated for the withdrawal of all American forces. During those lengthy negotiations in Paris, Secretary of State Henry Kissinger reminded the U.S. military in Vietnam that "we are playing the most complex game with the Soviets involving matters which extend far beyond the battle in Vietnam, as crucial as it is." Two years after the truce was signed, the North Vietnamese occupied Saigon, and today Ia Drang and other battlefields are part of the Socialist Republic of Vietnam.

The American operation in Afghanistan began nineteen years ago as a response to the 9/11 attacks. The U.S. and NATO allies sought to punish Osama bin Laden and his Al Qaeda militants and replace the Taliban government that supported them. Their invasion began in October 2001, and a month later, this coalition and the Afghan Northern Alliance captured Mazar-i-Sharif and then Kabul and Kunduz. The remaining Taliban forces slipped back to their homes or retreated to Pakistan.

American goals then expanded to more political ones to assure a stable and "democratic" government in Afghanistan and to engage in a "war on terror." The military launched civic action plans and economic development programs. And the fighting continued. Today, the Taliban have reorganized and are essentially controlling the area around Mazar-i-Sharif and negotiating as equals at the table with Americans and the Afghan government.

Sixteen years ago, in November 2004, American Marines led a force into Fallujah, Iraq, to defeat the Iraqi resistance forces that controlled that city. After nearly a week of door-to-door fighting and heavy casualties, the Marines were largely in control of the city. This battle followed the decision in the spring of 2003 to topple the government of Saddam Hussein and to remove his putative weapons of mass destruction. As in Afghanistan, the war aims then expanded, adding some of the same civic and economic goals, again overseen by the military. In 2014, ISIS (Islamic State of Iraq and Syria) forces took over Fallujah; two years later, the Iraqi army retook the city.

One can draw some lessons from all of these wars and those specific battles. First, the American military forces fought bravely and well. But these wars were finally not about winning battles as a step toward victory or even satisfactory resolution. They lacked a clear and consistent military goal and an overarching strategy to accomplish it. And as Sun Tzu wrote some 2,500 years ago, tactics without a strategy are a road to defeat.

These four wars have been costly in American treasure and lives: more than 101,000 servicemen and -women died in them and nearly 310,000 were wounded. And they were even more costly for the local civilian populations.

Many will recall and some ridicule the photo of President George Bush on the carrier *USS Abraham Lincoln* in May 2003 with the huge "Mission Accomplished" banner behind him. It is hard to reconcile that sense of victory with the fact that Americans remain engaged in Iraq over seventeen years later. But the irony is that the military had accomplished its mission then—as they had in Korea by the early fall of 1950 and in Afghanistan in 2001, only to lose earlier gains. Vietnam's mission proved a more elusive one—and the most costly of all these wars.

As happens in life and in war, the goals evolved and political negotiations overrode military engagement. Military engagement and the inevitable casualties that follow must be more than a political bargaining chip. In the summer of 1953, Americans and their NATO allies suffered heavy losses in the battle for Pork Chop Hill in Korea, even as negotiators were completing the final truce. U.S. soldiers in Korea talked of "dying for a tie." We need to recognize on Veterans Day, as we should every day, who holds that bargaining chip and who pays the price.

It is crucial on Election Day to recognize the consequences of electoral choices. It is unfortunate that we have spent little time in this campaign considering and debating what these might be for our national security policy. As we proclaim a widely desired end, the withdrawal of American forces from Afghanistan, let us also consider that those things that got them there too often involved tactical considerations rather than strategic goals. So it might be good now to think strategically about withdrawal. And at this time, it is essential to think strategically about engagement with Iran rather than rattling sabers there. We have seen this movie before.

V

CHALLENGES

How America's All-Volunteer Force Reshaped the Military— and the Country

March 2021

OVER THE PAST YEAR, the pandemic—with all its human tragedies and socioeconomic consequences, as well as the November election and its contested and violent aftermath—has dominated the nation's attention.

But there were two events in 2020 that deserved more discussion. First, the National Commission on Military, National, and Public Service, established by Congress in 2016, issued a significant report on March 25 urging a renewed emphasis on a culture of service. And 2020 marked the year when men born in 1955 became eligible for Social Security. Those men were the last Americans eligible to be drafted into military service. Now, no American under 65 has faced a draft notice.

The All-Volunteer Force was implemented in 1973. During the twenty years of war in the Middle East, few of us have known those who have served there. Moreover, these have been the first extended wars in our history without a dedicated tax to pay for them. Most citizens have only a passing understanding of, or interest in, these military operations.

The All-Volunteer Force was recommended in 1970 by a commission chaired by former Secretary of Defense Thomas Gates, and members included economist Milton Friedman, Notre Dame President Father Theodore Hesburgh, and NAACP Director Roy Wilkins. Their recommendations had broad support by groups ranging from antiwar and antidraft demonstrators to libertarians to senior military leaders, and they were approved by liberal Democrats and conservative Republicans alike—as well as by President Richard Nixon. All were seeking to distance themselves from the draft controversies of the Vietnam War.

In this century, these volunteers have served in the most professional, highly educated, and diverse military this country has known. They have conducted themselves well—with multiple deployments under trying circumstances in wars without end. They deserve the thanks of the nation.

A smaller volunteer force has consequences. In the over-75 age group, 44 percent of the men and 1 percent of the women are veterans. In the under-34 age group, among men it is 3 percent and women less than 1 percent. The military today is represented by enlistees from rural areas more than urban, and the South and the West more than the rest of the country. Over 40 percent of enlistees are Black, Hispanic, Asian, Native American, or Native Hawaiian/Pacific Islander. Sixteen percent are women. Many enlistees come from a military family.

A disproportionate number of those arrested following the January 6, 2020, attack on the Capitol were veterans. This should be troubling. There are a few factors that might partially explain this: The twenty-first–century military has been more successfully recruited from rural areas, as well as in the South and Southwest—notably "red state" areas.

Politically, veterans have tended to be more Conservative, and they were more supportive of President Donald Trump—although that support has declined in the last four years. Enlistment processes have not screened for racists; and military commands often have ignored white supremacist and neo-Nazi views among those in their ranks. Extremist groups, especially the para-military organizations. have explicitly sought to recruit military veterans. The consequences of these circumstances were visible on January 6. A CNN analysis shortly after the riot found that 14 percent of those charged with criminal conduct were veterans.

What needs to be equally apparent is that many of the voices who have spoken out against the January 6 assault on democracy were also veterans. A study in 2012 indicated that the Capitol Police Force had over 20 percent veterans. Brian Sicknick, the police officer killed in the attack, was a veteran.

The problem with the Republic today is not a problem with military veterans. To be sure, some veterans, along with many nonveterans, joined in actions contrary to our democratic values. They must be held accountable. But there has been something more fundamental at work in this country in the last fifty years: a decline in civic culture, an erosion of trust in government, in its representatives, its democratic processes, and a contagion of conspiracy theories.

Those born in 1955 heard it later when President John F. Kennedy insisted, "Ask not what your country can do for you—ask what you can do for your country." They watched siblings and friends enlist in the military or the Peace Corps. Despite the controversy over the draft, nearly 80 percent of those who served in the military during the Vietnam era were enlistees. Children of the World War II generation, they grew up in a culture that emphasized service.

This culture was not sustained. In the last half century, this nation has watched the release of the Pentagon Papers and the revelations of Watergate, detailing deceit at the highest levels of government. President Ronald Reagan argued that government is not the solution but the problem. This attitude has evolved from a campaign slogan to a conviction that the government cannot be trusted—that career public servants are deep-state swamp dwellers.

Many politicians and political commentators today reject bipartisan statesmanship. They shout that politics is about tribal loyalty and call opponents untrustworthy and disloyal. Expressions of racism and intolerance of "others" have become too common. Political leaders have refused to accept the results of a democratic election. Fringe views have become mainstream, and cynicism, hatred, and fear are stoked on cable television and social media. Schools are far less likely to require basic civics courses.

If veterans were represented disproportionately among those arrested for invading the Capitol on January 6, I would observe they were far from proportionately represented among those Republican leaders and media personalities who lied to them and encouraged them. Although it is the case that of the fifty-three veterans serving as Republican members of Congress, thirty-five of them voted to reject the certified Arizona electoral votes.

The importance of dedicated service and sacrifice has been celebrated during the Covid-19 crisis. We need to build on the example of those who cared for us. The National Commission on Military, National, and Public Service urged an effort to build upon this, to affirm a "widespread culture of service."

Starting with our leaders and representatives, all Americans need to acknowledge that our republic depends upon mutual trust, volunteerism, and civic values. People who insist they are "patriots" should start acting like it. The vast majority of our veterans already have.

Reflections and Observations:
The Twenty-first–Century
All-Volunteer Force

September 2021

THIS BOOK PRESENTS some ideas and suggestions that reflect my training as a historian and my work for the past fifteen years meeting with,
supporting, and explaining and advocating for veterans. In the essays and
lectures included here, I have described the changing nature of war in my
lifetime, taking into consideration the lag in the changing public understanding of how wars are fought and a more distant knowledge of those
who fight them and how we support them.

But in addition to the insights of a historian and the experience of an
advocate, my views are also framed more personally by the memories of
my own experiences and the values that I have come to hold. The world of
the veterans of Vietnam, of Iraq, and of Afghanistan was different from the
world in which I grew up. The wars they fought and are fighting were not
the wars for which I was trained to fight. And the diversity and issues and
challenges of the All-Volunteer Force are different from the ones my generation faced. Or perhaps the real difference is that we did not face them.

*IN THE COLD WAR MILITARY in which I served in the 1950s, we were train-
ing and planning for a global confrontation with the Soviet Bloc, for potential
engagement with a professional army in uniform on a battlefield with front lines.
Our strategic planning, maneuvers, and drills presumed a repeat of the type of
conflict that marked World War II. Marines still climbed down cargo nets into
small landing craft, sailed on LSTs (Landing Ship, Tank) with ramps prepared
to land troops and equipment on the beaches where we would engage an enemy
force in combat in order to secure and hold a physical place.*

During my tour with the 1st Marine Brigade at Kaneohe Bay, Hawaii, in one large-scale maneuver including some units of the 1st Marine Division from Camp Pendleton, we successfully "captured" the beaches of Kauai from their defenders. In a real-world scenario we deployed thousands of miles in an LST from Pearl Harbor to Yokosuka, Japan, to provide back-up support for Marines who had gone to Taiwan—then typically called Formosa—in order to defend the small offshore islands of Quemoy and Matsu from a potential Chinese Communist threat. My base in Japan, Atsugi Naval Air Station, had been the home of Japanese kamikaze units in World War II. Underground hangars and maintenance areas were still there. But in 1958 it housed a "secret" CIA squadron, officially listed as an Air Force "Weather Reconnaissance" unit, that was flying U-2s over China and the Soviet Union. In so many ways, this symbolized the era. World War II was always in our consciousness and a potential World War III framed our preparedness.

I served with NCOs (non-commissioned officers) and officers who had liberated Pacific islands from the Japanese just fifteen years earlier and some who had fought off the Chinese in an epic battle at the Chosin Reservoir in Korea. I recall one night in our barracks in Hawaii being startled from sleep by a duty sergeant shouting to get up and get ready because an air raid was expected shortly. Our barracks were just down the hill from the landmark Kansas Tower where, on December 7, 1941, Japanese attack planes had come over this windward side of the island before they arrived at Pearl Harbor. They destroyed most of the Navy planes on the runway at Kaneohe Bay, but one Japanese plane crashed on the hill near Kansas Tower. We were always aware of the latter as a symbol of that horrendous day.

On that night, in preparation for our presumed attack, we were moved to Pennsylvania Battery, an old World War II gun emplacement on Mokapu Point, named after the battleship, the USS Pennsylvania, which had been damaged while in drydock during the Japanese attack at Pearl Harbor eighteen years earlier. During the Second World War, the Pennsylvania Battery had two fourteen-inch turret guns reclaimed from the USS Arizona. After we were moved there during the night of the erroneous belief of impending attack, the Marine Corps decided to reclaim the old hollowed-out mountain. We moved in temporarily and I explored some of the cavernous rooms and facilities there.

We were trained to fend off a massive attack and we were prepared to launch our own assault on an enemy force. Prepared—and perhaps eager! Near the end of my infantry training at Camp Pendleton in the fall of 1957, we had a wrap-up mock battle—a day dug in and defending our positions and then a night assault on a hill that was controlled by "enemy forces." It was all very real—some live firing around us, many explosions, and flares lighting up the California sky. When we were commanded to attack the enemy, I found myself caught up in the action, enthused and ready. Shouting loudly, I raced out up the hill ahead of the other Marines in my unit, who were moving forward together. I was finally stopped by a sergeant who told me to slow down and advance with my platoon: "Who in the fuck do you think you are, John Wayne attacking Iwo Jima?" I guess maybe I did. That was our world.

As I WRITE THIS in September 2021, the twentieth anniversary of the 9/11 attacks served as a harsh reminder of the origins of the wars of this century. And the intrusive images of the chaotic withdrawal of U.S. forces and personnel from Afghanistan provide cruel bookends for a generation and for what, at least for now, can claim to be America's longest war.

I will look forward to scholars providing an assessment of the conduct of the wars in Afghanistan and Iraq. But at this time it is hard to get a handle on the conductors. The air is filled with a lot of denials and assertions and finger pointing.

SOME WILL RECALL Senator John Kerry's statement in 2003 when voting against legislation funding the war in Iraq, "I actually did vote for the $87 billion before I voted against it." He had supported the original authorization for war in Iraq before opposing the war.

Pundits had fun joking then about Senator Kerry's glib explanation of his changing views. Now the nation's landscape has many who have followed the same path. The two recent American presidents who determined to end our military engagement in Afghanistan, Donald Trump and Joseph Biden, also supported the war in Iraq—and that in Afghanistan—before they opposed it. As did many, many Americans.

When President Biden announced in the spring of 2021 that he was going to complete a withdrawal of all troops by September, he followed a goal of his two predecessors. In fact, President Trump had earlier agreed with the Taliban to complete a total withdrawal by May 1. Some military leaders expressed concern about his plan and Biden's intention to complete it. Many worried about the stability of the Afghanistan government and the fate of the many Afghans who supported the United States and its allies—as well as the future for women and girls if the Taliban should again take power. But by and large most Americans supported the proposed end of the nation's longest war.

Then came the actual withdrawal. In mid-August Afghan President Ashraf Ghani left the country and the central government essentially folded even before the Americans fully exited. By August most units of the Afghan army had melted away, back to their homes. Few remained to resist aggressive Taliban offensives. Given their long-standing problems with corrupt leadership and conflicts, they recognized the consequences of the loss of American military support. Perhaps the speed of this demise was unexpected, but the surprising thing about the collapse is that it seemed to surprise people.

The last few days of August 2021, marked by the chaos at the Kabul airport, the suicide bombing that killed thirteen American service members and at least 170 Afghans, the mistaken drone attack that killed ten innocent Afghans, the sight of the evacuation plane leaving with Afghans clinging to it—and falling to their death—all of this tainted badly the process of doing something that was popular in the United States: bringing the troops home. Hypocritical blaming countered by exaggerated claims of a good exit replaced any sense of shared grief and shared responsibility, any resolution to learn what happened and how to avoid such tragedies in the future.

In his testimony before a Senate hearing on September 28, Chairman of the Joint Chiefs General Mark Milley said the war in Afghanistan had "an outcome that is a strategic failure, the enemy is in charge in Kabul—there is no other way to describe that." And he reminded Americans, "that outcome is the cumulative effect of twenty years, not twenty days."

The twenty-first–century wars in Afghanistan and Iraq remind us of the timeless warning that it is easier to get into a war than it is to get out of one. Engaging in war is generally a clear unilateral decision. Disengaging is seldom unilateral, nor is it clear—or clean. Troops on the ground inevitably alter the shape of that ground and the views of those who reside there. The local population, friends and foes alike, have increasingly important roles in the chain of events. Allies have a stake in the decision and the process.

These twenty-first–century wars also stand as solid evidence that the old twentieth-century watchword that "politics stops at the ocean's edge" has no standing in this century. Needless to say, it was also of limited value in describing politics during the Vietnam War. Despite this disjunction, down through the end of the Cold War there was at least some strategic consensus on America's role in the world—even if there was not always tactical agreement on how to pursue that role.

The armed forces have not been immunized from the intense politics of recent years. The American military has been among the most popular institutions in the nation for the last forty years. Political parties and candidates wrap themselves in assertions of support for servicemen and -women and for veterans. Not surprisingly, even if these affirmations continue for "the military," current military leaders have not been immune from the partisan and ideological crossfire. Sometimes they have led with their chin: there has been a sharp increase in retired officers signing on to partisan efforts.

General Mark Milley has received criticism from all directions—first for his participation in President Trump's June 2020 photo-op clearing of demonstrators to walk across Lafayette Square, and then for the reports of his response to concerns that President Trump may have been planning some military action in order to overturn the 2020 election results. His regret for the former and his explanation of the latter have had little impact on his critics.

In recent months, conservatives have criticized the military for its willingness to change the names of bases named after Confederates and expressed their alarm that somehow the military and the service academies were pressing "wokeness" and teaching about race. They have sought a history untainted by any criticism—except that they have sought to make iconic some Confederate officers who engaged in the most aggressive acts of criticism of the republic in our history.

Progressives have challenged the military for its inability to address sexual harassment and sexual assault, for the failure to have senior leadership represent a cross section of the society. So far, these partisan criticisms have not been tangled directly with the conduct of the wars of the century. It is time, though, as the wars, their conclusions, and the ways they have been conducted have now become part of the political arena.

Ideology and partisanship and unfettered political fights have led to a world where foreign policy engagements are sublimated to calculations of image and partisan advantage. These calculations have resulted in some pretty clumsy proclamations and criticisms. And some equally clumsy shifting positions. Facts and memories have become malleable. The result has been a partisan circular firing squad in which policy goals are secondary to political advantage. It is impossible to develop a sustainable and successful military plan with shifting civilian leadership with shifting goals—and when partisan advantage seems to be a primary objective.

In 2019, retired Marine Corps General James Mattis, who had stepped down as secretary of defense on a matter of principle, wrote in *The Atlantic*: "And now, today, we look around. Our politics are paralyzing the country. We practice suspicion or contempt where trust is needed, imposing a sentence of anger and loneliness on others and ourselves. We scorch our opponents with language that precludes compromise. We brush aside the possibility that a person with whom we disagree might be right. We talk about what divides us and seldom acknowledge what unites us. Meanwhile, the docket of urgent national issues continues to grow—unaddressed and, under present circumstances, impossible to address." (December 2019)

Few would have disputed him then. And few would dispute that this paralysis is even worse now. Very urgent national issues remain unaddressed.

All of this is disheartening to anyone eager for a good policy debate that will recalibrate and make clear America's role in the world. The stakes here are far more consequential than most of the sparring that we see. And it is far more than disheartening when young service members are caught in the middle of shifting public opinion and partisan scrums. Servicemen and -women who fought and suffered and watched colleagues die at places like Fallujah and Kandahar joined Vietnam veterans who had the same experiences at Khe Sanh and Dak To and the Mekong Delta. Their anger and frustration and sense of despair were understandable. As was the fact that few of them insisted the response was to up the ante, to send in more troops. Those who proclaim the latter is the only action that will assure that those who died did "not die in vain" generally will not deploy themselves.

Following President Biden's May announcement of a total withdrawal over the summer, Afghanistan veteran and quadruple amputee, Travis Mills, shared in *USA Today* a feeling that many veterans of the wars of the post–World War II era have expressed: "This was not a war we could win, really. How many more good men and women should go through what I've gone through? Not one." (May 2, 2021)

Over the summer of 2021, as the Afghanistan drawdown began, I was reminded of the period during the last months of the Korean War in the summer of 1953, when the negotiated truce was in sight. American troops who engaged in heavy fighting on Pork Chop Hill allegedly said they just wanted to survive because no one wanted to "die for a tie." That negotiated truce continues, sometimes rockily, nearly seventy years later. Korean War veterans insisted they had accomplished their mission: repel the North Korean invasion and protect the Republic of Korea. Veterans of Vietnam, on the other hand, confronted in 1975 the news that the North Vietnamese had occupied Saigon. There was no tie there. But as one Vietnam veteran argued, emphatically, after the fall of Saigon: "We. Didn't. Lose. We were withdrawn." Now veterans of Iraq and Afghanistan wonder about the results—even more fundamentally, the meaning—of their wars. Even though troops remain deployed in Iraq it is clear that American military engagement there is ending. Veterans of these wars share the frustration of those who came before them. They know they had prevailed in the field. They can remind us: they did not lose.

A decade ago I had a conversation with a U.S. Army veteran who had served as a senior officer in Vietnam. He, along with Colonel Harry Summers, met a North Vietnamese veteran officer after the war and said to him, "You know, you never defeated us on the battlefield." The North Vietnamese response was, "That may be so, but it is also irrelevant."

This summarizes so well the nature of American wars after World War II—they are not about battlefield victories. This has never been more the case than it was in those engagements in Iraq and Afghanistan. They were tactical more than strategic. Ending terrorism is an essential national—international—goal. But the means to this are elusive and surely involve more than military force. Especially when there is seldom a clear enemy in the field against whom to direct that military force.

Combat operations that are not primarily about defeating an enemy in the field, wars with complex rules of engagement, armed deployments in the midst of tribal and political and religious differences, these are difficult wars for our military to fight and difficult engagements for our democracy to sustain. The U.S. domestic political environment changes—as does that of the nation in which we are engaged. It is often but a small step from being perceived as a liberator to being an occupier. Objectives shift to nonmilitary goals, many certainly quite desirable, and conclusions remain elusive and finally inconclusive.

How does a heavily armed military force fight when the only strategic goal is not military but an elusive "war on terror"? Terror is a violent attitude, an ideology, fostered in cells and secret enclaves. It relies on stealth rather than marching to battle with an army in uniform in the field. Opposition to terror and terrorists requires many tools, and while military force may be one of these, it is seldom the primary one. We saw previews of the use of the military to convert hearts and minds in Vietnam. And in Iraq and Afghanistan these previews had morphed into a long feature film. Many American service members had multiple deployments and found themselves walking the same ground seeking to protect it, but ironically, in order to do this, almost inviting an assault from an enemy that had no clear base.

The final days in Afghanistan provided stunning examples of the difficulty of combat operations against enemy forces who were able to slip in and out of the civilian population. The suicide bomber who killed thirteen Americans and 170 civilians at the Kabul airport was but one of the larger tragic examples of the difficulty of defending against such murderous assaults. And three days later the drone strike that mistakenly killed ten innocent Afghan civilians in an effort to head off another such assault tragically underlined the limits of the most modern military technology and the fatal consequences of many efforts to preempt attacks.

In many ways these last weeks were the war in microcosm: U.S. military forces were functioning as police, as guards, as processors in a swelling crowd. It was a concealed bomb that killed them and large numbers of Afghans. In an effort to preempt another attack, all of the modern technology was unable to distinguish friend or foe. And so friends, innocents, died.

Efforts to modernize Afghanistan agriculture and its economy, to provide more representative governments in the villages, to provide education for young women as well as men, to insist upon a democratic society, were all laudable. But there were cultural and religious and tribal and historic cross currents at work that few Americans understood. Young American service members functioned as agricultural extension agents, civil mediators, economic development advisors—and finally as security forces. As many as three million Americans served in Afghanistan and Iraq over the past twenty years, over half of them deployed more than once. And they did this in an environment where the government was too often corrupt and many people just wanted to be left alone. I think one of the remarkable stories of the war is how well these young volunteer soldiers and Marines performed their assignments in these circumstances.

In the future many will try to sort out the rationale, the conduct, and the consequences of these wars. One thing we do know is that, including the thirteen who were killed in August 2021, 7,049 American military died in these two wars. A Brown University Watson Institute analysis put the overall death toll in those wars, civilian and military, at as high as 800,000 individuals. A 2020 study placed the number of Americans wounded in action at over 53,000. Needless to say, the figure only includes the battle-field count—significant numbers of medical and emotional deployment injuries remain untallied and often unknown. And the Watson Institute study projects that, including obligations for veterans' care for forty years, these wars will cost some $6.4 trillion.

The wounded from these wars often have far more significant wounds than those carried by veterans of the twentieth-century wars. New pro-tective gear and modern battlefield medicine saved tens of thousands who might have died in earlier wars. But this major advance also has resulted in veterans now dealing with far more significant injuries than those older veterans who survived their injuries.

In Vietnam, small-arms fire, bullets directed at the head or upper torso, were the most lethal battlefield wound. Iraq and Afghanistan have not been wars with frequent fire fights. In these wars it has been mines and booby traps and bombs, sniper fire, explosives, and improvised explosive devices, all left by an unseen enemy. These have resulted in more survivals, but survivals of men and women with amputated limbs, burn damage, and other extensive injury. Explosions with flying shrapnel and a concussive impact, particularly for those inside a vehicle, have resulted in large num-bers of traumatic brain injuries. And the nature of multiple deployments in these twenty-first–century wars have meant many more cases of post-traumatic stress.

A striking statistic should give pause to all discussions about these wars and those who serve in them. The Watson Institute has calculated that over 30,000 active-duty personnel and veterans of the global war on terror have died by suicide—over four times the number killed in combat operations.

By no means were all of these deaths the result of combat experience. Each had its own story. And each of these is more than a statistic, it is a young life whose dreams have shifted to despair. As with the deaths on the battlefield, the heavy weight of grieving for these young lives is one felt by only a small section of the population. As deployed servicemen and -women have been saying since early in these wars, "We're at war while America is at the mall." Ironically, shopping patterns over the first twenty years of the century shifted more than did the patterns of these wars.

It is not possible adequately to assess the cost of these wars on the men and women who have served in them. Nor the cost for their families. And even as we treat the wars in the past tense, it is important to remember that U.S. forces remain in Iraq, and in fact an estimated 40,000 are deployed in the Middle East and in east Africa as part of the global war on terrorism.

As the Pentagon assesses its resources, stretched and depleted by these engagements, and as political attention shifts once more to strategic challenges from China and Russia, many are assessing the state of the military force today. Political and military leaders are considering many questions having to do with weaponry and aircraft and ships and preparedness and deployment and alliances. These questions await resolution.

Along with these matters of hardware and strategy, after fifty years some fundamental questions relating to the composition and the culture of the All-Volunteer Force (AVF) also remain unanswered. These may be considered twenty-first–century issues regarding race and gender and inclusiveness and opportunity. But they are twenty-first–century issues largely because they were not really addressed in the twentieth century. There is, as there always is, a history lesson here.

IN 1960 the U.S. armed forces had about 2.5 million men and women on active duty—170,000 of us were Marines. The Marine Corps and all service branches were essentially all-male institutions. There were fewer than 32,000 women on active duty in 1960, and they served essentially in administrative and medical roles. They had just recently been officially integrated, but they remained far from fully integrated. Women service members encountered a military culture in which sexist stereotypes, misogyny, harassment, and assault were prevalent. Certainly the post-World War II Marine Corps was aggressively masculine, macho. And white.

Black soldiers had fought with distinction and valor in the American Revolution and in the Civil War. Nearly 190,000 of them served in Union blue uniforms by the time of Appomattox. The Confederacy, short of manpower, ironically had also started to mobilize Black units in the final weeks of the war. Following the Civil War the U.S. Army had four Black regiments, two cavalry and two infantry, posted on the Great Plains, where they fought with distinction in the wars with Native Americans, who called them the Buffalo Soldiers.

Two general observations about these Black regulars in the first century of the Republic: they fought with pride and served well. And they largely served in segregated units. But as Southern racist assumptions and fears followed by Jim Crow restrictions came to dominate the country, the common racist theme was that these troops would not fight. If this was contrary to the record and the Medals of Honor held by Black soldiers, it made it more convenient to consider them second-class citizens, and importantly to keep weapons from their hands.

The military was largely very comfortable with this racism, always accepting and too frequently leading. In 1925 the Army War College issued a report based on racist pseudoscience arguing that Black soldiers lacked the courage, the intelligence, and the character to be dependable soldiers. On the eve of World War II, Major General Thomas Holcomb, the commandant of the Marine Corps, made it clear that he did not want Black Marines: "If it were a question of having a Marine Corps of 5,000 Whites or 25,000 Negroes, I would rather have the Whites."[1]

Remarkably, this racist view held in many quarters through the World Wars, even in the face of the record of units such as the Harlem Hellfighters, who spent more time on the front lines than any American unit during the First World War, and the exemplary Tuskegee Airmen and the 761st Tank Battalion in World War II. And despite General Holcomb's prejudice, the Black Marines from Montfort Point, a segregated training facility, joined Marine forces in the Pacific. Naturally, they were assigned to segregated service units. They served and served well—*and* in combat. They died on beaches that are part of Marine Corps lore. In January 1944, the new commandant, Lieutenant General Alexander Vandegrift, emphatically declared, "The Negro Marines are no longer on trial. They are Marines. Period."[2] Individual Black Marines received medals and their units received citations in the Pacific island campaigns.

In 1948, President Harry Truman issued an executive order ending discrimination on the basis of "race, color, religion, or national origin." All service branches sought, quite imperfectly and too often reluctantly, to follow this order during the Korean War and its aftermath. This was my time in uniform.

THE MARINE CORPS in which I served was still wrestling with and working on integrating Black Marines into the regular units. I served with a number of Black Marines. We personally got along fine, and I developed friendships with some of them, but clearly the races were separate on most nonmilitary occasions.

In the late 1950s I was stationed briefly at Keesler Air Force Base in Biloxi, Mississippi. Mississippi at that time was certainly not a welcoming place for nonwhites. Black Marines or airmen and I could not share a cab to go into town. And even if we could, there were no places where we could go together. In Biloxi there were "colored" areas in movie theaters, and in most public places like restaurants, there were not even those options. Drinking fountains and rest rooms and entrances were designated by race.

When I was in the Territory of Hawaii a few months later, there were no rigidly segregated places by law, but there were by culture. Black Marines went to certain places on Hotel Street on liberty. White Marines were comfortable going to Waikiki. And it was race, indeed Blackness, that was the determinant. I served with Native Americans and Mexican Americans, and in fact had a Mexican American top sergeant who was a World War II veteran. These Marines faced discrimination and demeaning stereotypes. But they were always above Blacks on the racist hierarchy.

These separate paths, and the awareness of them, was clearly part of our culture on the base. We had base boxing matches, "smokers," that we all attended, and I recall well the times when a Black Marine boxer and a white Marine boxer clashed. The rebel yells for the latter were clear. These were serious fighters in serious boxing matches. One, Amos Johnson, a Black Marine in my air group, fought while we were in Japan, where he was the Far East heavyweight champion. As a result, he came back to the states to compete in some matches. In May

1959 he defeated a young rising star from Kentucky, then known as Cassius Clay, in the Pan American Game trials in Madison, Wisconsin.

In Japan in late 1958, white Marines and sailors at Atsugi Naval Air Station went on liberty out the gate that led to the village of Yamato and Black servicemen went out another gate to the village of Sagami-Otsuka. There were no Japanese or U.S. military laws that restricted our options. We followed our customary—racist—patterns.

And these were as confining, as exclusive, as segregated, as Mississippi. Race was defining. This was not consistent with the basic values and principles for which we were trained to fight and for which others would fight—and die. The military did not construct a racist society—although they surely far too readily accepted it, and far too often facilitated it.

I recall one serious racial incident. At Kaneohe Bay, after a beer party, a white and a Black Marine got into a heated argument in our barracks. Tempers flared and language deteriorated. Pushing and threats followed. Some friends of each pushed into the scrum. I approached them and said to cool down just as someone hit another on the head with a full beer bottle. With warm beer, the bottle exploded. I was bleeding, with pieces of glass in my leg. The person who was hit was dazed. He and I and a few others went to the Sick Bay medical unit, where I had my wound cleaned and stitched. Some of those involved had major disciplinary action. Tensions remained high for a time.

Reflecting on this incident, I realize those tensions did not appear to interfere with our interaction in uniform or our operations. I observed in my study of the troops in Vietnam that they had sometimes serious racial tensions, but when they were in the field most acknowledged these were left behind. I sometimes played pickup basketball with Black Marines in my unit. We might then go to chow together. And a Black sergeant friend would occasionally give me a ride into town. But we never went to the same off-base places. This distancing was never explicit, surely not required, but it was the way that it was. And being that way had to have had serious consequences, whether we noticed them or not, in the way we functioned. "Semper Fidelis," the cohesion that follows mutual trust and interdependence, must be earned. And lived.

By any perspective, women and Blacks were still excluded from the mainstream of the ranks during the period in which I served. The problems of gay and lesbian Americans were far more isolating than entry to the mainstream of the ranks. They were not accepted, even on the margins. In American society, they were generally closeted and cautious. They clearly could not be "out" and join the military. Or remain in it. Homosexuality was considered a psychological disorder and gay sexual conduct was criminal. Gay and lesbian service members who were discovered received undesirable or dishonorable discharges. Homophobia defined the culture. The U.S. military embraced this stance and, with its traditionally "masculine" image, asserted it.

I recall one sergeant in our unit who allegedly made a sexual pass at another sergeant, a close friend. The friend reported him and the sergeant was escorted out of the barracks by MPs. We never saw him again. Another time one of the Marines in my unit came back from the enlisted club upset because he said a gay sailor at the club had propositioned him. The Marine was very angry and then unfortunately the sailor walked by. Our Marine assaulted him, punching him in the face repeatedly until I grabbed him and pulled him away and told him that he had to stop. I asked the sailor if he was okay but he said nothing and moved on, bloodied and clearly hurting. We never heard any more about this. And I have often wondered why I didn't do more about it. Why I didn't report it.

OVER SIXTY YEARS LATER, compared with this baseline, the AVF has made some real strides in addressing these chronic issues of racism, sexism, and homophobia. Real strides—but inadequate ones.

A 2020 Pentagon report described the composition of the current active-duty force. Among the enlisted ranks, 53 percent were white, 18 percent were Black, 19 percent were Hispanic, 4 percent were Asian, and 6 percent were multiracial, Native Hawaiian/Pacific Islander, and Native American. Blacks and Hispanics were overrepresented in this population. Among active-duty officers, 73 percent were white, 8 percent were Black, 8 percent were Hispanic, 6 percent were Asian, and 4 percent were multiracial, with less than 1 percent Native Hawaiian/Pacific Islander, and less than 1 percent Native American. Whites were overrepresented among officers.

In 1973 when the draft ended, women were about 2 percent of enlisted personnel and 8 percent of officers. Today the figures are 16 percent and 19 percent. Fifty-three percent of the enlisted men are married, 45 percent of enlisted women are married, and 68 percent of the officers. The average age of enlisted men and women is twenty-seven, and of officers it is thirty-four. The military is not representative in terms of gender or of geography—it is more southern and western in origin. It surely is not our father's—or mother's—force any longer.[3]

Vietnam disproved—once again—the racist stereotype that Black servicemen would not fight. They did. Time and again they fought bravely, and despite the prevalence of significant racist views in the ranks and in leadership, and the racial conflicts of American society in the 1960s. In the Vietnam War, 7,243 Blacks died, 12.4 percent of the total deaths. I am not aware of anyone raising the old hurtful claim about the combat record of Blacks who have served in Iraq and Afghanistan. But racism is more than a single cruel stereotype.

As we enter the third decade of the twenty-first century, the Pentagon and the service branches have undertaken serious inquiries and studies about continuing racism and about the disproportionately—the embarrassingly disproportionate—low numbers of women and Blacks serving in the senior officer ranks. It remains to be seen if serious inquiries and studies lead to serious results. We have learned, or should have learned, through experiences, civilian as well as military, that changes in structure and law and programs and training are essential, but they are not sufficient if there is not a change in individual attitude and interpersonal behavior.

Women in the services face an even more serious personal problem than any glass ceilings closing off their leadership tracks: sexual harassment and assault. There have been a number of accounts of individual cases, including the horrible story of the murder of Vanessa Guillen at Fort Hood following a pattern of sexual harassment by a young soldier. She became symbolic of the problem and of the failure of military commands to address this problem.

Many now insist on the need to remove from the military chain of command the authority over cases involving allegations of sexual harassment or sexual assault. Clearly things have to change, despite what some claim would be the negative consequences of removing command officers from ultimate responsibility for the conduct, the welfare, of their troops. Many have taken this responsibility seriously. Too many simply have not.

This proposed legislation enjoys bipartisan support. While senior military officers are uncomfortable with this change in the process, Pentagon opposition to this fundamental modification has lessened. And in March 2021, Secretary of Defense Lloyd Austin established the Independent

Review Commission on Sexual Assault in the Military. This is potentially a very important initiative.

In 2015 the Department of Defense ordered that women be allowed in all combat units. Serving in a combat role is an important affirmation of equality—and it also is a means to promotion. Combat experience counts when a promotion board considers cases. And some pioneering women have passed the difficult physical training and tests that some of the elite units require. They have successfully taken on this macho ceiling to their service. But beyond access to combat units, one of the underlying issues is the changing nature of combat. War fighting is no longer solely focused on a designated unit fighting in a specific geographic place. In fact, the nature of these modern wars is the absence of front lines. There are encounters with enemy fire, or with the devices planted and detonated by enemy, throughout the deployed areas. A 2020 congressional study reported that 173 women had died in the fighting in Iraq and Afghanistan. Very few if any of them served in traditional ground combat units.

Along with the treatment of women in the AVF and their narrow advancement paths, the military faces a major challenge in fully accommodating and accepting LGBTQ troops. "Don't Ask, Don't Tell" was a condescending and humiliating policy for twenty years—although perhaps not as humiliating as the total banning of homosexuals before that.

In 2009 or 2010 I met with a senior general serving at the Pentagon and we discussed the repeal of "Don't Ask, Don't Tell." He opposed doing this. I argued with him that it was a necessary and too-long-delayed step. He never once indicated any sense of homophobia but insisted that he was fighting a war and he was not certain of the effect this change would have on the morale of his troops. When we were leaving, he said to me that his children shared my view. I replied that they were the age of his enlisted troops and their generation would not find this a major issue. A few years later, after President Obama repealed the policy, this officer told me that he was mistaken, that it turned out not to be a big deal.

By the end of the second decade of this century, the focus had turned to transgender individuals serving in the military. In 2016 President Obama and his Secretary of Defense Ash Carter overturned the long-standing policy of not allowing anyone who identified with a gender different from their birth identity to enlist or remain in the armed forces. Their order represented a major recognition of the service and contributions of trans-gendered men and women. But the recognition lasted only until July 2017, when President Donald Trump announced on his Twitter account that transgender individuals would not be allowed to serve "in any capacity." On his fifth day in office, on January 25, 2021, President Joe Biden announced that as "Commander in Chief of the Armed Forces," he had determined that "gender identity should not be a bar to military service."

Jason Lyall recently published his impressive study analyzing wars and armies historically and globally. He determined that military forces that practiced inequality were less effective on the battlefield. He concluded,

In the United States, we still hear echoes of official concern about the inclusion of homosexual, female, and transgendered individuals in combat roles. Yet marginalizing or outright excluding these groups throws away military power. Removing structural barriers to their full inclusion in society and the military will muster new skills, produce new diversity bonuses, decrease intergroup biases and prejudices, and build more cohesive teams with superior problem-solving capabilities. Rather than misplaced fears about unit cohesion, political and military leaders should be devoting their efforts to harnessing the advantages unleashed by tearing down remaining obstacles to full, meaningful inclusion for these groups.[4]

Two important points warrant emphasis: first, the military has too often failed to be the accepting, inclusive force that represents our democracy. It has too often tolerated if not encouraged racist, sexist, and homophobic stereotypes and prejudices. Second, and more fundamentally, our republic has failed to be the accepting, inclusive place that should frame the culture of our military forces. And of our society. It would be hard to imagine the armed forces moving independently too far from the political restrictions and the social and cultural norms of the nation.

In the examples on inclusion that I have discussed here, American presidents Harry Truman, Barack Obama, Donald Trump, and Joe Biden issued the executive orders that directed the military to take action. These orders in turn were typically issued in the context of broad social, cultural, and political forces. Military units may be situated in enclosed, secure bases. But they are not apart from their civil society. Our system depends upon civilian control of the military. This is as it should be, but this also means political control. Needless to say, political control results in an absence of consistency and too often imposing and winking at decisions that allow prejudice. This is not a pass though: the military must demand, as only this institution can, more adherence to our highest values.

At the time of this writing the military is in the center of a controversy over the names of military bases. This should not be controversial. In this century we should not ask men and women serving their country to do so stationed at military bases that are named in honor of men who engaged in rebellion against the United States in defense of slavery, many in direct violation of their own oaths to the military. In fact, we should not have asked them to do this in the last century either. The military command seems largely supportive of these long-delayed changes. It is troubling to see political leaders push back in support of "lost cause" role models.

The controversy over the base names underlines the question of the role of the military vis-à-vis the broader society. Critically, the disparities described earlier that exist in the All-Volunteer Force, the scarcity of women and men of color in the highest military ranks, are not distinctly military problems. One need only look at business and corporate culture, at Congress, at the major media, at universities. Look everywhere at the most influential institutions in this country. There are not many civilian examples of leaders like Colin Powell and Lloyd Austin in the military forces. There are too many places where no such examples are apparent.

A Pentagon study a few years ago indicated that one third of Black servicemen and -women had encountered racial discrimination while serving. A 2020 poll of the civilian population revealed that 63 percent of Blacks reported being treated unfairly due to their race.

In a period of our history when we are confronted with tragic police killings of George Floyd and Breonna Taylor and so many others, when the "Me Too" movement forces us to see endemic sexual harassment and sexual assault, it is hard to describe racism and sexism and sexual abuse as problems isolated to the military forces. Some recent analyses have in fact concluded that rape is more of a civilian than a military problem.[5] Again, there is no free pass for the military: when young women volunteer to serve their country, they should not *ever* expect to encounter chronic sexual harassment and sexual assault.

LGBTQ Americans are struggling, in society as well as in the military, for acceptance and not condescending prejudice. This struggle is always caught up in the politics of the moment. In 2021 the Biden administration overturned a Trump order that the antidiscrimination provisions of the Affordable Care Act did not extend to transgendered individuals. At the same time many political figures, fanning the culture wars, have become apoplectic over the thought of transgendered high school girls playing field hockey. As a result, they have sought to protect the republic by passing laws to prohibit such a thing happening.

Few if any civilian counterparts exist equivalent to the decisive authority of the military chain of command. Senior commanders can order actions. But changing culture and attitudes requires more than issuing orders. In all areas of American life, a stronger effort is needed to gain public understanding of social problems and support for efforts to correct them. Such efforts are compromised in the military—and in our schools—by the current pushback by some politicians on any critical orientation program or instruction regarding matters of race. Or by political challenges to including women in combat roles. Or by establishing cultural boundaries around LGBTQ Americans.

The American military has the standing, the respect, and the means and authority to be a leader, a role model, in providing an environment where recognition and promotion are based on merit. Sexism, racism, and prejudice are problems for *all* of us, but the armed services need to lead and demonstrate how an inclusive and open society can operate better, more cohesively. They need to provide equal opportunities and address these problems. And, *emphatically*, our society needs to show the way.

U.S. Army Chief of Staff, General George Casey said in an interview in 2009, "Our diversity not only in our Army, but in our country, is a strength. And...if our diversity becomes a casualty, I think that's worse."

AS THE AMERICAN MILITARY wrestles with issues of inclusion and equality and opportunity, we need to remember that they are also organized to fight our wars. Or to be prepared to fight them. And the 99 percent who are bystanders to this process need to understand better what this assignment means.

Many parks in American cities that include cannons also have stone monuments identifying the local citizens who served in a war that is memorialized, probably with special notations saluting those who did not come home from that war. It should be a simple lesson to better relate the artifacts to the memorials.

Perhaps our parks in the future will have displays of twenty-first–century military equipment in them, maybe drones, embedded near the silent cannons. Perhaps. If so, I would hope that the children can squeal and laugh and play on them. But if they do, let us be sure to recognize that, like the cannons that symbolize earlier wars, these are not toys, and that before they were in the park, they were not in a game. Nor was the veteran sitting on a bench watching them. He or she could tell the story.

NOTES

1. Bernard Nalty, *The Right to Fight: African American Marines in World War II* (Washington, D.C.: Marine Corps Historical Center, 1995), 1

2. Nalty, 21.

3. Council on Foreign Relations, "Demographics of the U.S. Military," July 13, 2020; Department of Defense Board on Diversity and Inclusion Report, 2020; Department of Defense, "2018 Demographics: Profile of the Military Community."

4. Jason Lyall, *Divided Armies: Inequality and Battlefield Performance in Modern War* (Princeton, NJ: Princeton University Press, 2020), 428.

5. Jill A. Rough and David J. Armor, "Sexual Assault in the U.S. Military: Trends and Responses," *World Medical and Health Policy*, 9, no. 2 (2017): 206–24. See also David A. Schlueter and Lisa M. Schenck, "National, Military, and College Reports on Prosecution of Sexual Assaults and Victims' Rights: Is the Military Actually Safer Than Civilian Society?," *Gonzaga Law Review*, 56, no. 2 (2021): 285–350.

Sources for Previous Publications and Presentations

"Introduction: Semper Fidelis," "The Old Corps: Boot Camp Memories," and "Reflections and Observations: The Twenty-first–Century All-Volunteer Force" are published here for the first time.

REFLECTIONS

"Cannons in the Park": Excerpt from the Introduction to *Those Who Have Borne the Battle: A History of America's Wars and Those Who Fought Them* (Public Affairs, 2012).

"Visiting Vietnam": Excerpt from the preface to *Enduring Vietnam: An American Generation and Its War* (Thomas Dunne Books, 2017).

"A Generation Goes to War": Excerpt from the introduction to *Enduring Vietnam: An American Generation and Its War* (Thomas Dunne Books, 2017).

"Veterans Day 2009 at the Vietnam Veterans Memorial Wall": Remarks delivered in Washington, D.C., on November 11, 2009.

"Walking the Hill They Died On": Previously published in the magazine *Vietnam* (June 2019).

ADVOCACY

"Honoring Veterans": Previously published in the *Boston Globe* (October 6, 2007).

"The New GI Bill: It's a Win-Win Proposition": Previously published in the *Chronicle of Higher Education* (May 7, 2008).

"The Yellow Ribbon Program and Private Colleges and Universities": Excerpt from remarks delivered at the annual meeting of the National Association of Independent Colleges and Universities (NAICU) in Washington, D.C., on February 2, 2009.

"Veterans Day Is for Remembering—and for Looking Ahead": Previously published on *Huffington Post* / huffpost.com (November 11, 2012).

"What Does America Owe Its Veterans?": Excerpt from a lecture at the Abraham Lincoln Presidential Library and Museum in Springfield, Illinois, on November 14, 2012.

"The Challenge of Memorializing America's Wars": Previously published in *The Atlantic* (May 29, 2017).

"American Veterans and the National Obligation": Excerpt from remarks at a symposium organized by the National Institute of Corrections at the Library of Congress in Washington, D.C., on May 17, 2018.

"Welcome: Fall Meeting of the Ivy League Veterans Council": Excerpt from remarks delivered at Dartmouth College in Hanover, New Hampshire, on October 5, 2019.

HISTORY LESSONS

"We Are Always Rewriting Our Past—We Must": Previously published in the *Valley News* (July 11, 2020).

"War Veterans and American Democracy": Excerpt from the Jefferson Memorial Lecture at the University of California in Berkeley, on February 2, 2010.

"Veterans Day in America: The Place of the Korean War in a National Day of Memory": Excerpt from Shinhan Bank Lecture presented at Yonsei University, Underwood International College, in Seoul, Republic of Korea, on November 11, 2010.

"What We Learned From the Korean War": Previously published in the *The Atlantic* (July 23, 2013).

"The Baby Boomer War": Previously published in the *New York Times* (April 11, 2017).

"The Real Lessons of Vietnam—and Afghanistan": Previously published on DefenseOne.com (October 13, 2017).

"Remembering Vietnam": Excerpt from remarks at the Wardroom Club, a Boston organization whose members have served as officers in the Navy, Marine Corps, Coast Guard, or Merchant Marines, on November 15, 2017.

"Enduring Vietnam: An American Generation and Its War": Excerpt from remarks for the Lemnitzer Lecture Series of the Association of the United States Army in Arlington, Virginia, on May 16, 2018.

"How Modern Wars Are Changing the Definition of Heroism": Previously published on MilitaryTimes.com (September 21, 2018).

"As We Remember Normandy, Let's Not Forget Hamburger Hill": Previously published on MilitaryTimes.com (May 20, 2019).

"The Capture of Hamburger Hill": Previously published in the magazine *Vietnam* (June 2019).

RESPONSIBILITIES

"Bearing the Cost of War: Why the U.S. Should Raise Taxes—Just As It Has in Previous Conflicts": Previously published in *Foreign Affairs* (August 8, 2011).

"The Forgotten 1%": Previously published on *Huffington Post* / huffpost.com (October 4, 2012).

"War in Afghanistan: The Unseen Sacrifice": Previously published on *Huffington Post* / huffpost.com (December 13, 2012).

"Have Americans Forgotten Afghanistan?": Previously published in *The Atlantic* (March 25, 2013).

"Ten Years After 'Mission Accomplished,' the Risks of Another Intervention": Previously published in *The Atlantic* (May 1, 2013).

"Remember: Those Who Fight Wars Die in Wars": Previously published in the *Pittsburgh Post-Gazette* (July 3, 2013).

"Remembering Those Who Wore the 'Boots on the Ground'": Previously published in *The Atlantic* (May 30, 2016).

"The Human Face of War": Previously published on MilitaryTimes.com (June 27, 2019).

"Nixon's Leniency After My Lai Hurt Veterans. Trump's May, Too": Previously published on DefenseOne.com (December 15, 2019).

"We've Learned to Thank Those Who Serve, Whether It's in War or During a Pandemic": Previously published in the *Los Angeles Times* (May 25, 2020).

"The Election without a Debate Over War": Previously published on Defense One.com (November 1, 2020).

CHALLENGES

"How America's All-Volunteer Force Reshaped the Military—and the Country": Previously published on CNN.com (March 31, 2021).

ABOUT THE AUTHOR

JAMES WRIGHT is President Emeritus of Dartmouth College. A historian and a former Marine, he has been an advocate for veterans and has served on the boards of several veteran service organizations. The Secretary of the Army, the Commandant of the Marine Corps, and the Veterans of Foreign Wars have recognized him for his work. His previous books include *Those Who Have Borne the Battle: A History of America's Wars and Those Who Fought Them* (2012) and *Enduring Vietnam: An American Generation and Its War* (2017). He and his wife Susan live in Hanover, New Hampshire.